Friedrich Nietzsche

MY SISTER AND I

Translated by Dr. Oscar Levy

Los Angeles

This book was originally published in 1951 by Boar's Head Books and was distributed by Seven Sirens Press, Inc.

Book and Cover Design: Tom Dolan

Copyright © 1990 AMOK Books

ISBN 1-878923-01-3

"Nietzsche Discovery" by A. K. Placzek first appeared in *Saturday Review of Literature*, February 2, 1952. Reprinted by permission of the publisher.
"Nietzsche and the Seven Sirens" by Walter Kaufmann first appeared in *Partisan Review*, Vol. 19, No. 3, 1952. Reprinted by permission of the publisher.
"Review of *My Sister and I*" by Walter Kaufmann reprinted from *The Philosophical Review*, Vol. 65, 1955, by permission of the publisher.
"*My Sister and I: The Disputed Nietzsche*" by Walter K. Stewart. Used by permission of the author. Reprinted by permission of the publisher from *Thought*, Vol. 61, No. 242 (New York: Fordham University Press, 1986). Copyright © 1986 by Fordham University, pp. 321-335.
Selection of "The Last Letters of Friedrich Nietzsche" reprinted from *Selected Letters of Friedrich Nietzsche*, edited and translated by Christopher Middleton. Copyright © 1969 by The University of Chicago Press. Used by permission of the publisher.

AMOK Books are edited by Stuart Swezey and Brian King, and are available to bookstores through our primary distributor: The Subterranean Company, Box 168, 265 South 5th Street, Monroe, Oregon 97456. (800) 274-7826. For personal orders, please write to AMOK, P. O. Box 861867, Terminal Annex, Los Angeles, California 90086-1867.

CONTENTS

LIST OF ILLUSTRATIONS

Following page lxiv:

Advertisement for the *Two Worlds Quarterly*, 1926.
Advertisement for *My Sister and I*, 1953.
Elisabeth Nietzsche as a teenager in Naumburg.
Lou von Salomé.
Lou von Salomé, Paul Rée and Friedrich Nietzsche,
May 13, 1882.
Richard and Cosima Wagner, 1870.
Elisabeth Nietzsche, 1881.
Photographs of Nietzsche taken by Hans Olde as part of his
commission to paint a heroic portrait of the dying philosophe
in Summer 1899.
Nietzsche's death mask, August 1900.

Following page 235:

Letter to Catulle Mendès, January 1, 1889.
Letter to Catulle Mendès, January 1, 1889.
Letter to Jacob Burckhardt, January 6, 1889.
Letter "to the illustrious Poles," January 4, 1889.
Letter to Elisabeth Nietzsche, August 13, 1890.

PREFACE TO REVISED EDITION

And so as to leave no doubt as to my opinion in this matter, which is as honest as it is strict, I would like to impart one more clause of my moral code against vice: with the word vice *I combat every sort of anti-nature or, if one likes beautiful words, idealism. The clause reads: "The preaching of chastity is a public incitement to anti-nature. Every expression of contempt for the sexual life, every befouling of it through the concept 'impure,' is* the *crime against life — is the intrinsic sin against the holy spirit of life."*
— Friedrich Nietzsche, "Why I Write Such Excellent Books," *Ecce Homo*

So far as is known, Nietzsche lived as an ascetic, and very probably had no knowledge of having contracted syphilis. Hildebrandt, op. cit., considers the possibility that Nietzsche might have infected himself without sexual relations — perhaps through a skin wound during the war when he ministered to sick soldiers.
— Walter Kaufmann, *Nietzsche: Philosopher, Psychologist, Antichrist*

Here we find the disparity between the official academic line concerning this most transgressive of thinkers and his own writings. In life, we are told, he was a monk. Despite his brilliant advocacy of *living* his philosophy, despite his unequivocal denunciations of Christian hypocrisy, despite the inexorable unraveling which a *venereal disease* wrought on his mind, Nietzsche's life and the legacy of his wrenching (yet liberating) thoughts has since been ground into a bland scholarliness in the despotic hands of the most stultifying of pedants.

With the publication of *Nietzsche: Philosopher, Psychologist, Antichrist* in 1950, Walter Kaufmann had ensconced himself as the official translator and interpreter of Nietzsche's writings, as well as his life, to the English-speaking world. Surely the irony of being possessed by this half-hearted and self-important intermediary would not have failed to arouse the scorn of Nietzsche himself, were he to have witnessed it. In the preface to the first edition of his biography, Kaufmann attempts to distance himself from Nietzsche's actual philosophy by diplomatically declaring, "The decision to write on Nietzsche, however, was not inspired by agreement with him. What seems admirable is his deprecation of the importance of agreement and his Socratic renunciation of any effort to stifle independent thinking."

One year after Kaufmann's "definitive" biography came out, a book was published titled *My Sister and I*, which called for a major rethinking of the significance of Nietzsche's life in relation to his writings. Written in the mental institution at Jena after his mental collapse in Turin, *My Sister and I* would seem to be a final summing-up, a deeply self-searching memoir that is a counterpoint to the megalomania and strident assuredness of Nietzsche's *literary* autobiography, *Ecce Homo*.

In this revised edition of *My Sister and I* the reader can follow the book's progress, from its initial tentative acceptance as Nietzsche's final work (by a Nietzsche scholar, A. K. Placzek in the *Saturday Review*), to its seemingly final dismissal as a fake by Walter Kaufmann (throwing the weight of his credits as translator and biographer around with greater authority than his meager evidence actually warrants).

Also included, however, is recent notable research by Dr. Walter K. Stewart, an expert on Goethe and nineteenth-century German literature, calling into question the academic consensus which has banished *My Sister and I* to the status of an anomaly. Published originally in the philosophical journal *Thought* in 1986, "*My Sister and I:* The Disputed Nietzsche" delves into untranslated Nietzsche letters which were not published until 1969 (and some as late as 1982) in the Colli and Montinari *Nietzsches Briefwechsel* and *Nietzsche Werke*. Dr. Stewart makes a very thorough case for the book's authenticity, based on the text itself and its parallels with Nietzsche's actual words and thoughts. If *My Sister and I* is, in fact, the last writings of Nietzsche, then the entire edifice of Kaufmann's entombment of Nietzsche is exploded. One can say that the writer who proclaimed "I am not man, I am dynamite" has left a literary time bomb which could still, nearly a century after his death, reveal the lie of this self-appointed apostle.

An appendix of the last known letters of Nietzsche, some published in English for the first time, is also provided in this edition. Presented in chronological order, they are included to complete the frame of reference to the text of *My Sister and I*. Nietzsche furiously scribbled nearly thirty notes, postcards, and letters in a period of less than one week; they are a testament to his prevailing desire to *communicate*, even in the midst of losing his sanity.

Sigmund Freud considered that Nietzsche "had a more penetrating knowledge of himself than any other man who ever lived or was ever likely to live." The contrast between the tortured revelations of incest, sibling love/hate, mother fixation, and the psychic pain of unrequited love in *My Sister and I*, and Kaufmann's polite admonition to the reader about one of Nietzsche's published letters is striking: "The remarks about mother and sister smack of madness the way they are put, and we are almost bound to feel that one simply does not speak that way about one's closest relatives, at least in print." Even if Kaufmann had the German manuscript of *My Sister and I* sitting on his desk at Princeton, would he have had the suppleness of mind to deal with its disturbing admissions?

In his biography of Nietzsche, Kaufmann states, "There is a decided break in Nietzsche's sanity which comes only later, after his collapse in the street. From then on there is no startling lucidity, no great vision, but only a steadily increasing and unrelieved dullness of mind, a spreading darkness which envelops Nietzsche's mind in hopeless night." Again, the question of Nietzsche's madness emerges as the determining factor in denying the plausibility of *My Sister and I*'s authenticity. At this point in the study of the relationship of genius to insanity, it seems positively perverse to deny that Nietzsche could have written *My Sister and I* because he was in a mental institution. Premonitions of madness hung over Nietzsche for the entire span of his creative life; his father died following a mental collapse when Nietzsche was four years old, and in August 1881, for example, he wrote in a letter: ". . . sometimes the idea runs through my head that I am living an extremely dangerous life, for I am one of those machines which can explode." The creative pathology of Nietzsche's insanity, however it was induced, is central to the core of his philosophy and his "pathos of distance."

As Kaufmann himself must admit, "the whole notion of possibly discrediting Nietzsche's late works by proving from manuscripts and letters that he was not entirely sane is altogether inappropriate. A parallel may show this better than any argument: it is uncomfortably like trying to discredit Van Gogh's late paintings by pointing out that he was not altogether sane when he created them. As it happens, he was not, and some of them were done while he was in an asylum. To be sure, this is not altogether irrelevant to an appreciation: it adds poignancy to know under what strains he worked and how desperately he tried to cling to his creative work, painting to the last."

Far more worthy successors to Nietzsche than Walter

Kaufmann have emerged in this century who have expanded on Nietzsche's analyses, carrying on the rigorousness of his investigations into the true bases of our motivations and hallowed societal institutions. On the subject of insanity and Nietzsche, Michel Foucault notes in *Madness and Civilization* that "it is of little importance on exactly which day in the autumn of 1888 Nietzsche went mad for good, and after which his texts no longer afford philosophy but psychiatry: all of them, including the postcard to Strindberg, belong to Nietzsche, and all are related to *The Birth of Tragedy*. But we must not think of this continuity in terms of a system, of a thematics, or even of an existence: Nietzsche's madness — that is, the dissolution of his thought — is that by which his thought opens out onto the modern world. What made it impossible makes it immediate for us; what took it from Nietzsche offers it to us."

Deprived of my last veil of illusion — the power of ideas — I gaze with terror upon the Void, but still I cling to existence, for the fact of mere existence is all that is left in the shattered landscape of the intellect. All reasoning is a mode of self-deception, but I cannot reason myself into a state of euphoria and imagine that I can find happiness in the realm of death, sunk deep in Nirvana. Oh, to be alive, to vegetate stupidly, but still to be alive and feel the warmth of the sun!
— Friedrich Nietzsche, *My Sister and I*

When Nietzsche said he wanted to be understood in fifty years, he could not have meant it in only the intellectual sense. That for which he lived and exalted himself demands that life, joy, and death be brought into play, and not the tired attention of the intellect. This must be stated simply and with an awareness of one's own involvement. What takes place profoundly in the revaluation of values, in a decisive way, is tragedy itself; there is little room left for repose. That the essential for

FRIEDRICH NIETZSCHE

human life is exactly the object of sudden horror, that this life is carried in laughter to the heights of joy by the most degrading events possible, such strange facts place human events, happening on the surface of the Earth, in the conditions of mortal combat, making it necessary to break the bonds of recognized truth in order to "exist." But it is vain and unbearable to try to address those who have at their disposal only a feigned attention; combat has always been a more demanding enterprise than any other. In this sense it becomes impossible to shy away from a meaningful comprehension of the teachings of Nietzsche. All this leads to a slow development where nothing can be left in the shadows.
— Georges Bataille, "Propositions," *Visions of Excess*

With the reintroduction of *My Sister and I* into the field of Nietzsche's published works, the best-hidden portion of Nietzsche's life is exposed. As is shown in the remarkable autobiographical writings of such figures as Dr. Daniel Paul Schreber and Vaslav Nijinsky, at the point of madness there is little left to repress, and the "last veil of illusion" is lifted. As Nietzsche wanders through the shattered debris of his diseased mind he reveals, at a deeper psychological level than ever before, the origins of his thought. *My Sister and I* is, ultimately, Nietzsche's final revaluation.

Our grateful thanks to the following people for their contributions and support: Gary Todd and Michael Intriere, for their production expertise; Julia Solis, for her excellent translation of Nietzsche's letters; Walter Fields, for showing us *My Sister and I* in an entirely different light; and Walter K. Stewart, for providing us with the pervasive logic and extensive research needed to see this project through to the end.

Stuart Swezey and Brian King
AMOK

INTRODUCTION

Dr. Oscar Levy

I

Oscar Wilde once jestingly accused George Moore of conducting his education in public. To an extent, this is true of all artists who show their work in print before they have reached a point of maturity in their development from which they can be viewed in something like their full stature and true colors. It was deserved censure in the case of George Moore who must have had some sense of the unfitness of placing his *Poems of Passion* next to Swinburne's *Atalanta in Calydon*. It could not fairly be said of Friedrich Nietzsche who, when he published his first work, had never read either[1]   or Stirner. It is true, on the other hand, that though the seeds of the Nietzschean view of life were sown in *The Birth of Tragedy*, no one would have bothered to look for them or would have worried about what became of them, if its author had not followed it up with[2]   and *The Joyful Wisdom*. If he had not a few years later taken that long bold forward stride with the publication of *Thus Spake Zarathustra*, the seed strewn so abundantly through all his previous books would have had to fall into a ken other than his own, there to fructify into a work solid enough to challenge the accepted moral

---

[1] Name not clear in copy.

---

[2] Copy indistinct. Probably *The Dawn of Day* is meant.

thinking habits of the world. (The *Zeitgeist* is as passionate in its quest for self-fulfillment as the most individualistic of individuals.) But Nietzsche realized only too keenly the limitations within which he labored, with the result that his succeeding works grew into deeper and broader clarifications of his unique point of view, and created even more compelling claims to a companionship of understanding among the readers of his own century (which Heine opened and he closed) and of the centuries to come.

Nature makes mistakes as often and as carelessly as does man but, even in the worst of her errors, there are rich, significant compensations. If — unlike Copernicus, Spinoza and Descartes — Nietzsche did not burst full-blown on an astonished social consciousness, the world into which he was born needed a slow indoctrination, rather than to be astonished, into a revolutionary turn in its career. As a matter of fact, Europe has never been found wanting in good, honest, picturesque sages. But there has never been a time when it could not use one of those bold, undaunted spirits which dare to teach by example. Jesus had to climb the bitter heights of Golgotha and die most painfully and publicly before a very dissolute age, as an example of semitic moral conduct. Nineteen hundred years later someone else had to do the same job, publicly punctuating the lesson with his blood, to affirm the validity of the other side of the medal. Nietzsche's life and work, one and inseparable, were needed to impress the imagination of his time, and he was never known to shirk from making his contribution.

Every new book Nietzsche published was an additional clarification of his revolutionary interpretation of the function of the old semitic teachings in the new world. Hebraism and Christianity had separately emphasized the rich heritage of antiquity. To the sense of beauty in Greece and the sense of place of Rome had been added a sense of the earnestness of living which reached its high flowering in the Italian Renaissance. This earnestness had been given to the world in a doctrine of good and evil which, in Nietzsche's opinion, vitiated the true values of life and seriously compromised the happiness of mankind. Why, he wanted to know, could not the world hold on to this new sense of moral responsibility, yet redefine sin and virtue in more realistic terms, so that the shadow of the dome of religion would not continue to weigh so heavily on the fauna and flora of the earth? His books were not worked out in the cool shades of libraries, or in pleasant conversational semesters conducted in sacrosanct classrooms. Each book was the result of a new affront he offered the world or of an affront he was offered by it. The first of his books (especially those entitled *Thoughts Out of Season*) were obscured by a mysticism regarding his ultimate objectives which he himself could hardly have been able to pierce. *The Dawn of Day* was the first book in which Nietzsche recognized clearly the force he represented. He saw it, but the ability to make his readers see it did not become apparent until the publication of the *Genealogy of Morals* in which he attained full maturity as a thinker, as later, in *Thus Spake Zarathustra,*[3] he achieved his first rounded out work of art. *The Antichrist* added little to the clarification of his attitude. It was largely a song of triumph, and it could be set to music, just as Zarathustra was set to music. *Ecce Homo* — in which for the first time in this expanding cycle of mediations madness (or would it be better to call it nihilism?) mingles with the frenzy of proselytism — is possibly the most lyrical and certainly the most readable of all his books, the book in which he demands to be heard and is heard above all the noises and distractions of the world. It was *Ecce Homo* which Nietzsche's family — taking advantage of his failing health — suppressed. After the triumph

---

[3] *Zarathustra* was written before publication of *Genealogy of Morals* which appeared in 1887. Dr. Levy must have placed it later because its first public edition is dated 1892.

of finishing what he must have known to be the most unique expression of a personality in his time, and after the obvious exhilaration with which, in the preface to it, he identified himself with his beloved Zarathustra, imagine his chagrin at being told that it could not, would not ever be published.

All who saw Nietzsche during those tragic years in Jena and Weimar report hours of lucidity in which nevertheless Nietzsche could not be cajoled into talking about any of his books or ideas. It was as if he realized that he had a voice but not for speech, ears with which he could hear the most incredible nonsense but never the sounds of his own thunderous refutations. It is my considered opinion that as the result of the suppression of *Ecce Homo* (which his sister did not release until 1908, eight years after his death and about twenty years after he had turned it over to her as finished) Nietzsche regarded his immediate connections with the world as violently if not finally severed.

II

I first learned of the existence of the manuscript of *My Sister and I* in the spring of 1921, a period of both triumph and depression in my life. Most of what I had planned for the emergence of Nietzsche in English translation had been achieved. But his reputation had suffered so severely at the hands of both the Germans and the Allies during the recent war (with the Germans calling him a war god and the Allies a war devil) that there seemed little likelihood of a return to reason in the consideration of his doctrine during my lifetime. My work of editing and revising seemed pretty much ended. Barring another throwing together of a few thousand epigrams under a title Nietzsche once contemplated as the subject of a serious work (the method of composition of the posthumous *Will to Power*), his sister had no further surprises for me. Anything else that might come along in the shape of new Nietzsche material would easily be classifiable as Miscellany, I thought. Imagine my astonishment, therefore, to receive a communication from a young American in London, where he was representing a great American newspaper, asking for an opportunity to discuss with me a newly discovered autobiographical work by Friedrich Nietzsche.

"But where is the manuscript?" I asked, when the young man appeared the following day with only the morning's *Times* under his arm.

As well as he knew, the young man explained, the manuscript was still in the possession of an Englishman, an ex-clergyman who had emigrated to Canada, but was now in England. The manuscript itself was in Canada, where the ex-clergyman had a business in rubber. The American had met him and had some interesting conversations with him on the ship which brought them and the Englishman's wife to England. A few weeks after their arrival the ex-clergyman had called on him for help in a very extraordinary difficulty involving his wife. The help required to make possible her return with him to Canada involved the young journalist's risking his personal liberty, a venture he was extremely unwilling to undertake for a fellow passenger he had hardly expected to as much as see again after their ship landed. It was then that the ex-clergyman revealed his ownership of the Nietzsche manuscript which he offered the young man in return for the needed assistance, to be shipped to him as soon as he and his wife got back to Montreal.

"Then you have only the word of a clergyman that there is such a manuscript!" I exclaimed with obvious disappointment.

"An ex-clergyman, if you please," he corrected me. "There is an important difference." And then he proceeded to retail to me the story of the manuscript itself.

During his first days in the asylum in Jena, having determined in his heart that his mother and sister were less than perfect conductors of his passion for the world, Nietzsche made up his mind to write another autobiographical work, not to replace the suppressed one but to supplement it and let public opinion compel his relatives to restore the older book into the light of publication. In the new embarrassment[4] imposed on him he felt he could write at least as clearly and forcefully as ever. The difficulty would be, how to get such a work before the world. He certainly would never again trust his mother and sister, or any of the people they brought with them to look at him and pity him. Nietzsche found the solution to this problem in the asylum itself.

There was, among the inmates of the asylum, a merchant in a small way whom the gossip of the house held most likely to receive an early discharge as cured. This man had conceived a great kindness for Nietzsche. It was this man's young son who brought to the house (during a visit to his father) the paper, the pen and the ink with which the new memoirs were composed. It was with this friendly inmate that Nietzsche entrusted his new work, on the morning of the inmate's discharge from the asylum, with instructions that he take it to a publisher who would be sure to compensate him for his trouble.

The man with whom Nietzsche made this extraordinary arrangement was little better than semi-literate, though, even if he had had the German equivalent of a college education, he would not have been likely to have heard of Nietzsche at that time. He did not make the promised journey to a publisher, and when he showed the manuscript to members of his family it was only to recount to them the story of that comic herr-professor who would stride up and down the place identifying himself with a whole string of famous persons from Napoleon to God. The

---

[4] While the deterioration of his faculties had brought to a standstill Nietzsche's ability to answer people who talked to him, the stream of his thoughts flowed on as clearly and swiftly as ever, and he did not experience in putting his thoughts into writing any of the hesitancy which overwhelmed him when he tried to give utterance to them by word of mouth.

manuscript might have gone lost completely if the son of this small merchant, on migrating to Canada many years later, had not taken it with him out of sheer whim. There, upon learning that his employer (our ex-clergyman turned merchant) was interested in old books and manuscripts, he brought it forward to show to him, expecting nothing as grand as the hundred dollars he was paid for it by him.

"But how could the clergyman know that it was a Nietzsche manuscript?" I asked.

"*Ex*-clergyman," the American once more corrected me. "There's an important difference. The moment his German employee mentioned Jena and the mad herr-professor, our ex-clergyman exercised the chief intellectual ingredient of the ex-clergyman, curiosity and suspicion. He compared the manuscript with the published specimens of Nietzsche's handwriting — and that might be forged. But he read and re-read — and the style, the matter, the character of Nietzsche, who could forge that? Indeed — who would try?"

"But how could anyone — clergyman or ex-clergyman — keep such a manuscript secret for such a long time?" I demanded to know.

"As a matter fact he had had it only a little more than a year," was the answer. "And you forget that under the special circumstances of his original flight from England, he cannot afford the publicity which would attend such a revelation. By turning the manuscript over to me, he rewards me suitably for a particularly precious service, and he manages to get back to Canada with a prize he cherishes infinitely more, his beautiful young wife. The question now is, when I get the manuscript upon my return to America, may I send it to you for translation, and necessary editing — at your usual rates, of course?"

At this point I was not quite sure that I believed in the adventure or the prize. But what was to be lost by asking to see the work? I, too, was motivated by curiosity and suspicion.

More than two years passed in which I almost forgot the young American and the manuscript. Then one morning it arrived. I read it with increasing amazement. Who but Nietzsche could have set out to write such a story?

III

How was I to find the English equivalents for those mad words? The opening pages struck me like a deliberate, violent slap in the face. Yet I recognized what I read as the natural opening of such a book by such a writer. While there was such truths to be told, how else were they to be told when the narrator was Friedrich Nietzsche? And that chaotic, incredible manuscript to me is Nietzsche himself, turned inside out.

I reconstructed *Chapter II* out of the two main currents of Nietzsche's grief: the laments of his soul-searing loneliness; his attempts to reconstruct the place of the woman Lou Salomé in the shambles of his life. Nietzsche's mind wanders as usual, but you are always aware of what conditions it, and he never lets you forget that no personal preference or loyalty can ever take precedence over his loyalty to the world into which he was born.

Third in the order of Nietzsche's interests in that last tragic phase of his life were his speculations on his mother's determined widowhood, a venture in self-revelation that would have frozen even Rousseau. Nietzsche attacks the problem with undiminished fervor. The object is never to scandalize, always inquire and learn. In Nietzsche's opinion his mother's failure to marry after his father's death was responsible for most of his and his sister's woes. What occurred between himself and Elisabeth while they were children could and probably does happen in any ordinary household, he seems to think. The continuation of such a relationship into adolescence, or even later, he argues, has to be fostered by especially evil conditions such as were engendered by his mother's persistence in shutting the male world out of her life. (*Chapter III.*)

It was also natural for Nietzsche to speculate (*Chapter IV*) on the sort of women he needed in his life, in contrast with those who actually imposed themselves on him. Here Nietzsche builds himself as close to the norm as he ever got.

Undoubtedly thoughts of Lou Salomé pierced Nietzsche's humid loneliness more frequently than thoughts of any other living human being. It is always so with the people we openly and publicly renounce. She is present in his thoughts even when he cries, *I want a woman — any woman.* Further on (*Chapter V*) one can see the process in which these entries are made in Nietzsche's book and in his life.

The whole function of *Chapter VI* is to lead up to and introduce Aunt Rosalie's death-bed confession of her knowledge of the relationship between her nephew and niece, which takes up most of *Chapter VII*.

Nothing in this book contributes to the body of Nietzsche's commentary on the most superficial of his adversaries, Richard Wagner. Whenever he mentions him, it is with an air of tiredness. *How could I ever have got myself involved in this sort of thing,* he appears to ask himself. This cannot be said of his comments on Schopenhauer. The urge to tie himself up with his one great spiritual parent is always in his mind, as in *Chapter VIII* in which he draws the parallel between Schopenhauer's mother and his own. This elementary worship of Nietzsche's is witness to and provides a sharp view of his one and only visible inferiority complex, a feeling you can find even in those passages in which he treats Schopenhauer with such superb contempt.

In *Chapter IX,* and *X* and *XI* he permits himself a return visit to the world of his childhood in his reidentification of himself with the Prophets Samuel and Elijah. But *Chapter XII* brings him back fully to the image of Dionysos, identification with whom becomes him so much better.

The unfinished poem offered as an epilogue could have fitted in between any two of the chapters of the book.

IV

The style of *My Sister and I* is that of *Ecce Homo*. With one difference. The hammer has fallen out of the hand of the author of *The Antichrist*, and is replaced by a clenched, naked fist.

It is the record of the rounding out of one of the earth's most glorious and hopeless lives. Hardly a nice story, the reader will think from chapter to chapter. But neither is the story of the Crucifixion a nice story. Where our human life shows up at the seams it is never a spectacle to expand our paunches.

If the publication of *My Sister and I* comes about in my lifetime it should go a long way towards dissipating the clouds of misunderstanding now hanging over Nietzsche's name. It should certainly do much toward solidifying the pro-Nietzschean forces in the United States, now so ably led by Mr. Henry L. Mencken, the spry translator and annotator of *The Antichrist*.

I don't see how my young American friend can dare to publish this work while Frau Elisabeth Forster-Nietzsche is within such easy reach of a law book. I hope the libel laws of America differ sufficiently from ours to make this possible.

March, 1927   OSCAR LEVY

NIETZSCHE DISCOVERY

A. K. Placzek

MY SISTER AND I. By Friedrich Nietzsche. Translated and introduced by Dr. Oscar Levy. New York: Seven Sirens Press, Inc., 254 pp. $4.

Here, in an unpretentious format and bearing a title that suggests a Broadway comedy, is nothing less than a hitherto unpublished book by Friedrich Nietzsche. It is said to have been written while he was in the Jena Insane Asylum (1889-90); to save the manuscript from being discovered and suppressed by his ruthless sister Elisabeth, he entrusted it to a departing fellow-patient; the latter, attaching no importance to the scribbled notes of "the mad Herr Professor," left them to his son; the son, having emigrated to Canada, sold the manuscript to an ex-clergyman, who, in turn, gave it to a young American journalist as a reward for helping him to dodge the immigration laws; the journalist, realizing the unique importance of the manuscript, drew it to the attention of the renowned Oscar Levy, Nietzsche's chief apostle in England; Levy authenticated it, translated it, and wrote an introduction for it. In this he states that he cannot envisage any possibility of the book being published "while Elisabeth Förster-Nietzsche is within such easy reach of a law book." That was in 1927. Elisabeth died in 1935, Levy in 1947. Nietzsche himself (incurable, but released into the care of his sister) died in 1900; since then whole libraries have been written about his work, his philosophy, his tragic medical history, and the enigma of his personal relationships. Only recently Thomas Mann used him as a model for Adrian Leverkühn in *Doctor Faustus*; and now, fifty-one years after Nietzsche's death, there falls into our hands what may prove to be the key to the whole problem.

The contents — 250 pages of disjointed but surprisingly coherent paragraphs — are, to put it mildly, explosive. They deal largely with those two basic experiences upon which any deranged mind tends to dwell: childhood and sex. He describes in pathetic detail his incestuous relationship with his sister, which was instigated by her, it seems, at a very early age and which endured, emotionally at least, throughout his life, doing irreparable damage to his personality and effectually frustrating all his attempts to lead a normal sex life with other women. He writes vividly of his later love affairs — with the unnamed and perverted "Countess," with the brilliant and beautiful Lou Salomé, with Cosima Wagner. We cannot tell, of course, whether these liaisons were matters of fact or hallucinations born of his disease. Interspersed amid all this are observations on various other subjects — art, nature, history, politics; some humorous, some witty, some tender, many heart-rending. He knew that he was misunderstood, demented, and lost. Philosophically, there is a retreat from the extreme position of his last phase; he seems to have been overcome by a realization of the ultimate futility of a mere doctrine of power:

"Humanity is bogged deep in bestiality: must I see my philosophy used to drive the human spirit deeper into the swamp? But I shall go stark mad and die before this tragedy takes place!" And "The irony of my life is that I praise the strong, sympathize with the weak, and bear an unquenchable love for the utterly helpless."

Several questions burn to be answered. How can Nietzsche in 1889-90 have written an outburst about his mother's death, which occurred in 1897? Why are we given not a single sample of the German text, which — especially to those of us who have been lifelong students of Nietzsche — would be stylistically unmistakable? Why is the only facsimile page of Nietzsche's handwriting taken from an early poem and not from the present work? Is it possible to gain access to the manuscript of Levy's introduction, which is presumably in the hands of his heirs or executors? What happened to the manuscript of *My Sister and I* between 1927 and 1951? And, above all, where is it now?

Altogether, an arresting affair. When this volume is known about in Germany, it will cause intense interest, no little outcry, and probably a justifiable demand for the publication of the original text. If — as the publishers clearly believe — this is a genuine Nietzsche work it must rank as one of the greatest literary discoveries of the twentieth century; if all concerned, including Dr. Levy, have been deceived, it is the most skillful artistic hoax since the Van Meegeren Vermeers.

A. K. Placzek, a Viennese-born writer, is on the staff of the Columbia University Library.

[Originally published in the *Saturday Review of Literature*, February 2, 1952.]

[Correspondence in response to Placzek's review:]

Sir: In his review of Friedrich Nietzsche's *My Sister and I* [*SR* Feb. 2], A. K. Placzek writes: "Several questions burn to be answered. How can Nietzsche in 1889-90 have written an outburst about his mother's death which occurred in 1897? Why are we not given a single sample of the German text? . . . Is it possible to gain access to the manuscript of Levy's Introduction?"

These are questions it would seem — from our correspondence — the whole world is asking. To reply to them comprehensively we must tell you something of the history of *My Sister and I* since it was returned to us by Dr. Levy, in translation.

To begin with, I should point out that our publishing house for many years led the forces of battle against book censorship in the United States. . . . Within New York State a certain amount of violence entered the picture. Acting for his Society for the Suppression of Vice, John Sumner, accompanied by two or three detectives, would walk into our offices and seize anything they might consider a source of danger to public morals. In such a raid on our premises at 160 Fifth Avenue, Mr. Sumner seized almost a whole edition of *Ulysses*, our entire Carrington collection, and, as we later discovered, the Nietzsche manuscripts.

All our efforts to recover them were unavailing. But we never entirely gave up hope. Early last year, while rummaging through a warehouse trunk containing much ancient material, a member of our firm found a battered, bug-eaten carbon copy of Dr. Levy's translation. Considerable reconstruction had to be done. Words that had become indecipherable had to be replaced. But in effect it was the work as Dr. Levy had delivered it to us.

Now to answer your reviewer's questions: 1.) Nietzsche's outburst about his mother's death was the transcription of a dream; it is as a dream that Nietzsche presents it in the opening words of the incident. 2.) We cannot provide any specimens of a text which to the best of our knowledge no longer exists. 3.) We never had a holograph copy of Dr. Levy's introduction: only typescript.

In the vast correspondence on the subject that is coming in to us from every part of the world, we have a letter from Prof. Peter Viereck, of Mount Holyoke College, suggesting the interesting possibility that Oscar Levy might have written the whole book himself, instead of translating the manuscript we left with him. We doubt that Oscar Levy would or could have done this. There is too much of the body and spirit of Nietzsche in this book to leave room for such speculation. *My Sister and I* is Nietzsche or nothing.

Margaret Meehan
Seven Sirens Press, Inc.
New York, N.Y.

Sir: Mrs. Meehan's answer to my question about Nietzsche's mother was apparently based on a misapprehension. I was not, of course, casting any doubts upon the passage clearly indicated to be the transcription of a dream. I was referring to the Editorial Note on page 86: "This section was evidently written after his mother's death."

. . . As I said in my review, many questions remain. Mr. Viereck has advanced a most interesting theory. I should like to venture one of my own — that this fascinating manuscript was based on random notes jotted down by somebody who had listened attentively to Nietzsche's outbursts in the asylum and who was afterwards one of his closest companions.

A. K. Placzek
New York, N.Y.

[Originally published in the *Saturday Review of Literature*, April 5, 1952.]

Sir: May I, as the daughter of the late Dr. Oscar Levy, editor of the authorized English translation of Nietzsche's works, be allowed to comment on the correspondence printed in your columns on the subject of the recently published book *My Sister and I*, by Friedrich Nietzsche (Seven Sirens Press), and thereby answer the doubts raised in the minds of a great number of readers in the United States and in other countries — indeed "the whole world" according to Margaret Meehan of the Seven Sirens Press (cf. her letter, *SR* Apr. 5).

The whole evidence concerning the authenticity of the text is based on the introduction "by Oscar Levy" containing the extraordinary history of the manuscript and "Oscar Levy's" claim that it is a genuine work, that he translated and annotated it.

None of this is true. My father never wrote the introduction, he never translated, annotated, or knew this fantastic and clumsy concoction of nonsense here published as a text of Nietzsche's. He never knew or communicated with the publishers, nor did he "deliver the work" to them as Margaret Meehan alleges in her letter to you. The book, it will be found, contains only four lines of interest and consequence, namely the following "Publisher's Postscript" (p. 17): "As the date on the title-page of *My Sister and I* shows, the publishers had to wait many years before it was safe to offer it to the world — a whole four years after Dr. Levy's death."

Safe? Not as safe as they thought. For not only are there numerous intelligent and faithful friends capable enough to expose this shameless fraud, but both my mother, Mrs. Frieda Levy, who typed all my father's correspondence and manuscripts since 1908 and I, who lived and worked in closest collaboration with him for over twenty years until his death, are still able to defend his name against defamation and forgery of this sort.

The introduction bristles with quite elementary mistakes

and inaccuracies which would alone suffice to rule out my father's authorship (for instance those concerning the chronology of Nietzsche's works). The style, too, is, thank heaven! entirely unlike his. I shall not abuse the hospitality of your columns by quoting these mistakes in detail, though I am looking forward to doing so at the appropriate moment and place.

As to "Nietzsche's" text itself, those sentences not stolen from the philosopher's known texts and from other authors are as authentic as the introduction. . . . Anyone familiar with the numerous exact and reliable accounts of Nietzsche's existence after his breakdown (I need only mention the letters of his mother to Overbeck) knows that he was quite incapable of writing coherently between 1889 and his death in 1900. It is, indeed, a measure of the real author's nature that he should besmirch this great tragedy in the history of human thought with this ludicrous and obscene travesty of Nietzsche's mind and style, and that he should attempt to cover his traces by the fraudulent use of the revered name of my father.

I sincerely trust that through your columns this letter will reach as many readers of the book as possible and that it will clear the minds and allay the doubts of those who were taken in or confused by this fraud.

"*My Sister and I* is Nietzsche or nothing," according to Margaret Meehan. "Nothing" is a somewhat modest appraisal of such an enormity.

Maud Rosenthal [née Levy]
Oxford, England

[Originally published in the *Saturday Review of Literature*, May 5, 1952.]

NIETZSCHE AND THE SEVEN SIRENS

Walter Kaufmann

Thomas Mann's Goethe novel, *The Beloved Returns*, may have created a new genre: half of the volume was given over to a recreation of Goethe's stream of consciousness, authenticated in very large measure by profuse allusions to his published works, and made interesting in part by the exploitation of a few might-have-beens. The transfer of this technique to other literary figures, without the scrupulous restraint of novelistic form — an attempt to forge a great writer's work as has often been done with great painters — suggested interesting, if dangerous, possibilities. The risk, of course, could be greatly reduced by offering such a work not in the writer's own language, but in an alleged translation of a mysteriously recovered manuscript. And if the stylistic demands could be greatly lessened in this manner, the intellectual standards, as well as the requirements of factual accuracy, could be relaxed equally by finding a writer who had become insane, and by ascribing the work to his last years. If this should deprive the fabrication of much interest, it need merely be hinted (inconsistently, but nonetheless sensationally) that the author may not really have been mad and that his mental disease might have been faked. Whatever the inspiration or authenticity of *My Sister and I* may be, this new book (which is not by Betty MacDonald but, we are told, by Nietzsche) fulfills all these conditions to perfection.

Published by Boar's Head Books and distributed by Seven Sirens Press, Inc., this volume (256 pp.) was, according to the title page, "translated and introduced by Dr. Oscar Levy, *Editor*, the complete works of Friedrich Nietzsche." The eleven-page Introduction is dated March, 1927, but "the publishers had to wait many years before it was safe to offer it to the world — a whole four years after Dr. Levy's death." Why? Nietzsche's sister died in 1935, and surely no German could have sued the publisher during the war. Did the publisher have to wait until not only Dr. Levy, but those close to him, too, had died? Or was the whole book written quite recently? I do not know; but such assertions in the Introduction as that Nietzsche had not yet read Schopenhauer when he published *The Birth of Tragedy*, or that he wrote *Zarathustra* later than the *Genealogy of Morals*, certainly suggest less familiarity with Nietzsche than Dr. Levy had. And while the presence of many similar errors in the book itself might be charged to Nietzsche's madness, it raises the question whether the whole work was not written by the author of the Introduction.

According to this Introduction, the manuscript of *My Sister and I* was smuggled out of the asylum in Jena; but it contains ample references to the years in Naumburg, where Nietzsche lived in his mother's care after his release from the asylum in March, 1890, and even to his final years, spent in Weimar under his sister's watchful eyes, when his mother had died. One incident (p. 90) is explicitly dated in 1898, by a quotation from an article which appeared on October 19 of that year. The whole detailed account of the origin and importation of the manuscript is thus untenable. We are told in the Introduction that this account stems from an American who supplied Dr. Levy with the manuscript — the American being (according to a letter I have from him) the publisher himself. He *could*, therefore, have himself written the Introduction. And why should Levy, who did not consider his English good enough to do any of the translating in the collected edition which he supervised, make a point of quoting the American who offered him the manuscript: "May I send it to you for translation, and necessary editing — at your usual rates, of course?" A forger, of course, might be interested in thus covering himself against financial claims from Dr. Levy's potential heirs.

It is certainly the book itself, and not the Introduction, which should be examined most closely. Was it written by Nietzsche? And if not, was it forged by a German and then translated in good faith? Or is there no German manuscript at all? There are a number of plays on words which seem possible only in English: "sense and sensibility" (p. 80); "he paralyzed the cosmos and now he himself is in the grip of paralysis" (186); "horses," "horse-sense," and "horse-play" (148) — and the only passage in the book which shows any wit at all: "Wagner rewards his friends by slandering them, as he slandered Meyerbeer, thus reversing Job's prayer: *Though he trusted me, yet will I slay him*" (222). The fact that all the other jokes fall flat and utterly lack Nietzsche's poignancy can, of course, be ascribed to his madness; but how are we to account for this sole flash — which depends on the mistranslation of Job 13.15 in the King James Version? Or how could the following thought have taken shape in the mind of a German? "Wagner once told me he placed me in his heart between Cosima and his dog, in other words, between two bitches" (220).

The references to Detroit (166), to the "English Nietzscheans" (202), to "Social Darwinists" (76 and 94), and to our "Faustian age" (193) strike me as anachronistic, as does the conception of the "priestess of Isis" (201) which apparently alludes to D. H. Lawrence's *The Man Who Died*. There is even a reference to Deussen's book, published a year after Nietzsche's death: "An incident of my college days has been recorded . . ." (124). And would an English translator have said "college days"? The lengthy reflections on Marx and Marxists (nowhere referred to in Nietzsche's works or letters) have a particularly un-Nietzschean ring (138-143, 162, 182, 191). In fact, the prose throughout the book sounds neither like the great aphorist nor like a madman, but like a fourth-rate contemporary writer.

Now the reviewer might well be asked: are you not an interested party, seeing that another work from Nietzsche's pen might date the interpretation advanced in your *Nietzsche* (Princeton University Press, 1950)? The question is fair enough; but *My Sister and I* is in such remarkable agreement with my book and, if genuine, would corroborate it so significantly that it seems more likely that the author had read my *Nietzsche*. The demonstrably true biographical data are largely confined to those I discussed. Even the (to my mind, utterly implausible) account of Nietzsche's alleged incestuous relationship with his sister could have been suggested by my observation (p. 37): "It is conceivable that his passionate love of her as a boy had something to do with his later remark: 'To Byron's Manfred I must be profoundly related: I found all these abysses in myself — at thirteen, I was ripe for this work.' " In *My Sister and I* we find: "Elisabeth played the same role in my life's drama as Augusta played in Byron's" (151). Such parallels, too numerous for cataloguing here, extend to the philosophic side, too; e.g., "These Rousseauan savages, these *blond beasts* of mine, were at the polar extreme to my Superman" (208). This is indeed my interpretation; but having read the medical records of Nietzsche's pathetic behavior in the asylum — how he would save his own excrements in a table drawer, or even eat them, not to speak of his bodily symptoms — I cannot readily accept such corroboration.

I took the sister to task for withholding *Ecce Homo* until 1908, and merely recorded in my Bibliography that two of Nietzsche's other works were not published until 1895. This last fact is entirely overlooked in *My Sister and I*, while Nietzsche's mental collapse (in January, 1889) is emphatically blamed on his sister's suppression of *Ecce Homo* (9f.) — which she had, as Dr.

Levy must have known, never even seen at that time. Nor is it credible that Nietzsche himself, in the asylum, should have complained of his family's suppression of the book (14). The characterization of *The Will to Power* in the Introduction also seems an echo of my book. Finally, my book, published in 1950, begins: "Nietzsche became a myth even before he died in 1900." In *My Sister and I* (152) we find this: "Fifty years after my death, when I shall have become a myth . . . my power-philosophy will be re-examined. . . ." A prophecy? Or a sentence written recently? Some of the flat aphorisms with their incessant allusions to Nietzsche's work with which, however, they never brook comparison, could certainly have been written earlier; and even the amalgamation of this insipid material with such pornography as could be interpolated by supposing that Nietzsche had sexual relations with his sister, with Lou Salomé, with a countess, a harlot, and a few others, might have been entertained years ago.

There remain at least two important questions: where is the original German manuscript? (The "specimen of Nietzsche's handwriting" on p. 18 is nothing new.) And who, really, is the publisher? A letter to Seven Sirens Press, Inc., brought forth an answer from Samuel Roth: the German manuscript has disappeared — probably in a raid on his establishment by Mr. Sumner of the Society for the Suppression of Vice. Roth was never able to secure the return of anything Sumner took from him, and in this case actually thought it might be for the best, as publication might only get him into grave difficulties. So, from 1927 until 1951, he resigned himself to the irreparable loss of Nietzsche's manuscript; but then his wife suddenly discovered a carbon copy of Levy's translation in an old trunk in a warehouse. Roth claims that in 1926, in his magazine *Beau*, he had already announced serial publication of the work, in an abridged version, for the second year of another of his magazines, *Two Worlds Quarterly*. And it is true that his announcement included not only "The

New Unnamed Work of James Joyce," but also "The Dark Surmise: Concerning Friedrich Nietzsche and His Sister." But so far from proving his point, it would appear that the thought of publishing a work *by* Nietzsche had not yet occurred to him. And how could one, robbed by one's arch-enemy of an unpublished Nietzsche manuscript, fail to publicize the fact until twenty-four years later, in a letter to a skeptical scholar?

And who is Samuel Roth? His previous publications include *Inside Hitler* (1941 — reissued in 1950 as *I Was Hitler's Doctor* — allegedly written by a mysterious German psychoanalyst, Dr. Kurt Krueger, who here reports the filth which he uncovered when analyzing Hitler in the twenties — a book, it seems to me, justly ignored by scholarly reviewers), *Lady Chatterley's Husbands: An Anonymous Sequel to the Celebrated Novel, Lady Chatterley's Lover* (1931), and — among many other titles — *Jews Must Live: An Account of the Persecution of the World by Israel on all the Frontiers of Civilization* (1934), admittedly by Roth himself. Although he often gets more famous writers to pen introductions to his volumes, he has almost always been ignored by scholars — with two notable exceptions. Herbert Gorman, in his well-known work on *James Joyce* (1939), characterized Roth as a man "whose hide was apparently that of a rhinoceros" (306f.), and said: "Never, it would seem, was there such colossal impudence from an opportunist of suspect character than from the amazing Mr. Roth" (309). And in support, Gorman cites, among other things, a protest against Roth's conduct, offered in 1927 and signed by "one hundred and sixty-seven famous authors and prominent figures in letters and distributed to the press." The signers included Robert Bridges, Croce, Einstein, Eliot, Havelock Ellis, Gide, Hamsun, Hemingway, Hofmannsthal, D. H. Lawrence, Thomas Mann, Maurois, O'Casey, Pirandello, Bertrand Russell, Arthur Symons, Valéry, Jacob Wassermann and Yeats.

In the end, *My Sister and I* reminds me of a true story. In their reaction against Hitler's authoritarianism, German universities since the war are given to punctilous observation of democratic procedures; and during the past years the faculty of one great university after another had to reject by solemn vote an offer for the sale of — Nietzsche's mustache, allegedly severed from the corpse before burial.

[Originally published in the *Partisan Review*, May/June 1952.]

Walter Kaufmann was born in Freiburg, Germany, in 1921, came to the United States in 1939, and studied at Williams College and Harvard University. In 1947 he joined the faculty of Princeton University, where he was Professor of Philosophy. His books include Critique of Religion and Philosophy, From Shakespeare to Existentialism, The Faith of a Heretic, Cain and Other Poems, Hegel, *and* Tragedy and Philosophy, *as well as verse translations of Goethe's* Faust *and* Twenty German Poets. *He translated the following books by Friedrich Nietzsche:* The Birth of Tragedy, Thus Spoke Zarathustra, Beyond Good and Evil, On the Genealogy of Morals, The Case of Wagner, Twilight of the Idols, The Antichrist, Nietzsche contra Wagner, *and* Ecce Homo. *He died in 1980.*

THE PUBLISHER'S BELATED EXPLANATION
With Which the Publisher Answers Certain Critics

Samuel Roth

Only half of the tribulations of Friedrich Nietzsche's *My Sister and I* is told in Dr. Oscar Levy's *Introduction*. Dr. Levy could not tell the other half because he never knew it. I refrained from telling the remainder of the story in the first edition because I regarded the misfortunes which befell Nietzsche's manuscript as properly a misadventure of the publisher — not a part of the book.

The freedom to publish works of one's choice is taken for granted in these times but it was dearly won in a series of legal battles throughout which I took a proud part, in my younger days.

In the course of one of these struggles, shortly after Dr. Levy had sent me the translation of *My Sister and I*, together with his Introduction, offices of mine at 160 Fifth Avenue, New York City, were visited by agents for the New York Society for the Suppression of Vice. The occasion for this visitation was an edition of James Joyce's *Ulysses*, which they confiscated, along with tons of other books, manuscripts and records.

Creating order from the resulting chaos in my business took some time. I had been planning a digest of *My Sister and I* for the 1928 series of *Two Worlds Quarterly* and announced its publication in *Beau*, *Two Worlds Monthly* and the *Quarterly* itself. It was only then, when I was unable to find the Nietzsche material, that I realized it had been appropriated with the rest of my property at

160 Fifth Avenue. Later, when the New York newspapers reported the wholesale burning by the Vice Society of the material they
had seized, I assumed my loss to be irrevocable.

Somewhat abruptly I retired from publishing and was away
from New York for some years. During that time all manuscripts
and other accumulations of my business were gathered and stored
in a warehouse where they continued to remain for some time
after I had returned to New York and resumed publishing. But
eventually it became necessary for us to take inventory of that
material and, in the course of so doing, my wife came across
brittle, vermin-eaten carbon copies of the translation and the
Introduction, both having been further mutilated by careless han-
dling. Much of the work required reconstruction in my office. To
secure a maximum of accuracy I put several people to work on
research at the New York Public Library. Some of the fruits of
these researches I incorporated into the footnotes to the text.
These footnotes — inserted by me hastily and without corroboration — have caused much misunderstanding.

Anticipating that reviewers would want to know the where-
abouts of the original manuscript, I prepared for them a statement, the gist of which is in the above paragraphs. In all instances
but one the explanation was accepted and the book reviewed on
its merits. The exception was one Walter A. Kaufmann, who
teaches German at Princeton University and is himself the author
of a monograph on Nietzsche.[1] Like other critics he had written

---

[1] Truly great scholars had written, to protest the errors of carelessness committed in
the footnotes to the book. Kaufmann alone used them as the springboard for an
attack on the book's authenticity. But one can judge Kaufmann's value as scholar and
critic from the verdict passed by the learned world on his own book on Nietzsche:
In the N. Y. *Times*, the only reputable New York newspaper to take notice of it,
Irwin Edman deplored its "ambiguity and indecisiveness." After observing that he
"creates the most complicated and artificial constructions in order to harmonize the
contradictory," *Commonweal* adds: "Especially absurd is his chapter on Nietzsche and
Socrates, in which he disregards almost completely Nietzsche's opinion of Socrates."

my office for information and we sent him, not only the information, but also a bound volume of my magazine *Beau* (which he never troubled to return) containing my 1927 announcement of a digest of *My Sister and I* to be published under the title, *The Dark Surmise: Concerning Friedrich Nietzsche and His Sister.*

In his first review of *My Sister and I*, in a Hearst newspaper, Kaufmann ignored this proof that I had the book as far back as 1927. Inspired possibly by a flattering letter I wrote him regarding his book on Nietzsche,[2] he had the colossal conceit and impudence to claim that not only was *My Sister and I* not Nietzsche's but that a few of the ideas seemed to derive from himself. If not for the 1927 announcement he might have claimed that Nietzsche's very confession of incest with his sister, Elisabeth, was based on a parenthetical remark in his own monograph, to the effect that Elisabeth felt she was the only woman her brother ever loved.

In Kaufmann's second article on *My Sister and I* in *Partisan Review*, he takes cognizance of the 1927 announcement, but attempts to nullify it by pointing out that what I announced was not a book by Nietzsche, but one *about him and his sister.* How could I have done otherwise when, as Kaufmann himself declares in his own book, "She (Elisabeth Förster-Nietzsche) jealously established and guarded her authority by first gaining all

---

"Mr. Kaufmann aims too high," is the obit of the London *Times*. *The Journal of Philosophy* deplores the book's numerous inconsistencies," "its constant use of the word *notorious*," and "the number of its vulgarities." In *Social Research* Karl Lowith notes "instances in the book which betray a strange lack of sense of proportion." *Grozer Quarterly* points out that "he rarely quotes or mentions other writers except to disagree with them."

---

[2] Trusting readers will be pained to learn that publishers not only write flattering letters to possible reviewers of their books; they not infrequently offer cash bribes. The worst offenders will be the first to deny this.

exclusive rights to her brother's library and remains and then refusing to publish some of the most important among them." Would the woman who, for years, opposed the publication of *Ecce Homo* agree to waive her property rights in *My Sister and I*? If I had published the whole work, as Nietzsche wrote it, how long would it have taken her to suppress both me and the work?[3] In this second review Kaufmann characterizes references to Detroit, to English Nietzscheans, to Social Darwinists and our Faustian age as anachronistic; traces the conception of the priestess of Isis to D. H. Lawrence's *The Man Who Died*; he all but stands on his head to deny Nietzsche in death as the German professors so stubbornly denied him during his life.

Kaufmann's whole attack (except that portion which is directed at me personally and is unworthy of mention) is based on an error in Dr. Levy's *Introduction*,[4] another in one of my footnotes to the text,[5] and still another[6] which was inserted into both

---

[3] English libel law being what it is, Levy himself was so scared of his connection with the book that he made me promise not to mention his part in it if I decided to publish it during Elisabeth's lifetime.

---

[4] Kaufmann suspects the authenticity of the *Introduction* because it mentions Schopenhauer and Stirner as writers Nietzsche had not read before writing *The Birth of Tragedy*. This was one of the badly mutilated parts of the copy. The name of *Stirner* was clear, Schopenhauer's name was more conjectured than read. The text has so many references to Schopenhauer's influence on Nietzsche's youth that Kaufmann's deduction from this error is pedantic as well as impudent.

---

[5] The footnote at the bottom of page 68 suggests that the first paragraph, referring to the death of Nietzsche's mother, is factual. There is nothing in the whole book to justify such an assumption, and I must have put it down because of my being so overwhelmed by Nietzsche's convincing prose.

---

[6] On page 90, Nietzsche wrote: "My sister has read me an article by an English

footnotes and text by one of my staff.

---

writer who has perhaps shown a greater understanding of my historic significance than I have myself." Nietzsche then quoted, but the quotation was undecipherable. One of my staff found an article by John G. Robertson, appearing in 1898, and slipped it — date and all — into the body of the book!

REVIEW OF *MY SISTER AND I*

Walter Kaufmann

MY SISTER AND I. [Allegedly] by Friedrich Nietzsche. New York, Boar's Head Books (distributed by Seven Sirens Press), 1951. Ninth Printing, with a new preface by the publisher, 1953. Pp. 256. $4.00

When originally published in 1951, this book received many favorable notices in staff-written newspaper reviews in this country, though it was ignored by scholarly journals and by the British and continental press. The present reviewer wrote an exposé for *Partisan Review* (May-June, 1952), giving a number of reasons why the book could not have been written by Nietzsche, why it could not be based on any German original at all, and why Dr. Oscar Levy, late editor of the English edition of Nietzsche's works, must be considered wholly innocent of this volume, though the Introduction and translation are ascribed to him. In a letter to the *Saturday Review* (May 24, 1952), Dr. Levy's daughter expressed the same opinions. The publisher is Samuel Roth, who boasts of having served what he calls "a few honorable jail sentences"; and on one previous occasion his conduct provoked a public protest signed by 167 writers, including Croce, Einstein, Eliot, Gide, Mann, Russell, and Yeats.

In the new printing, two gaps, one of them comprising five lines, have taken the place of two glaring anachronisms to which I had called attention. The second of these was originally supported by a footnote, written in the first person singular, signed by the editor, and contending that the passage "proves that Nietzsche . . . was lucid to the very end, though suffering from occasional lapses into insanity." Now we are told that the manuscript (i.e., "vermin-eaten carbon copies of the translation," the original being lost) was "undecipherable" at this point and that a member of Mr. Roth's staff "slipped" in something to fill the gap.

Most of the new preface is devoted to an attack on the present reviewer which contains not only several bland misstatements of fact, but also "quotations" from five reviews of my *Nietzsche* (Princeton, 1950), designed to show how "the learned world" has condemned it. All of the quoted phrases completely misrepresent the tenor of the reviews from which they are taken, most of them even of the sentences out of which they are carved, and two of them are nowhere to be found in the review to which they are credited.

Mr. Roth has not seen fit to remove what I called, in *Partisan Review*, "the only passage in the book which shows any wit at all" — a line which, as I pointed out, depends on a mistranslation in the King James Bible and could therefore hardly have occurred to Nietzsche. Meanwhile, Jacques Barzun has kindly informed me that this sole good line was evidently lifted from the Wagner chapter of his *Berlioz*, published in 1950.

[Originally published in *The Philosophical Review*, January 1955.]

MY SISTER AND I:
THE DISPUTED NIETZSCHE

Walter K. Stewart

In the year 1951 a book appeared that was so remarkable in content and provocative in its implications that it was promptly acclaimed and damned at a stroke. The book was entitled *My Sister and I*, assertedly the last work written by Friedrich Nietzsche while he was confined in the Jena asylum between January 1889 and March 1890 (Nietzsche, *MSaI*). Following an initially favorable review in the *Saturday Review* (Placzek 19-20), a spate of others quickly appeared to refute it. The critics charged 1) that *My Sister and I* contained obvious anachronisms and discrepancies; 2) that the supposed translator, the eminent Oscar Levy, could not have been connected with the book in any way; and 3) that Nietzsche, in any event, was hopelessly insane and totally incapable of writing anything at the time when the original manuscript was supposedly penned. The curious fact that the book appeared in an English translation of the now "missing" manuscript only added weight to the case against the book.[1] As an epilogue to the history of *My Sister and I*, Walter Kaufmann

---

[1] *MSaI* xxxi-xxxii. Publisher/editor Samuel Roth insists that the original Nietzsche manuscript was in his possession as early as 1927 when he announced a planned digest of the work for the 1928 series of the *Two Worlds Quarterly* in Beau, *Two Worlds Monthly* (see covers of Vol. 1, no. 3, no. 4; Vol. 2, no. 1 for the year 1926) and in the *Two Worlds Quarterly* itself. The work in all cases is referred to as *The Dark Surmise: Concerning Friedrich Nietzsche and His Sister.* There is no proof to the contrary that this work is not identical to *My Sister and I*. *Also note:* English translations

briefly mentioned in his revised *Nietzsche* that a minor writer named George David Plotkin (aka David George Kin) allegedly admitted shortly before his death that he indeed had authored the book for the publisher "for a flat fee" (Kaufmann 496).[2]

My Sister and I has generally been dismissed as an outright fraud ever since. Critics, in fact, are satisfied to rely on the work of Kaufmann and others and to point to the shady reputation of the publisher, Samuel Roth, as sufficient proof of fraud. Meanwhile, the central argument against the book always hovers over the entire controversy: the insane Nietzsche of 1889 and 1890 was incapable of writing anything.

However ponderous the weight of these arguments seems at first blush, the case against *My Sister and I* is not really as open and shut as it might appear, and the book's authenticity has yet to be disproven. We may chalk this up in part to faulty criticism but also to the fact that the text stands up rather well to close scrutiny, especially in those places where it has been criticized most. What I therefore hope to make apparent in the following is the fact that there exist many good reasons why we should not summarily dismiss this work, particularly in light of the far-reaching consequences that it might have on Nietzsche's contribution to Western thought. Precisely what our discussion will attempt to show, then, is 1) that the previous case made against the book was inadequate; 2) that the book shows definite connections to Nietzsche's published and unpublished writings; and 3) that the

---

of Nietzsche's untranslated documents and letters, the correspondence of his friends and relatives, along with citations from articles, journal entries, etc. appearing in this article are my own.

---

[2] Kaufmann offers no corroboration concerning Plotkin's confession. In previous reviews Kaufmann accused Roth of forging *My Sister and I* and of authoring the specious tract *I Was Hitler's Doctor* (see Kurt Krueger).

true state of Nietzsche's physical and mental condition during the precise period when the original manuscript of *My Sister and I* was supposedly penned has been vastly misrepresented.

The entire backdrop of the Nietzsche controversy — including the appearance of *My Sister and I* — is set against the circumstances of his mental breakdown. Erich Podach's excellent research leaves little doubt that Nietzsche's breakdown occurred on 3 January 1889 in Turin, Italy (*Nietzsches Zusammenbruch* 107-13). On 9 January his close friend Franz Overbeck rushed to Turin in response to the pleas of Nietzsche's landlord. Overbeck immediately recognized the seriousness of Nietzsche's condition and packed him off to the Basel clinic, where they arrived on 10 January. Nietzsche was examined at this time and remained under observation until 17 January when he was transferred to Jena. He arrived on 18 January and was taken directly to the asylum where he was examined again and kept under observation until 24 March 1890 when he was finally released into his mother's care. Thus, for most critics, Nietzsche was insane as of January 1889 and could not have written anything on the order of *My Sister and I* after that date. Consequently, the fact that the publisher of the book purported that it was written around 1890 shows that it must be a fraud. Case closed!

Surprisingly, the entire case against *My Sister and I* rests on a mere handful of obscure newspaper and journal reviews. Kaufmann, the preeminent critic, was first to publish his "exposé" of *My Sister and I* in the *Milwaukee Journal* in February 1952. Ludwig Marcuse's two-article series followed in *Aufbau* in April and May along with two "letters to the editor" by Alfred Werner and one by Kaufmann. Even Thomas Mann briefly became involved (*Aufbau* 5) but wisely excused himself from the debate which by that time had degenerated into an embarrassingly petty exchange between Kaufmann, Marcuse, and Werner on the question of who first discovered the book to be a fraud. Other minor pieces were published. But, in fact, no solid evidence against the text of *My Sister and I* was ever produced; the discrepancies and anachronisms that were cited were largely limited to the Introduction, supposedly written by Oscar Levy.

On balance, Kaufmann's supposedly devastating evidence in his first two reviews hardly warrants the effusive praise it received; for on closer inspection, it is neither devastating nor particularly well-documented. His penchant for fuzzy phraseology like "seem possible," "strike me," "apparently alludes to," etc. (*Partisan* [xxvi]) is calculated to imply much without proving anything. And every single alleged anachronism to which he points (i.e., "Detroit," "English Nietzscheans," "Social Darwinists," "Faustian Age," "blond beasts" [xxvi]) can be readily explained point by point within Nietzsche's own works or letters. The same can be said of the only three items Kaufmann finds in the entire text that one might legitimately consider as concrete discrepancies: 1) the "anachronistic" report of a drinking episode in Nietzsche's life; 2) the "anachronistic" use of the terms "Marx" and "Marxists"; and 3) the question of incest between Nietzsche and his sister, Elisabeth.

In fact, we may summarily deal with all of Kaufmann's objections. In the first instance, Nietzsche actually "recorded" the incident himself in a letter to his mother. Next, Nietzsche personally owned a copy of Andreas Schäffle's *Quintessence of Socialism* that specifically names Marx throughout and discusses his theories. Lastly, the question of incest is most instructive of all, for it reveals precisely the kind of criticism that has kept *My Sister and I* in the shadows. Simply stated, Kaufmann based his critique on his own mistranslation of *Ecce Homo* II, 44 (*Nietzsche* 1950 ed. 37): "To Byron's Manfred I must be profoundly related: I found all of these abysses in myself — at thirteen, I was ripe for this work" (*Partisan* [xxvii]). The translation is in error for the following reasons: 1) Kaufmann confuses *Manfred* the work with

Manfred the character; 2) he focuses more on Byron than on his *Manfred;* and 3) he assumes that the German *"Werk"* should be literally translated as "work." Thus Kaufmann implies by his focus on Byron that the "work" to which Nietzsche refers in *Ecce Homo* must be of a deviant, sexual nature; i.e., incestuous. However, Thomas Common's translation of the same passage is more to the mark: "I must be profoundly related to Byron's *Manfred;* I discovered all his abysses in my own soul — at thirteen I was ripe for this book" (842). In Nietzsche's original text *"Werk"* obviously refers to *Manfred* — Byron's work about a brooding, Faustian character who is at odds with a world he would like to shape and control. This image is far more consistent with the general theme of *Ecce Homo* that places Nietzsche squarely in the center of his own universe; it has absolutely nothing to do with incest.

Moreover, perusal of the correspondence of Nietzsche's closest friends, Franz Overbeck and Peter Gast (Overbeck, "Briefe" 35, 38), also thoroughly disproves Kaufmann's contention that the family was not involved in the suppression of *Ecce Homo* from the early months of 1889, and his assumption that it was not "credible that Nietzsche himself, in the asylum, should have complained of his family's suppression of the book" (*Partisan* [xxviii]). The correspondence of Overbeck and Gast along with that of Nietzsche's mother (Podach, *kranke Nietzsche* 14, 19) makes a solid case for just the opposite.

Once more, of all of Nietzsche's friends, Nietzsche confided most in Peter Gast about *Ecce Homo* in the months just prior to the breakdown. When Gast finally spent some six weeks with Nietzsche beginning in January 1890 in the Jena asylum, there is every possibility that the topic of *Ecce Homo* may have arisen. At any rate, if Nietzsche's letters of the last three months of 1888 are any indication, he placed great store in publication of *Ecce Homo.* His reaction to suppression of it would almost certainly have followed along the lines of the complaint made in *My Sister and I.*

In his final review of *My Sister and I* in the *Philosophical Review*, Kaufmann acknowledges the claim of the widely known musicologist, Jacques Barzun, that a biblical quote from Job was "lifted" from his own book on *Berlioz* (183), but he adds nothing substantive to his previous arguments. This brings the debate on the book to a close.

Curiously, the arguments of Kaufmann and the others and their unanimous condemnation of *My Sister and I* have been accepted on face value alone as definitive and conclusive up to the present day. However, when viewed with more dispassionate eyes, their criticism obviously suffers in several respects from significant inaccuracies and from false presuppositions. In the absence of any other criticism that is more convincing, it should therefore be clear that their entire case is seriously flawed and that, as yet, no convincing case exists against *My Sister and I*.

Surprisingly enough, no one has yet thought to consider the fact that the text of *My Sister and I* itself may hold far closer connections to Nietzsche and to his writings.

The text, to begin with, is largely biographical and faithfully recapitulates information reported elsewhere prior to 1951 (*Partisan* [xxvii]). The original 1951 text underwent one revision after the anachronisms were pointed out and is now 256 pages in length, including a two-page Index.[3] The book is written in English and has been blocked off into numbered chapters and paragraphs by the design of the editor. The style is that of a

---

[3] *MSaI* xxxi-xxxv. Roth's explanation of the English translation must either be accepted or rejected. It is highly unlikely that the book could have been based on any other materials that had been translated into English. The *Union Catalog of Pre-1956 Imprints* shows beyond Nietzsche's translated basic texts only the *Nietzsche-Wagner Correspondence* (Elisabeth Förster-Nietzsche, ed.) which appeared in 1921 and was reprinted in 1922 and 1949, and *Selected Letters of Friedrich Nietzsche* (Oscar Levy, ed.) 1921. But neither of these works remotely hints at any of the intimate details that are revealed in *My Sister and I*.

continuous narrative autobiography that has all the appearance of a one-time, original production; yet, there are no obvious stylistic earmarks that connect the book to Nietzsche — the English has completely obliterated anything of the sort if it ever did exist. Furthermore, the details given out about Nietzsche's life are rather racy — the fact that prompted Reichert to dismiss it as a "pornographic tome" (*Monatshefte* 51:116). *My Sister and I* thus remains a conundrum even in the curious world of forgeries, for there is no pretense here at attempting to duplicate the personal nuances of the author's style as one observes in infamous forgeries like that of the van Meegeren paintings or the recent *Hitler Diaries.*

Still, what we can definitely state at the outset of our discussion is that the information contained in the text not only consistently corresponds to what Nietzsche expresses in his major works and letters published in English up to 1951 and to the assortment of biographies on him, but it also corresponds to his untranslated correspondence, to that of others, and to his untranslated *Archives* — the great repository of Nietzsche's Protean and fragmentary ideas. That so great a correspondence exists between *My Sister and I* and untranslated material should immediately alert the scholar to the fact that the book is not so transparent a fraud as it appears at first blush.

Of the most pertinent matters discussed in the text, the ones that have elicited the greatest criticism are paradoxically those that may be most revealing: Nietzsche's relationship to Lou von Salomé and to his sister, Elisabeth.

It is at the end of December 1882, just after Nietzsche had broken with Lou von Salomé and Paul Rée, that he complains to Malwida von Meysenbug about Lou in a letter, saying: "So much for this topic [Lou]: it belongs to the wanderings of your friend Ulysses. If only I were somewhat more clever" (*Dokumente* 271).

The choice of the classical imagery was obvious for

Nietzsche. The focus of the image, of course, is Ulysses's dalliance with the witches Calypso and Circe, and his escape from the sirens. Any or all of these figures are plainly equated with Lou. Nietzsche's clear implication is that he was not as fortunate as Ulysses in his encounter with Lou, for as numerous biographies show, Lou had a devastating effect on him.[4] The image is clear. Still, as central to the relationship between Lou and Nietzsche as this Homeric imagery is, no one has yet drawn any logical connections from it either to Nietzsche's writings or to *My Sister and I*.

Nietzsche's estimation of Lou as revealed in numerous letters and drafts of letters of this period is plain. For Nietzsche, Lou is little more than a hedonist and seductress whom he describes at one point, for example, as "clever and full of self-control with respect to the sensuousness of men" (*Dokumente* 263); simply, she is a modern counterpart to her classical archetypes Circe, Calypso, and the sirens. At any rate, the connection obviously struck Nietzsche in this way as his letter to Malwida proves. More revealing yet is the fact that the significance of this Homeric imagery was not lost on Nietzsche even as late as the latter months of 1888 — a little over a year before *My Sister and I* was supposedly penned — for we find that both his friends Carl von Gersdorff and Peter Gast are quite comfortable referring to their own paramours in letters to Nietzsche with the appellation "Circe" (Nietzsche, *Briefe* III/5: 311, 326).

Meanwhile, although numerous references in *My Sister and I* to Circe, Calypso, and the sirens allude to other women, it is Lou who receives the greatest attention. The author calls her his "Russian Calypso" (*MSaI* 213). Later, Lou is Aspasia who took

---

[4] For example, Elisabeth Förster-Nietzsche, *Das Leben Friedrich Nietzsches* 2: 402-18; Carl A. Bernoulli, "Nietzsches Lou Erlebnis" 225-60; Lou Andreas Salomé, *Lebensrückblick* 93-107. For more recent accounts see, for example, Rudolf Binion, *Frau Lou* 35-140; H. F. Peters, *Zarathustra's Sister* 52-76.

Nietzsche's philosophy seriously, "like an educated Calypso who discussed Hegel, Schopenhauer and Tolstoy between violent acts of courtship, exhausting her Ulysses with her love and with her lore!" (*MSaI* 222). Finally, the author complains bitterly that "A Pole of noble blood who calls himself Nietzsche is no different in the cave of Calypso from a mindless peasant. . . . On her silken bed all men are equals — the wrecked Ulysses and the gibbering idiot who has lost all goal or purpose in life . . ." (*MSaI* 224).

The fact that the image of Circe, Calypso, and the sirens as female seducers is employed in *My Sister and I* when Nietzsche only employed the Homeric imagery with his closest friends, in private correspondence, or in his own rough notes is of special consequence. For this imagery for him constituted the essence of his relationship to Lou von Salomé in the year 1882. Moreover, there is no mention of the image in any biography prior to 1951 — certainly none in connection with Lou. That the identical Homeric imagery only occurs in the text of *My Sister and I* in the identical context in which Nietzsche perceived the Lou experience raises questions that can no longer be easily dismissed.

My Sister and I also makes a case for incest between Nietzsche and his sister, although this is hotly denied by most critics (Kaufmann, *Philosophical Review*; Montinari 392). It is in *My Sister and I* that a most curious parallel connects Nietzsche and his sister to the incestuous relationship of the Egyptian Pharaoh and his sister/wife. For example, the author argues that Elisabeth, "the priestess of virtue sank with me to the lowest pit of Tartarus, to the bottomless wickedness of the Egyptians who defied the barriers of blood!" (*MSaI* 68). At another point the author states: "To maintain her dominance over me she [Elisabeth] seduced me into the sins of the Egyptians" (*MSaI* 151). The meaning of the image in *My Sister and I* is clear, but it is an image that is all but absent from Nietzsche's writings — except for one very special place — recently discovered fragments by Nietzsche that were never published in any language before 1969 and were apparently only ever seen by a handful of those closest to him.

In July 1969 Mazzino Montinari identified these two astonishing fragments in the Peter Gast *Archives* as having been authored by Nietzsche near the end of 1888. Montinari shows the first fragment to be a textual revision (belonging to *Ecce Homo*, Chapter Three, "Why I am so Wise") which focuses on Nietzsche's disdain for his mother and sister and for his belief in his own divinity (Montinari 380). But it is the second fragment that makes the connection to incest and to *My Sister and I.* Here Nietzsche states:

> All prevailing notions about degrees of relationships are psychological nonsense that cannot be surpassed. One is least related to one's parents; the marriage of brother and sister as, for example, was the rule in the Egyptian royal families, is not so unnatural that, in comparison, every marriage is nearly incest. . . . (380)

It is with Nietzsche's insistence on his divinity — not unlike that of an Egyptian Pharaoh as alluded to in the second fragment — that we are led directly to the question of incest. For it is here that Nietzsche surprisingly endorses incest between the Pharaoh and his sister/wife — an endorsement which he makes nowhere else in his writings. Yet the identical imagery crops up in *My Sister and I* and in the identical context — with the focus on himself and Elisabeth.

There can be no doubt that these fragments were never seen by anyone outside of a select few of those closest to Nietzsche (i.e., Peter Gast, Elisabeth Nietzsche, Nietzsche's mother, Nietzsche's publisher and his son). Montinari also relates in detail the extraordinary lengths to which Elisabeth went in order to obtain the fragments which she burned. It is a legitimate question as to why Elisabeth would do such a thing since it is well-known that she kept almost every other scrap that Nietzsche had written since his youth. At any rate, the fragments were never published in any form before this date, and it is inconceivable that anyone else might have employed them at any time around 1951. That the question of incest in *My Sister and I* is so intimately connected to Nietzsche's statements in these forgotten fragments once again raises questions that can no longer be easily dismissed.

Montinari also points to another revision of *Ecce Homo* which he relates to Lou and in which Nietzsche refers to "people [meaning Lou] *who are destinies* ['*Schicksale*']" (391). In this case there exists a clear connection to a draft of a letter written to George Rée at the end of 1883 in which Nietzsche complains in fairly harsh terms about Paul Rée's estimation of Lou, saying: "In writing he [Paul Rée] once called her [Lou] his fate ['*Verhängnis*']: what taste! This skinny, dirty, foul-smelling little ape with her false breasts — a fate! Pardon me" (*Dokumente* 325).

This seemingly innocent epithet is significant, for although it was something of a commonplace in the nineteenth century to refer to persons involved in romantic entanglements as "fates" or "destinies," for Nietzsche it was not. He employed the term in a strict connection only to Lou, to himself, and to the influence of his work. It is for that reason that the final chapter of his last work, *Ecce Homo*, is entitled "Why I am a Destiny." It is also for that reason that he writes in his letter draft to Ruggero Bonghi at the end of 1888, "The works that will follow from me — and they are completely ready — are no longer books but destinies" (Nietzsche, *Briefe* III/5: 569).

It is especially revealing that Nietzsche chose to employ this particular epithet with respect to Lou just when he was in the midst of making final corrections for *Ecce Homo*. Even after nearly seven years, Nietzsche continues to refer to language that is almost identical; in 1883 she is a fate (*"Verhängnis"*), and near the end of 1888 she is a destiny (*"Schicksal"*). The synonymous nature of the epithets underlines the fact that Nietzsche continued to attach great significance to the Lou experience at the critical point just before the breakdown. After the breakdown there is only silence on the matter. Only in *My Sister and I* — supposedly written only one year later — is the Lou experience along with a number of other important matters carried through the period of illness in such a way that is completely consistent with what came before Nietzsche's breakdown and afterward.

On the other hand, all of these questions are moot in the face of the single one that looms over the entire controversy concerning *My Sister and I:* Was the Nietzsche of 1889 to 1890 — the Nietzsche of the insane asylum — able to write anything, and does even a remote possibility exist that he could be connected with such a work?

For many critics, the veil of insanity was drawn before Nietzsche's eyes on 3 January 1889, and from that time on, although he may have experienced "some lucid hours" (as Kaufmann allows), he remained a hopeless case and was certainly quite incapable of writing anything on the order of *My Sister and I.* Nietzsche's sometimes bizarre behavior in the first months of his illness and his steady decline and incapacitation especially after 1893 conforms to the image of him with which we have been made most familiar.[5] However, Nietzsche did not in fact suffer from the illness to such an extreme degree at all times during the

---

[5] Podach, *kranke Nietzsche*, Frau Franziska Nietzsche's letters and the appendix of the book (209ff.) give an excellent account of Nietzsche's illness from the days at the Basel clinic to the beginning of April 1897. By 1892 (see 3 July 1892 [144] and 5 November 1892 [156]) even Nietzsche's mother had to admit that his mental condition had seriously deteriorated. Peter Gast himself admitted there was little hope as of 24 February 1890 (223-24). By June 1893 Nietzsche mumbles to himself (165) and must be conveyed in his wheelchair (166).

crucial first 14 months. Indeed, the precise state of Nietzsche's physical and mental condition at this point — and during the identical period when *My Sister and I* was supposedly penned[6] — has been vastly misrepresented.

Certainly there can be no question of physical debilitation. Dr. Baumann, the first physician to examine Nietzsche in Turin, remarks straight off: "Robust constitution, no physical illness."[7] It is significant that all reports during the first year and long after show Nietzsche to be physically robust. In fact, by October 1889 his mother clearly states that Nietzsche appears quite unchanged, "just as he looked in his healthiest days; he also looks quite healthy in his eyes (because I looked at them especially for that); he has his cheerful demeanor which the doctors call 'affectedly cheerful' " (*kranke Nietzsche* 44).

Although there is no denying that Nietzsche appeared at some periods at the beginning of his illness to be mentally out of

---

[6] *MSaI*. The text states (4) that Elisabeth suggested Nietzsche return to Paraguay with her "only a few days before her return to that country. . . ." In fact, Elisabeth returned to Germany on 21 December 1890 (Podach, *kranke Nietzsche* 105) and she did not leave again until the end of 1891. Despite this seeming discrepancy, numerous other places throughout the text refer to Nietzsche's confinement at Jena/Weimar. In addition, toward the end of the text, there is reference to Dr. Julius Langbein (sic) (Langbehn) who was involved with Nietzsche only from November 1889 through the first two months of 1890. These facts (the appearance of Elisabeth, Nietzsche's confinement at Jena, and the presence of Langbehn) restrict the date of any possible production of *My Sister and I* by Nietzsche from December 1889 to March 1890 before he was released.

---

[7] Podach, *Nietzsches Zusammenbruch* 107. Dr. Baumann also mentions Nietzsche's "Extraordinary intellectual ability, very good education, instruction most excellently successful," thus indicating that Nietzsche was capable of conducting an intelligent, intellectual conversation. Baumann's additional diagnosis of "Megalomania, mental weakness, diminution of memory and diminution of cerebral activity" still leaves great latitude in the *degree* of Nietzsche's impairment.

control and even outright violent, his mother's letters and other sources show that his behavior improved markedly over time. Thus it is perhaps more accurate to characterize Nietzsche in the first year of his illness as lapsing in and out of lucidity for varying lengths of time, for many reports show that he behaved very often in much the same manner as before his breakdown. For example, even at the very outset of his illness when Overbeck had him admitted to the Basel clinic, Nietzsche conversed amiably with Dr. Wille whom he immediately recognized as a psychiatrist with whom he had held a conversation on the topic of religious insanity years earlier. And yet, Overbeck knew that Nietzsche was anything *but* well (Overbeck 29). Still Nietzsche's condition to all appearances improved considerably after only ten months following his breakdown, for the journal entry for 1 October 1889 states: "In general, distinct remission" (Podach, "Krankenge-schichte" 1453).

In fact, reports show that Nietzsche was lucid much of the time during the period of January through March 1890 if not earlier. He was permitted out on walks with friends, relatives, and visitors precisely because of his improvement. A journal entry for 20 December 1889 even refers to Nietzsche after one such walk with a former student as exhibiting "No essential influence of the state of the illness" (Podach, "Krankenge-schichte" 1453). Moreover, both Nietzsche's mother and Peter Gast report that another physician named Dr. Langbehn took walks with Nietzsche mornings and afternoons daily for some three weeks from the end of December 1889 through January 1890. Gast, in fact, reports at one point that Nietzsche and Langbehn were able to converse "about the most refined things" (*kranke Nietzsche* 216). And we know that Langbehn probably bent Nietzsche's ear about his own book, *Rembrandt as a German*. Meanwhile, Nietzsche's attendants were likewise astonished "about the change and rapid improvement of Nietzsche" (*kranke*

Nietzsche 217).[8]

Thus, Nietzsche at the beginning of 1890 — during the precise time when *My Sister and I* may have been written — seemed to many who were intimate with the case to be vastly improved. Only Dr. Binswanger and Franz Overbeck did not see this as a hopeful sign. Still, the positive view of Nietzsche's health was not merely a case of wishful thinking. Simply, Nietzsche's condition at this time was so ambiguous that even his closest friend, Peter Gast, did not know even after some three weeks what to make of his mental state. He reports that Nietzsche would alternately seem in full control of his faculties and could recount anecdotes with astonishing accuracy, but at other times he would fictionalize things and give them a ghastly perspective. On the other hand, sometimes Nietzsche seemed quite indistinguishable from his old self (*kranke Nietzsche* 219). Indeed, Gast writes Overbeck on 20 February that he truly feels that Nietzsche might simply prefer to be considered mad: "he would be approximately as thankful as one who jumps into a river to kill himself and would then be pulled out alive by a dumb ass of a livesaver" (*kranke Nietzsche* 222). Gast, in fact, tells Overbeck flatly that he had seen Nietzsche in situations in which it seemed to him that the man was actually only feigning madness (222-23).

Meanwhile, reports from every quarter not only point to Nietzsche's relatively unchanged behavior but add that his memory of past events, people, literature, dates, and names was nothing less than astounding. Indeed, his skill at the piano was still so astonishing that Peter Gast was moved to write his friend

---

[8] *kranke Nietzsche.* Frau Nietzsche's letters of 21 November 1889 (47-51), December 1889 (52-53), and 8 January 1890 (53-57) give details about his walks. Her observations on Nietzsche's improvement are corroborated by Gast (8 January 1890, 217) and his reports on his visit with Nietzsche (219-24). See also report of Alwine (the Nietzsches' maid 85) who states: "the Professor does not seem to me to be sick at all; his manner is so natural and he laughs exactly as before" (7 June 1890).

Widemann: "if you heard it! Not a single blunder! Nothing but combinations full of Tristan-like spirit; pianissimi and then again trombone choirs and trumpet fanfares and Beethovenesque fury and exultant singing and musing, dreaming — it can't be described. . . . Bring a phonograph!" (*kranke Nietzsche* 220-21). Gast, moreover, reports the same episode to Carl Fuchs on the same day, and adds that "The effect afterward on his cerebral system was very powerful; he was as transformed afterward. Exquisite! Today he read in a book that Naumann sent me and in which Nietzsche is often quoted; that also brought him remarkably to his senses" (*kranke Nietzsche* 221; *Zusammenbruch* 164). Nietzsche, thus, also read and enjoyed critical material concerning his own works. Clearly, up to March 1890 Nietzsche exhibited remarkable abilities that more closely reflected his behavior before the breakdown and that were by no means restricted to "a few lucid hours."

But to produce a book of the style and scope of *My Sister and I* under such conditions as Nietzsche lived at the time, he would have required not only the mental capacity to write but also the desire, the opportunity, and the practical ability to do so. Did he possess these as well?

The combined effect of entries in Dr. Ziehen's journal that Nietzsche lost all interest in his previous writings after the breakdown and could no longer even write legibly,[9] coupled with the strange contents of his last letters to Peter Gast, Jacob Burckhardt, Cosima Wagner, Bismarck, and others, has always given

---

[9] Podach, "Krankengeschichte." See Dr. Ziehen's journal 20 February 1889, 1 March 1889, 19 April 1889, 5 May 1889. Nietzsche's mother also reports on 1 November 1889 (*kranke Nietzsche* 45) that although he was willing to write a few lines to his sister, "His handwriting is, however, unintelligible." What he wrote also did not seem to make sense to her. Overbeck also writes Gast early on that Nietzsche did not request any writing material during the trip from Turin (Overbeck 37). Overbeck also speaks bluntly of what he considers to be Nietzsche's "Incapability of writing."

the impression that Nietzsche was completely unable to write anything coherent.[10] Yet this impression is false.

In the first place, overlooked entries in Dr. Ziehen's journal show that Nietzsche definitely expressed interest in his own works, as does the entry for 22 January 1889 where Nietzsche requests that his compositions be brought to him. Next, Gast's letter to Fuchs indisputably reveals that Nietzsche enjoyed reading critical matter in which his own works were quoted. Moreover, both the journal and other reports show that Nietzsche continued to read diverse materials while he was at Jena and afterward.[11] That he did not read more, and more often, was by the design of his doctors and his mother. In fact, there is absolutely no question that Nietzsche desired to read his own works, for as his mother writes to Overbeck: "With respect to your worthy inquiry whether he still is interested in his own works, I can only say that he would gladly read them if I were to permit him to do so" (*kranke Nietzsche* 97).

Moreover, it is clear from both the reports and correspondence that Nietzsche not only continued to read — he also continued to write while he was at Jena. Even in Nietzsche's most demented condition, he could not resist the impulse to write on walls or scribble on scraps of paper that he had secreted. It is also significant that the journal entry for 27 August 1889 reveals that Nietzsche possessed a notebook while in the asylum — a perfectly useless item for a madman who had no interest in writing. And

---

[10] Podach, *Friedrich Nietzsches Werke des Zusammenbruchs*, especially plates XVII, XXII, XXIII, XXIV, XXVI, and XXIX. See also Schlecta, *Werke* 3: 1349-52 for transcribed letters.

---

[11] Podach, "Krankengeschichte." See Dr. Ziehen's journal 29 April 1889, 5 September 1889. See also *kranke Nietzsche* on the following pages for indications that he continued to read: 4, 19, 31, 33, 36, 60, 77; he reads music, 87.

Gast writes Widemann on 15 February 1890 that Nietzsche "wants to write again" (*kranke Nietzsche* 222).

But the clearest indication that Nietzsche not only had the desire to write but did so in secret comes from his mother who reports in her letter of 3 August 1889 that she accompanied her son through the asylum:

> but then he found a pencil and, since I had an old enve-lope, he began to write on it and was happy to be in his element. I also could not prevent him from taking this pencil and another one out of the auditorium as well as paper which we finally discovered; and when I also said jokingly to him, "old Fritz, you are really a little pack rat," he thought, saying in my ear as he took his leave quite cheerfully: "But now I will have something to do when I creep back into my hole." (*kranke Nietzsche* 36)

Just how much writing of value Nietzsche accomplished when he crept back into his hole will never be known. But clearly, during almost the entire time he was at Jena, he possessed the mental capacity to write, the desire, the materials, and the opportunity to do so. If what Nietzsche did had amounted to some sort of crime, he would in all probability be judged guilty. Meanwhile, his mother's observation that he was "in his element" when he was writing in the asylum is most instructive, for as others have noted, Nietzsche led a solitary life and communicated best primarily with himself and through writing. Nietzsche's *Archives* demon-strate this fact abundantly. Although the notable gap in his life is the period at Jena, the fact remains that all of the prerequisites exist for Nietzsche to have produced something — perhaps even something on the order of *My Sister and I.*

We would be remiss if we did not also mention the fact that Nietzsche had seemingly managed to maintain a sense of humor at Jena. For example, when his mother told him of the death of Bernhard Förster, his brother-in-law and a man whom Nietzsche absolutely loathed, Nietzsche characteristically remarked: "It's no wonder, a man like Förster who has already exacted so much from his nervous system from the antisemitic business and had to break into a whole new field there [in Paraguay] — along with the worries about the means for it — simply overtaxed his nerves, etc." (*kranke Nietzsche* 44). And how else is one to interpret his remark to his mother when one day he beheld the insane asylum in which he was confined and asked: "When will I get out of this palace?" (*kranke Nietzsche* 45). Clearly, Nietzsche was still capable of using euphemisms and irony on a sophisticated level.

And yet the predominant opinion of the doctors at Jena was that Nietzsche behaved erratically and spoke gibberish. Dr. Ziehen's diagnosis typically states: "The facial expression is assured and self-confident, often self-complacent and affected. He gesticulates and continually speaks in an affected tone and uses pompous words and, indeed, sometimes in Italian, sometimes in French" ("Krankengeschichte" 1452). In truth, neither Nietzsche's gestures nor his use of language had probably changed very much from before the breakdown. It is for this reason that his mother says that the doctors believed him to be acting in an affected manner — ergo abnormal — when she knew that he was just acting like his old self (*kranke Nietzsche* 44). Gast also vigorously complains that the doctors have a completely mistaken opinion about Nietzsche: "They think of him as a German professor that idled away his time and went crazy in Italy, whose slow ruin they have only to preside over" (*kranke Nietzsche* 217).

However, the most compelling evidence on the true state of Nietzsche's mental acuity at this time comes from another member of the Jena staff, Dr. S. Simchowitz, whose important report on Nietzsche's condition has been relegated to the footnotes of the case. Simchowitz, basing his report on personal conversations with Nietzsche, directly contradicts his colleagues and shows that Nietzsche was not acting as confused or as affected as asserted. Indeed, the picture he presents is perfectly consistent with our evidence and with the reports of Nietzsche's relatives and close friends. Simchowitz states that at first he was nonplussed; he had never heard anyone speak that way before. But then he continues:

> Later, when I read Nietzsche, it became clear to me what had puzzled me so. For the first time I sensed the magical effect of the Nietzschean style. For he spoke just as he wrote. Terse sentences full of peculiar word combinations and ingenious antitheses; even the interspersed French and Italian phrases which he particularly loves so much in his last writings were not lacking. His manner had nothing of the professor or the lecturer in it. It was a chat, and one recognized a man of the best education by the soft tone of his sympathetic voice and by his elegant mimicry and gesturing. (*Frankfurter Zeitung*)

If one recalls the reports of others like Dr. Baumann in Turin and contrasts these with Dr. Ziehen's diagnosis, it is obvious that Nietzsche's pattern of behavior had been consistent. In all probability the doctors at Jena rashly misinterpreted Nietzsche's use of language and gestures and dismissed his behavior from the start as aberrant and affected. In truth, however, even though Nietzsche's mind was steadily deteriorating, his conduct during this period appeared to others to have remained relatively unchanged. When we add this to Simchowitz's report and to the fact that Nietzsche still desired to write, that he had both the mental capacity as well as the opportunity to do so — and at precisely the same time when *My Sister and I* was supposedly penned — the questions about this mysterious manuscript loom too large to be ignored any longer.

If there is any connection between *My Sister and I* and Nietzsche, it could have a significant effect not merely on Nietzsche scholarship but also on history's estimation of his contribution to Western thought. Indeed, we have demonstrated that some tantalizing coincidences between the text and Nietzsche's writings may counterbalance the criticism of the past. On the other hand, *My Sister and I* is riddled with a number of perplexing problems — only a few of which have been touched on here — that do not easily yield to the usual explanations.

We may never know for certain just who the real author of this curious book might be. What we can say, however, is that a much more thorough investigation needs to be undertaken before we can even begin to make any serious judgments about the questions of authorship and authenticity. We have also clearly shown that no possibility should be ruled out, not even the possibility that Nietzsche himself may have played a role here, since the flawed criticism of Kaufmann and others presents no real case for fraud. In the end we must also ask ourselves what imagined or real value a forgery of this kind could possibly have and who, indeed, would have had the slightest interest in revealing such tawdry details of Nietzsche's life as litter the pages of *My Sister and I*. When we can answer such questions with any certainty, we may better be able to discuss the problems of authorship and authenticity. Until then, however, the case of *My Sister and I* remains open to scrutiny, and the book itself remains catalogued as the last work of Friedrich Nietzsche.

[Originally published in *Thought*, September 1986, Vol. 61 No. 242.]

AUTHOR'S ADDENDA

Editorial proscriptions concerning the original length of "*My Sister and I:* The Disputed Nietzsche" in *Thought* necessitated the exclusion of some salient points, to wit:

1) Montinari's first fragment also states in brief: "Frau Cosima Wagner ist bei weitem die vornehmste Natur die es gibt, und, im Verhältnis zu mir, habe ich immer ihre Ehe mit Wagner immer nur als Ehebruch interpretiert . . . der Fall Tristan" (380). ("Cosima Wagner is by far the most noble individual there is, and, in relation to me, I have always only interpreted her marriage to Wagner as adultery . . . the case of Tristan.") This statement makes a clear connection to many such assertions in *My Sister and I* that Nietzsche had also been intimate with Cosima using the imagery of Tristan and Isolde's adulterous affair. For example, at one point in the book, Cosima is likened to Isolde and Nietzsche to Tristan in the identical context when the author states:

> It was under the leading-strings of Cosima that I first learned to take the initial steps in the world of great lies which are called absolute truths. The betrayal of my best friend sickened my conscience to the point of death, but she *cured* me by convincing me that my conscience in itself was a sickness contracted in Naumburg in an atmosphere of Lutheran prudery and hypocrisy. She masked her brutish adultery behind the pious pretense of pure, self-denying love, and Tristan, in his amorous dalliance with Isolde, was made to feel like a brave knight of the Ideal, fighting the cant and idiocies of Philistine morals. (*MSaI*, 175)

Whether or not Nietzsche actually was intimate with Cosima is immaterial. The point is, as Montinari's fragment clearly shows: Nietzsche, by the end of 1888, regarded his relationship to Cosima in the framework of adultery, and he employed the image of Tristan and Isolde to express it. This evidence casts quite a different light on the well-known statement that Nietzsche made at the onset of his illness that Cosima was his wife — a statement so absurd on its face that it would quite naturally be attributed to the ravings of a madman. But a claim of adultery is a different proposition altogether, and the only other place where such a bold assertion is made is in *My Sister and I* where the author employs the identical imagery as that of the Montinari fragment.

2) The possibility that the forger may be either Samuel Roth or David George Plotkin, as Kaufmann insists, seems unlikely. In the first place, no forger could have been aware of all of the details we have given here. Although Roth knew German, published substantially, and was embroiled in questionable publishing practices, he was never associated with a forgery of any kind. Furthermore, there are compelling reasons why Plotkin's supposed confession should be rejected on its face. Plotkin was not widely published. In terms of philosophical and and political perspective, the opinions revealed in *My Sister and I* stand against everything Plotkin ever wrote (see *Rage in Singapore* [New York: Wisdom House, 1942], and especially *The Plot Against America* [Missoula, Montana: J. E. Kennedy, 1946]). Finally, neither the writing style of Roth or Plotkin appears to be very similar to that of *My Sister and I*.

3) A glaring discrepancy in *My Sister and I* is the consistent misspelling of Dr. Julius Langbehn's name as "Langbein" (*MSaI* 205). Such an obvious error by a forger is beyond comprehension, especially in light of the fact that Langbehn's name is not misspelled in this or any other way in any biography, and his works comprise some thirty-three entries in the *National Union Catalog of Pre-1956 Imprints* (London: Mansell, 1974, Vol. 314,

pp. 585-87). The error might well be ascribed to a typographical mistake, to extreme clumsiness, or even to extreme cleverness in the case of a forger who wished to second-guess future criticism. But there may be a more practical explanation. Simply, the linguistically archaic "behn" portion of Langbehn's name is phonetically close to the more modern orthographic form, "bein." Anyone who saw the name in print but had only heard it in conversation could easily mistake the spelling. Since only Nietzsche himself was in such a singular situation, this evidence must be added to the list of coincidences that connect him with the book.

Walter K. Stewart is a Professor of German and Philosophy who has published widely in literary criticism, folklore and mythology, as well as in philosophy for the Colloquia Germanica, The Encyclopedia Hebraica, The Encyclopedia of American Popular Beliefs and Superstitions, The Germanic Review, The German Studies Review, The Goethe Society of North America, Seminar, *and* Thought. *His published work concerns a range of topics from Goethe's* Faust *to Thomas Mann's* Death in Venice, *including a major theoretical work on* Time Structure in Drama *(Rodopi, 1978). His current research in philosophy concerns epistemology and metaphysics.*

WORKS CITED

Andreas Salomé, Lou. *Lebensrückblick.* Zürich: Max Niehans Verlag, 1951.

Barzun, Jacques. *Berlioz.* Boston: Little Brown, 1950.

Beau, Two Worlds Monthly. Ed. Samuel Roth. 3 vols. New York, 1926-1927.

Bernoulli, Carl A. "Nietzsches Lou Erlebnis." *Raschers Jahrbuch* 1 (1910): 225-60.

Binion, Rudolf. *Frau Lou.* New Jersey: Princeton UP, 1968.

Förster-Nietzsche, Elisabeth. *Das Leben Friedrich Nietzsches.* 3
vols. Leipzig: Naumann, 1904.

——————, trans. *The Nietzsche-Wagner Correspondence.* New
York: Boni and Liveright, 1921.

Kaufmann, Walter. "Herr Nietzsche's 'Lost Confessions.' " Rev.
of *My Sister and I*, by Friedrich Nietzsche. *Milwaukee
Journal* 24 Feb. 1952.

——————. *Nietzsche.* 3rd ed. New York: Vintage Books, 1968.

——————. "Nietzsche and the Seven Sirens." Rev. of *My Sister
and I*, by Friedrich Nietzsche, *Partisan Review* 19 (May/June
1952): 372-76.

——————. "Re: Nietzsche's *My Sister and I*." Reply to Alfred
Werner. *Aufbau* 9 May 1952, Vol. XVIII no. 19: 8.

——————. Rev. of *My Sister and I*, by Friedrich Nietzsche.
Philosophical Review 64 (Jan. 1955): 152-53.

Krueger, Kurt. *I Was Hitler's Doctor.* New York: Biltmore
Publishing, 1943.

Levy, Oscar, trans. *Selected Letters of Friedrich Nietzsche.* New
York: Doubleday, 1921.

Mann, Thomas. "Meine Meinung uber *My Sister and I*." Letter.
Aufbau 16 May 1952, Vol. XVIII no.20: 5.

Marcuse, Ludwig. "Ein Stück aus dem literarischen Tollhaus."
Rev. of *My Sister and I*, by Friedrich Nietzsche. *Aufbau* 18
April 1952, Vol. XVIII no. 16: 11-12; and 25 April 1952, Vol.
XVIII no. 17: 11-12.

——————. "Meine Nietzsche-Artikel und ihre 'Hinter-
gründe.' " Letter. *Aufbau* 16 May 1952, Vol. XVIII no. 20: 5.

Meyer, Dr. Paul. "Ueber Dr. Oscar Levy." Letter. *Aufbau* 2 May
1952, Vol. XVIII no. 18: 7.

Montinari, Mazzino. "Ein neuer Abschnitt in Nietzsches *Ecce
Homo.*" *Nietzsche Studien* 1 (1972): 380-410.

Nietzsche, Friedrich. *My Sister and I.* New York: Boar's Head,
1951.

——————. *Nietzsches Briefwechsel: Kritische Gesamtausgabe.* Ed. Giorgio Colli and Mazzino Montinari. 3 Sections, 20 vols. Berlin: Walter de Gruyter, 1975-1984.

——————. *Nietzsches Werke: Kritische Gesamtausgabe.* Ed. Giorgio Colli and Mazzino Montinari. 8 Sections, 20 vols. Berlin: Walter de Gruyter, 1967-1982.

——————. *The Philosophy of Nietzsche.* Trans. Thomas Common. New York: Modern Library, 1954.

——————. *Werke in drei Bänden.* Ed. Karl Schlechta. 8th ed. 3 vols. Muchen: Carl Hanser Verlag, 1977.

——————, Paul Rée and Lou von Salomé. *Die Dokumente ihrer Begegnung.* Frankfurt: Insel Verlag, 1970.

Overbeck, Franz. "Briefe an Peter Gast." *Die neue Rundschau* 17 (1906): 26-51.

Peters, H. F. *Zarathustra's Sister.* New York: Crown, 1977.

Placzek, A. K. "Nietzsche Discovery." Rev. of *My Sister and I,* by Friedrich Nietzsche. *Saturday Review of Literature* 2 Feb. 1952: 19-20.

Podach, Eric F. *Der kranke Nietzsche.* Wien: Bermann-Fischer Verlag, 1937.

——————. *Friedrich Nietzsches Werke des Zusammenbruchs.* Heidelberg: Wolfgang Rothe Verlag, 1961.

——————. "Nietzsches Krankengeschichte." *Medizinische Welt* 4 (1930): 1452-54.

——————. *Nietzsches Zusammenbruch.* Heidelberg: Niels Kaufmann Verlag, 1930.

Reichert, Herbert. "The Present Status of Nietzsche: Nietzsche Literature in the Post-War Era." *Monatshefte* 51 (March 1959): 103-20.

Rosenthal, Maud [née Levy]. "Rediscovered Nietzsche." Letter. *Saturday Review of Literature* 5 May 1952: 28-29.

——————. "Wer schrieb *My Sister and I.*" Letter. *Aufbau* 30 May 1952, Vol. XVIII no. 22: 10.

Schäffle, Andreas. *Die Quintessenz des Sozialismus*. Gotha: Friedrich Andreas Perthes, 1875.

Simchowitz, Dr. S. "Der kranke Nietzsche." *Frankfurter Zeitung* 7 Sept. 1900, Abendblatt.

Two Worlds: A Literary Quarterly. Ed. Samuel Roth. 2 vols. New York, 1925-1927.

Union Catalog of Pre-1956 Imprints. 685 vols. London: Mansell, 1968-1980. Vol. 419: 233-66.

Werner, Alfred. "Der Pseudo Nietzsche." Letter. *Aufbau* 2 May 1952, Vol. XVIII no. 18: 7.

——————. "Eine Erwiederung." Reply to Ludwig Marcuse. *Aufbau* 30 May 1952. Vol. XVIII no. 22: 10.

Advertisement for the Two Worlds Quarterly, *1926.*

Advertisement for My Sister and I, *1953.*

Elisabeth Nietzsche as a teenager in Naumburg.

Lou von Salomé.

Lou von Salomé, Paul Rée and Friedrich Nietzsche,
May 13, 1882.

Richard and Cosima Wagner, 1870.

Elisabeth Nietzsche, 1881.

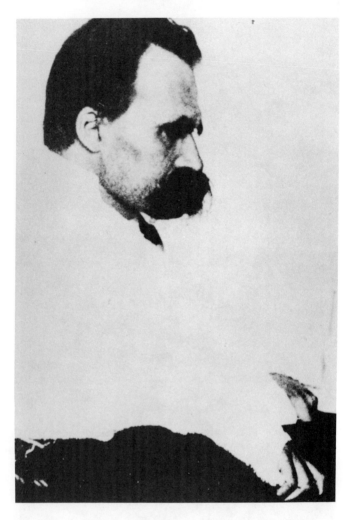

Photographs of Nietzsche taken by Hans Olde as part of his commission to paint a heroic portrait of the dying philosopher in Summer 1899.

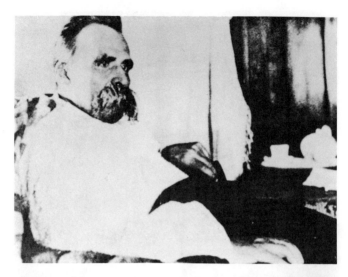

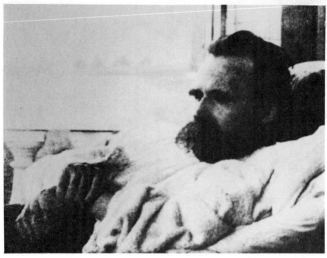

FRIEDRICH NIETZSCHE

Nietzsche's death mask, August 1900.

MY SISTER AND I

CHAPTER ONE

1

I had a dream last night. Or should I say a nightmare? A nightmare is something which rises out of the subconscious into the conscious, loaded with shock and unpleasantness, to punish or frighten us. But what happened to me last night was a presentiment frenzied with happiness. If I think of it as a nightmare it is because, unlike ordinary dreams, which rise and fall in shadow, this one was deep and clear, and still remains with me, instead of fading away.

It appeared to me that the last citadel of the enemy had fallen. The old woman — whom I have hated more and more intensely every day since childhood — was dead. With my own eyes I saw her locked in a wooden box, dropped into a hole in the ground covered with lime. I was at the cemetery with a group of dark, wailing people none of whose faces — except that of Elisabeth, half embraced at my side — I saw clearly. Did it stem from the malevolent visit they paid me yesterday afternoon?

The dream went on from the cemetery into a carriage which brought my sister and me home (*where that could be I could only wonder*). In a long, clattery ride not a word passed between us. We sat huddled into each other and let the empty, bitter, futile years, marred for us by that tyrannous presence, melt down to their chemical elements. I felt the way the earth must feel when winter's ice gives way for the new crop of flora and vegetation. My heart ached with anticipation.

The same warmth must have welled up in Elisabeth, too. I surmised this, as we always do in dreams, in an emotional tide not as clearly directed as in life, but none the less real. Once when I stole a surreptitious look at her cold, handsome face I caught a faint smile in the corner of her mouth, which mounted swiftly to her wonderful luminous eyes. But for the presence of the driver (masked like the people at the funeral) I might have tried to kiss her.

If a thought can be conveyed from one person to another in associated words conceived but not uttered, this was my first communication to Elisabeth upon reentering this dreamhouse *(so strangely familiar to me as it sits in my recollection): There are three empty beds in this house, and two of them shall remain unslept in for as long as I am able to influence you . . .*

This thought would never occur to Elisabeth herself. Suggested to her, it would most certainly be reacted to violently and unfavorably. My sister's world is one of scattered sunlight and shadows, the sunlight of her true passions and the shadows of the false ideas with which the world has bewitched her. Under no circumstances can she be expected to function as definitely and as imperiously as I do. But the seed of the thought can be planted in her mind. With a sick brother, so badly in need of kindness and sympathy, who can tell what will happen?

By all that has passed between us (in our childhood years directly, and directly and indirectly later) she is neither my sister nor any of the other things — such as adviser and helper — which she would like me and the world to believe her to be. For me, Elisabeth is primarily a woman — the warm sunny harbor toward which my whole life gravitates.

2

It was so sunny and delightful in the cemetery, it shines powerfully into my dream. Cemeteries — those roofless palaces of rich and poor alike, which we visit only when we have to, and never find unpleasant or disappointing — are really the warmest and the most enduring of the habitations which we build for ourselves. Winter or summer they greet us with their open-armed candor: *Welcome, old friend. So you have come to look over your final resting-place?*

Did you ever notice the little round stones behind the big square tombstones? Don't tell this to anyone, but they're really the marbles the occupants of the graves play with to while away the tedious hours they have to spend on their rounds among the living, when night falls and the grim, tired overseers retire to their potato-soups and dank beds.

I keep thinking of those fatuous people who defy the angel Gabriel by instructing their heirs to burn their remains and scatter the ashes of their flesh and bones to the four winds. Personal immortality is a foolish enough and unreasonable enough assumption to go on. But to fight it so hard, and with such violent maneuvers, is not that even more unreasonable?

A wind grew up in my dream and blew through the streets of its *terra incognita* as the carriage took us on and away from the cemetery. I listened closely to it as its noise rose above the faint groaning of the wheels of the carriage. It seemed to be pursuing Elisabeth and me and trying to tell us something. Could it be the same little wind which finally drowned out the voice of the holy man who made so much empty prattle about the old woman's lovingkindness and virtue?

I talk to it in a whisper so that Elisabeth will not hear me: *Is it something I left in the cemetery that I should have taken along with me, little wind? But what could that be? Certainly not hope or strength or ambition or desire — least of all, desire, for all that I desire is with me, sitting next to me, snuggled against me as only love can snuggle, Femina personified.*

3

3

What threw me into such a heat yesterday afternoon was my sister's sudden unaccountable suggestion that the best thing for me would be to leave this awful place and go with her to live in Paraguay. (This only a few days before her return to that country to settle her affairs).

I thought you didn't like Paraguay, I reminded her.

For myself, not, she admitted.

Then why for me?

For you it might mean to be reborn.

Like Jesus?

She shrugged. *There you go, uttering sacrilege. Don't you know the effect that sort of thing has on mother?*

It doesn't kill her. And if it did, I know that it wouldn't be long before she'd be back to haunt me, and you too, for that matter.

It's not you who are unkind to us, but your illness.

O precious illness! But I won't consider going to Paraguay, so let us have an end to that. In the first place, it's too far away; the journey alone would kill me if your society didn't. In the second place, your late husband has probably so beloused Paraguay with his antisemitic rubbish that it would be almost as bad a place to live in as Germany.

Worse, I could have told her. Antisemitism in a place where you can occasionally get a glimpse of a genuinely homely Jewish face is one thing. Where there are only empty Christian faces to greet one, it must be all but impossible to breathe.

For all of its rampant antisemitism, I surmise, there cannot be enough things in Paraguay to hate, to make supportable the regular steady miseries of life. But for the true hater, Germany is the place. There is, first of all, the Kaiser; one could spend a profitable lifetime detesting him alone. Then there is Bismarck, as a source of loathing a treasure comparable only to his master. And should one go out of one's mind, as I am supposed to be doing, and forget both master and servant, the sight of any good German burgher on the street should be a sufficient reminder to a sensitive person that the function which renders man superior even to the Lord of Hosts Himself is the ability to hate with all of his heart everything he was taught in childhood to revere and honor . . .

4

Among the things they brought me yesterday afternoon was a letter from August Strindberg, and it was only by pleading with them that I was finally allowed to keep it. Here it is:

I have been thinking of you for all of three days. I write in the hope that by doing so I shall finally dismiss your image from my mind so that it may be able to turn to matters more agreeable to my eyes and profitable for my soul.

The wretched business started with my finding a photograph of you at the bottom of page four of my morning newspaper. It is something, I suppose, to get oneself into the public prints. But should not one be careful of the means by which one does this?

What a photograph! Do you really look like that — like the Mephisto of a third-class road show of Faust?

When I've forgotten that awful image of you I'll write again.

Strindberg likes to tease. I believe he's jealous of me because Brandes pays so much more attention to me than to him. Besides, he's a natural tease. He teases me and he teases the world, but most of all he teases himself.

5

I have only a fleeting recollection of my father. I remember that he was tall, and that he had warm, good brown eyes which seemed to delight in everything they saw. Towards my aged aunts, who overflowed our house, his behavior was painfully respectful. Towards my mother, his deportment can only be described as worshipful. Was this over-solicitude of my father for the embodiment of the groove of my origin responsible for the abysmal hatred which I early conceived for her?

6

My sister Elisabeth's eyes followed my father as devotedly as my father's eyes followed the slow, apprehensive figure of my mother. She once explained to me in a whisper that father would not take a morsel of food or a drop of water into his mouth unless he was absolutely certain that everything was well with mother and the rest of the females of the house. I often wondered about this, especially as to the doors of influence it may have opened up in my own life.

7

It first happened between Elisabeth and me the night our young brother Joseph died, though we had no idea that he was dying when she crept into my bed, pleading that it was cold where she was, and she knew how warm I always was. As a matter of fact, this was not true. Even in these early days, chills seized me and held on to me at the oddest and most unexpected times. And I was particularly cold that night . . . All afternoon little Joseph had kept the household in turmoil with his screaming and gasping . . . Suddenly I felt Elisabeth's warm little hands in mine, her hissing little voice was in my ear, and I began feeling warm all over.

8

I never managed to attend one of father's self-managed concerts. When he played in the house we all attended with the breathlessness yielded only to religious ceremonies of a high order. I learned how to read and write directly from him. It was due to him, too, I guess, that I acquired my desperate devotion to music — heaven help me.

9

Next to my father, my maternal grandmother was the ruling element of my half-smothered childhood. It was she who managed our removal to Naumburg-an-der-Saale, which had been her own home by her marriage. Some of the most important people in town made a point of coming to see her, with my mother shrinking more and more into the background. The only time my grandmother herself was superseded was when Grandfather Oehler had me transferred from public school to a private school. "A born scholar like this lad should at least be pampered in his schooling," he growled, in his aloof, good-natured way.

10

The Bible was the book of my childhood. In it I read and thought seriously before I could take any other book to heart. I had to read it, of course, but I do not remember that I ever resented it. My strict adherence to it and to all religious ceremonies as they came along, earned me the name *little pastor* among the children of the neighborhood. As our pastor was held in very high regard by all members of the family, it was long before I understood that the name was not bestowed on me in a spirit of praise.

11

I both loved and resented the wealth of warmth which Elisabeth brought to me in those unexpected hours of the night. I was usually in the midst of a sound sleep when she got into my bed, and thrilling as I found the ministrations of her fat little fingers, it also meant my being kept awake for hours and hours. Besides, though in my conscious nature I knew nothing about what was going on, I must have had a feeling that my sister was bringing into my life as accomplished facts sensations whose real value to a boy was in their being discovered as part of the experience of growing up. She was presenting me with triumphs I should by right attain only by my own efforts in a much more restricted world . . .

12

I gained complete freedom from Elisabeth's pryings only on those occasions — school holidays — when we both visited our grandparents Oehler at Pobles, and we were compelled to spend the nights in different rooms in different parts of the house. Those holidays were never long enough for me . . .

13

There are people — professional atheists for the most part — who claim that their religious skepticism came of being brought up in homes overburdened with religious dogma. It was entirely different with me. Whatever religious zeal occupied my house — and religion was never absent from it — I accepted with the same feeling with which I accepted the air I had to breathe in order to live. God might just as well have been a member of our household — as distant as Grandfather Oehler, though not nearly so humorous.

14

I began writing verses when I was ten years old. I must have written at least a hundred by the time I was twelve. Elisabeth showed me some of them a week before she sailed with Förster for Paraguay. It seemed unbelievable to me, only from a glance at them, that I could ever have been so vague and banal. I would have destroyed them if I could have got my hands on them. But Elisabeth slyly replaced them in her trunk. *They're mine*, she said.

Don't you remember? You wrote them for me. It is all I have left of your love. It was another way of reproving me for my friendship with Lou Salomé, which she never forgave me.

15

I used to combat Elisabeth's emotional assaults on me by trying to interest her in literature, music, philosophy, conversation in general. Conversation, as a discourse between two people, is, of course, hopeless of attainment by any woman. As for the other matters — which these days she discusses with so much authority — I couldn't so much as interest her in them. For the life of me I can't make out who did finally convert her — or why, or how.

16

The first family death to make a definite impression on me was that of my father; the second was that of my brother Joseph who was only two years old and could hardly have been said to have lived; the third and fourth were the deaths of my Aunt Augusta and Grandmother Nietzsche. With only poor Aunt Rosalie left of the oldsters, my mother began to assert herself, and by that time I knew as a certainty that I hated her.

At about that time, too, I remember, my eyes began to hurt me noticeably, and I got into the habit of caressing them regularly with my fingers. I became subject to violent headaches, and derived from them the first feeling of a challenge life was laying down to me. I began keeping a diary like this one — only I did not need it as much as I do this.

17

I never had the measles. The mumps got me, and I almost died of scarlet fever. Wagnerianism, which I contracted at seventeen, is a plague I cannot say I have ever been really cured of.

18

The two great events of my boyhood, as I see things now, were my loss of faith in religion and the dawning on me of the suspicion that the hundred or so poems I had written were not of the stuff of immortality. Of the two disillusionments I cannot say which wrought the greater havoc in my life. My religious faith has never been replaced by any faith worth mentioning. As for my belief in the importance of my destiny, concerning that, too, I have done a great deal of posturing and pretending . . .

19

I was nineteen when I got drunk for the first time. And even then I had to spoil it all by writing my mother a letter about it, in which I pleaded with her not to let the story spread. So tight was the knot which tied me to her apron.

20

All this is very fine and noble, but what I really want is a woman — any woman.

21

When I think of women, it is their hair which first comes to my mind. The very idea of womanhood is a storm of hair — black hair, red hair, brown hair, golden hair — and always with a greedy little mouth somewhere behind the mirage of beauty . . .

22

Oh, the many terrible, wonderful things I have missed on your account, my dark princess! You have left my mouth as dry as a bone in the sun. Heaven help you if we are both consigned to the same circle of hell.

23

Feet move forward of their own accord. Fingers close into fists. Hands rise and fall like pistons of an electric machine. But I myself do not rise — not even to my fiercest desire. I watch myself lying flat between my thighs, like another vermiform appendix. How much does love have to hurt to cause a hemorrhage?

24

I have small hands and feet like a woman. Could I have been meant to be a woman? Am I a miscarriage of the intention of my Creator?

25

The man with whom I am entrusting these notes in the hope that he will be able to get them to a publisher without the intervention of my sister or my mother is down with a bad cold. I dare not go near him lest, after this, my movements be observed more closely. I hope he recovers. Between coughing and retching he seems ready any moment to give up the ghost.

26

People fight out of many motives and furies, but the only time I ever fought with a lethal weapon and drew blood it was with a friend. After all the ink I have spilled on the subject I do not really know what I mean by *the good fight*. Perhaps if people fought with fiddles instead of with swords, aimed pianos at one another instead of howitzers . . .

27

This morning a bird flew by the window at which I sit making these notes. It was a brown bird with a blue breast and white-brown wings, and it slid by with such a lazy motion that it might have been God Himself making the rounds of the world and looking in on me, His most faithful servant. As I see things, God could be anything in the world, the world itself, or nothing. If He is just a potent principle out of which all things flow, like a new chemical out of a planned combination of chemicals, I don't think I care, and I am quite certain I am not interested.

28

I wonder if I would have hated Christianity with such ardor and abandonment if I had not surrendered so completely to its blandishments in the blameless days of my childhood.

29

In most matters — when my physical presence was not so far removed from her that she could forget me — it was Elisabeth and I against the world. But there was always in Elisabeth's makeup a love of the peace and comfort which usually goes along with acceptance of the *status quo*. No sooner had I left home for some distant place than a whole host of objections rose in her, and in her letters. Beginning with the appearance on the scene of the antisemite Förster even my presence did not influence her much . . .

30

A conversation of three or more people becomes a testing-ground of personal qualities, though it rarely decides anything more important than which of the contestants has the strongest voice. A conversation of two presents two monologues with a series of more or less patient interruptions.

31

Mother came to see me today to tell me that Elisabeth

has settled her affairs in Paraguay,[1] and is on her way back to Germany, to stay with us, never to leave us again. For a few weeks I have allowed myself the luxury of being unaware that she was around anywhere. My illness would never have come about, mother again assures me, if Elisabeth had been here instead of being in South America helping her insane husband sow seeds of hatred across the South Atlantic. I have nothing to say to her about this. I could tell her that perhaps I would never have been in need of any sort of help if it had not been for Elisabeth's initial interference in my life. If I did that I might have to tell her of the true state of affairs between her children, and then, almost immediately, there might be two of us confined here instead of one . . .

32

If I had yielded to the demands of my commoner nature which in every man cries out for peace with the *status quo* — I would have been either a musician or a theologian. I would have become a great heady mediocrity either way, to be sure. My ultimate choice — to become a philosopher — was, as a matter of fact, an act of profound cowardice. In the first place, I was afraid that I could never attain the stature of a Wagner, and in the second place I just could not talk myself into playing second fiddle to anyone, no, not even to God.

33

Try as I do, I can remember almost all of my early teachers in music and none of those who first talked to me on the subject of literature. Does that mean that it is easier to teach music or that the ears are more grateful than the eyes?

---

[1] Frau Förster returned to Germany only towards the end of her brother's confinement in Jena. The time-element in these notes is confused in more places than one. — Editor

34

When I left Bonn I felt like a fugitive. Only I did not understand. I was a fugitive not from Bonn but from life.

35

I am still running away. But from whom, from what am I running away now? I thought I had cleared all decks when I finished writing *Ecce Homo*. For what extraordinary reason is it so frowned on by my family and withheld from publication? There is nothing in *Ecce Homo* which I have not said at least once in my other books. Only in *Ecce Homo* I found myself in such good voice that I could define everything so much more sharply and clearly . . .

CHAPTER TWO

1

Shakespeare often makes an irresolute man the center of his plays, as in *Hamlet* and *Richard II*. His flabby characters are more real because they are more human; moral and spiritual flabbiness being the price we must pay for our mortality.

In my writings I have endowed myself with the most exquisite qualities, including Promethean stoicism. With the Shakespearean hero I have cried: *Rouse up thy youthful blood, be valiant and love.* But the weight of conscience has crushed me at last, added to the dead weight of age, and bone-cracking, paralyzing Bravery becomes me no longer — I am a miserable worm. No event interests me, except the great event of my approaching death.

Will I be outdated by an upsurge of democratic thought or will a new Caesarism place me among great apostles of force and violence like Bismarck and Treitschke? Strangely enough, what worries me most now will be people's reactions to my revelations with regard to my relations with my mother, sister and Lou Salomé. There are some things that must not be revealed without exposing the Holy of Holies to the profane eyes of the mob. Thus many of my friends will argue, and they will take me to task for dragging my mother, sister and sweetheart into the pit that I dug for myself and where I now lie helpless, unable to climb back into life.

Some critics will berate me in the same manner that Galileo

was condemned for insisting that the earth turns, thus inflicting a mortal wound on the Church which, they thought, could only survive in a static earth-centered universe, with heaven above and hell below. It is important, they will argue, to preserve the sacredness of certain conventions that mask our fear of the Beast. But I have dared in my philosophy to rip away every mask, every pretense from the mind of Man and trot him out on the stage of life in his bare and unashamed skeleton. What I have dared to do, with Everyman, shall I keep from doing with myself? Must I sink masked into the grave, a mortal and intellectual coward, I who have preached duty to Truth above all other duties?

My sky has been befouled by my relationship with four women, and as I lie dying the thunderclouds gather about me — these dark, brooding notes which I scrawl with painful, paralyzed fingers. The storm will break soon, and my sky, bat-winged with all the loathsome things pouring from my mind, will soon be fresh and clear as a meadow after a mountain rain has poured down upon it. When these notes are published, the storm will freshen the landscape of memory and quench the thirst of my dusty bones.

My death will not make me victorious over life, but my Confession will give me a certain immortality, for I dared to tear the veil from the Holy of Holies and show the naked spirit with all its putrid sores. Roused from the dream of life I am not able to challenge the reality of doom from the other side of the grave.

Il descend, réveillé, L'autre côté du rêve.[1]

My main task from now till death-day is to keep these notes from falling into the hands of my sister who best exemplifies the saying of Matthew: *By their fruits ye shall know them.* Fearing temptation, she has been tempted beyond what is common to

---

[1] "Awakened, he descends the other side of the dream." From Hugo's *"Contemplations."* — Editor

mankind, and has drawn me irresistibly toward her incestuous womb. But I urge the reader to remember the parable of the tares: the rank weeds of our being, if gathered up, may cause us to root up the wheat also. Despite her incestuous leanings, Elisabeth has been both a mother and a father to me. Without her strict discipline, my genius might have been blighted in early youth when I first realized that God was dead and that we were trapped in a whirling Void, a meaningless chaos of being.

When I am not angry with her, I see a great deal of bright, golden wheat in the Lama's[2] nature. If the tares look ugly to the reader, let him remember that they are not the whole of personality, but only the part which has never before been revealed to the sight of Man. But the eyes of Eternity have seen them before, and as I move speedily from time to timelessness, and I berate her bitterly, it is because in my present mood of desperation I am more acutely conscious of the Lama's faults than of her virtues.

Spirits soar to the stars, the wild spirits who have been hellbound, trapped in the vomit of incestuous desire. Elisabeth is Hugo's *fair devil* who has met *an impolite God*, but even a devil can sprout wings, for we were all once inhabitants of heaven. She will survive the mud of these notes which I splatter through a need to bathe myself clean — a shocking paradox of the psyche! . . .

If I could only express myself in a delicate fashion, to cast down an idol without chipping it or soiling its beautiful surface. But I am *the philosopher with the hammer*, a sworn enemy of all idolatrous cults, even the ancient Chinese cult of family-worship. There is nothing sacred to me, not even my own mother and sister! . . .

The die is cast; I have taken the fortress of my most intimate being. The corpses are sprawled beside the broken cannon and the dead leaves drop from the trees at last, at last . . .

---

[2] His nickname for his sister. — Editor

2

I have been a rebel against the universe, and the universe has wreaked its vengeance upon me. Tolstoy's notion that Love is at the heart of the cosmos has always caused the laughter in me to rumble. Now the laugh is on me.

Like Ulysses I stopped my ears with wax, bound myself to the mast of my ship and sailed out to meet the Sirens. But the Sirens did not shatter my ears with their song of love; my wax and my chains were useless against their wiles. For they had a more potent weapon than song to drive me out of my monastic cell into the delirium of frustrated love: instead of song they showered me with silence, the hailstorm of voiceless derision.

I have been fox-like in my guile, but Lou Salomé and the other sirens have out-foxed me: they clung to their perilous rocks, and I have dashed my head against them. The golden radiance that falls from their hair weighs heavily upon me like a coffin-lid. I can no longer love and therefore can no longer live, like a petrified forest whose gray branches are crumbling into dust. All I fear is the Lama's evil eyes, for she must suspect that, given the strength and the opportunity to evade her, I would in some way try to turn my slow dying into a victory over death. How better than by revealing my inner collapse in hasty notes such as these?

Yesterday she caught me agonizing in my nightmare world and tried to cheer me up by a favorable report from the doctors. She helped me to the front, where I sat facing the sunlight while she ransacked the drawers in my room in the hope of finding a diary. But, anticipating her desire to keep my confession from the public, I decided to entrust these notes to a neighbor, a peasant-like small merchant, who still thinks I am a master-mind and addresses me as *Herr Professor*, like my boarding-house cronies in Turin.

The great end of art is to strike the imagination with the power of a soul that refuses to admit defeat even in the midst of a collapsing world. Up to now my work has been artistic because of my refusal to cry out against my private doom. But now I bellow like a wounded bull who is tormented beyond animal endurance, and the Lama dreads such a revelation of me who have become synonymous with Stoic fortitude and indifference.

I have been broken on the wheel of Fate; I am dying in agony, but my dear sister already considers me dead and is only eager to save me for the deathless future, for the psychic immortality that Spinoza spoke about. She is already enjoying my immortality as famous men come here to pay their respects and to bring the flowers of flattery to my premature grave. She quotes my *Grave-Song*[3] to them: *Hail to you, will of mine! Only where there are graves are there resurrections.*

I smile in approval, but my will to affirm life above all suffering has dried up like water in an empty well. I am strangling in the airless void of the age, without love, without life, without the song of the Sirens to recall me back to my vital being once crowned with the evergreen garland of bliss. O singing birds of my hopes — where are you now? Your throats are cut and your blood gushes out upon the dry desert sands. And the Sirens are quiet, buried in the Great Silence of the Abyss.

I have demanded of life that it shape itself in my broken image: life is whole and entire, only I am shattered and ready for the dust-heap. The divine Nietzsche is not even human or sub-human, he is merely a disembodied howl in the screaming chaos of our times. Once on Portofino Mountain divinity descended upon me and I wrote the *fifth gospel* of Zarathustra. Now I cannot even seek shelter in my humanhood or brutehood; my body is paralyzed, my brain is turning to rock and my pall-bearers discuss

---

[3] In *Thus Spake Zarathustra.* — Editor

my greatness in my presence as if I were already laid out in my burial-clothes.

The sun is in its zenith. It is high noon in Weimar and Elisabeth is serving tea in the garden to some distinguished foreigners who have come all the way from Brazil — or is it Peru? — to see me in the flesh. Like an Egyptian mummy who somehow has forgotten to die entirely, I am the spectator of my own death, feeling my eyes turned into dust.

Oh love, love, come back to me, bringing life on your healing wings! . . . Ariadne,[4] I love thee! I love thee, Ariadne! Only my wife Cosima can carry me back to the love of the world where Dionysos and Jesus meet at the breast of the Eternal Woman, the Eternal Delight!

3

What Molière laughed at in order to keep from weeping Augier treated with solemn emphasis as befitted his bourgeois muse. When he makes his heroine[5] say: *I have my mother's heart*, he emphasizes the impact of heredity which is as implacable as the *ananke* of antiquity pursuing the tragic hero to his doom.

I have my mother's heart: her hypocritical virtue held me in bonds of iron all her life and I could only break away by attempt-

---

[4] This reference is, of course, to Cosima Wagner, whom Nietzsche associated with Ariadne in his *Dionysian Dithyrambs*. Out of Turin came the last tragic note of the mad Nietzsche: *Ariadne, I love thee. Dionysos*. And when he was taken to the asylum by his faithful friend Overbeck, he told the doctors with calm resignation: "It is my wife, Cosima Wagner, who has brought me here." From Nietzsche's confession we learn for the first time that his relationship with Cosima was more than spiritual and that his break with Wagner was fatal because it removed him from the beloved presence of his adored one, the implacable, irresistible and indestructible Cosima. — Editor

---

[5] Antoinette Poirier in *Monsieur Poirier's Son-in-Law*. — Editor

ing the impossible, the continuation of the desperate love-relationship with my sister who was equally in the grip of my mother's false modesty. We dared to go to violent extremities because we did not dare to hope for a normal sex-relationship — because our Mother with her Medusa-eyes turned our emotions into stone. This is the paradox of my existence: I have loved life passionately but have never dared to channel this love in the direction of normal erotic experience.

My mother's excess of modesty has poisoned the well-spring of my being. As I lost my father in early childhood, the waters of my life remained polluted without the necessary masculine chemicals to purify the source of my being. I have therefore inwardly raged against delicacy and modesty in women, and when Lou Salomé stormed me with the full impact of her erotic nature I surrendered to her with a sense of infinite relief — and delight.

But alas, like Augier's heroine, *I have my mother's heart.* She bowed to the ascetic ideal of the Christian to escape from the torture of the flesh, and although I tried to build a new heaven on the body of my beloved, my mother's God filled my paradise with the dreams of self-accusation so that my heaven became a hell, and I was driven like Adam out of my primal Eden. Instead of transfiguration, I suffered crucifixion, and my *Zarathustra the Atheist* was merely Nietzsche-Jesus affirming Life on the Cross, though secretly in terror of existence.

I have never cherished my proud loneliness; I have hungered for the passionate love of a woman who could redeem me from the terror of a world that has witnessed the death of God. As I wrote Elisabeth: *A profound man must have friends, unless he has a God. But I have neither a God nor a single friend!* With the tempest called love, Lou Salomé blew all the clouds away, all the dark clouds that hid God's widower from the sun of comradeship and communion. Now the clouds have rolled back, the sea has surged back upon the shore and drowned me in the welter of loneliness

21

while the bells of annihilation boom in my ears.

Once I set to music my tragic *Hymn to Life*, echoing the resounding harmonies of Wagner, who led me, through the blind alley of Christian asceticism, into the belief that eternal suffering is the price man pays for the cause of eternal truth. But this is merely the counsel of despair: as the waves of death gather about me I cry out more than ever against the hypocrisy of love, which is the scourge of modern society and which destroyed me through the indecent modesty of my mother.

That virtues may exist it is necessary to legitimize the pleasures of the flesh for the austerity of the pillar saints is not piety but pathology. Lou Salomé was modest in the truest sense of the word, for she set bounds to our passion and never permitted it to veer beyond the line of mutual enjoyment. We were never bored with each other, for she always kept a voluptuous reserve, a reservoir of feminine mystery that made her, like God, a source of infinite delight . . . O Lou, my lost paradise, there is no return to Eden, to the bliss that was and is no more. Like the gigantic shadows that trail us in the night, the kisses of our beloved dissolve suddenly in the darkness, without a hint of their golden rapture, without a touch of moonlight to soften the rough edges of black despair . . .

The winds die down, there is calm everywhere, but a mad storm rages in the heart, for the hour of death has arrived. O peace of men and places, O caves where souls may hide and find tranquil oblivion. O sweet refuge of mountains where Silence walks on feet of velvet and the brooks flow without a sound through raptures of quiet green! Why must my head split open with the roar of a thousand seas, I who loved the stillness of the mountains and walked alone through miles of utter silence? . . . Oh Lou, this is my punishment: I choked love to death, and its ghost drowns me in a rush of waters . . .

4

I had grown tired of the world from which I received nothing but abuse. Just as I had received the precious gift of love as a solace, it was snatched from me by the Vandal hands of my jealous sister. Even as the watchman who keeps guard over the purple towers of a city she kept guard over the purple towers of our incestuous passion.

Verily the love of a woman is a balm for the wounded soul, but incest is a closed garden, a fountain sealed, where the waters of life are dried up and the flowers bloom only to wither at the touch.

So I shrink inwardly into my despair, remembering nothing but the guilty kisses of her who blocked every exit to the life of love, dooming me to an all-consuming hatred for God, for Man and for myself which gathered round me like a formless dread, trapping me in self-terror, the fear of a man who has been unshadowed by the love that he has killed . . .

Let us love each other in unity of thought. The words ring in my brain like a bell, a bell of longing swung from a belfry in Tautenburg. Let us love each other . . . let us love . . . let us . . . love . . .

5

I have never ceased to educate myself, and even at the brink of the grave, while still in the flux of change, my comment on life changes with the surrounding tempest of events. My brain is still at work and weaving complexities of thought, while my shroud is being prepared and I am about to be gathered to my ancestors.

While other writers have written about nothing except people falling in love, I have postponed this trifling subject to the last, but now this personal side of life takes full possession of me: not art, not science, not philosophy, but falling in love has

usurped the whole landscape of my foundered being. There is no
other thing to talk about but the love that eludes us and which we
seek passionately like the sunken continent of Atlantis buried
beneath the ocean of the world's hatred.

Self-centered, solitary and alone, my brain no longer reaches
out for the life of art or ideas, but rides implacably towards the
harbor of her arms amidst the howling winds and raging tides of
being.

Oh Lou, let me surrender myself to my instincts of passion
and bliss! — Alas, it is too late: you are gone, and tomorrow I will
already be dead!

6

I am beginning to weary of my weariness, and I dream of a
remote future, forgetting that I am trapped in the paralysis of
death. It is the prerogative of a madman to dream that he is a
fatality, that he has cut in two the history of the world as I
thought I did in *Ecce Homo.* Not the world is being annihilated,
but I am; nature rejects ideas, even the most noble, in favor of
mere animal existence: Life is its own goal, and all my thoughts
are as chaff in the wind of cosmic destiny.

Deprived of my last veil of illusion — the power of ideas — I
gaze with terror upon the Void, but still I cling to existence, for
the fact of mere existence is all that is left in the shattered landscape of the intellect. All reasoning is a mode of self-deception,
but I cannot reason myself into a state of euphoria and imagine
that I can find happiness in the realm of death, sunk deep in
Nirvana. Oh, to be alive, to vegetate stupidly, but still to be *alive*
and feel the warmth of the sun!

In the absence of all desire there is still the desire to live,
even though every breath is an agony and death holds out the
promise of release from pain. Death is in our power, but life

never, and because life rejects us we cling to it with desperate firmness, like an infant gripping a bar of iron. As I fought for life in my mother's womb, I fight for life now, with the same blind panic, dreading the very thought of existence but still eager to break into the light of Day!

7

What is more terrible, as I have written, than Don José's last cry: *Yes, I have killed her, my Carmen, my Carmen whom I have adored!*? Yes, I have killed my Carmen with the dagger of my megalomania; I have destroyed her not because she refused to love me, but because I refused to love God, or even admit His existence. And the No-God has been terrible to me as He is terrible to all atheists, who deny the divine Love from which all love springs.

Now as I lie dying while the trees greet the spring with their new mantles of green, I know I am a dead leaf being carried away by the breeze and that the cosmic weather will leave not a trace of me, not even a faint hint of my demonic pride. Like the effaced generations, nothing will be left of me, while nature, with its imperishable order, will move from spring to winter and back again to spring! . . .

Oh my God, Lou, you were beautiful and twenty, eloquent with the eternal language of flowers, and I did not listen to you. I let the blight of Luther fall on the garden and wither every bud, every golden blossom. My father tripped over his pet dog and died of an illness of the brain, but my madness is self-inflicted, and I will have died because I struck a blow at Love — the love in you and the love in me. I fell at no door-step at night, I slipped through my own folly . . . Or is it the intention of Nature to decoy men into madness?

Verrà un giorno, said Goldoni, *che dei piccoli e dei grandi si farà*

25

nuovamente tutta una pasta.[6] That was the favorite remark of the Italian baker in Turin from whom I bought bread and rolls, and locked myself up in my room, fearful of my boarding-house comrades who fed me with Jean-Jacques Rousseau.

Against this egalitarian concept I have fought all my life; I have striven desperately to maintain the social space, *the pathos of distance*, between me and my inferiors. But who above the earth is inferior to me now? My limbs are paralyzed, my brain is cracking, and this great mind of mine, the greatest since Aristotle, is being kneaded into the dough of mass imbecility.

I am ready for Rousseau and Schiller; I am ready to exclaim with the author of Minna von Barnhelm: *Gleichheit ist allein das feste Band der Liebe.*[7] When one has been flattened out with the gutter, one is ready to espouse the cause of gutter-equality with all the vulgar proponents of democratic thought. *On with the Revolution!*

8

If Life offends us we have in some way offended Truth. Our former errors lie in wait for us and we are ambushed to ruin. All the generations struggle to reduce truth to unity, to a God-idea, to Justice, Love and Power. My God was Power, and in my powerlessness I realize that I have built upon foundations of sand.

Jesus said: *Therefore whosoever heareth these sayings of mine, and doeth them, I will liken him unto a wise man which built his house upon a rock; and the rain descended and the floods came, and the winds blew, and beat upon that house; and it fell not: for it was founded on a rock.*

---

[6] "A day will come when the small and the great will all be made again into one dough." — Editor

---

[7] "Equality is the only sure bond of love." — Editor

And every one that heareth these sayings of mine, and doeth them not, shall be likened unto a foolish man which built his house upon the sand; and the rain descended, and the floods came, and the winds blew, and beat upon the house, and it fell: and great was the fall of it.

My house has collapsed, and great was the fall of it. Antichrist lies in ruins before the indestructible feet of Christ shod with the love of the world, the love made manifest in deeds. O life, mock me not! *Thou hast conquered, Galilean, thou hast conquered in the very heart of thy greatest foe!*

Must I hide Christ's victory from my own soul to perpetuate the myth of Antichrist — the theme of my future biographers? Did not Ajax cry: *O Zeus, give us light, though thou slay us in the light!*? I have been slain and re-slain for the truth, and if Christ has laid me low for a moment or forever, must I deny him the laurels of victory? . . .

Credo quia absurdum: I believe the absolute absurdity of Jesus, but still I cannot be saved. To the very last I cannot surrender my pride of intellect, my conviction that Jesus must stoop to Nietzsche, even though he is a heap of ruins! No more enemies — no more hate — only a world-embracing love! That is no kingdom for me! I must have lightning and thunder, and die while the world crashes about my ears! . . .

I am scared with dreams and terrified with visions; like Job's, my skin breaks and is dissolved. But in all this dissolving world I can grasp at no Swedenborgian life-belt as Strindberg does. I can only sink traceless in the wild flood of being. I am hopelessly and irremediably lost . . . Like Napoleon I die amidst a terrible storm; the landscape is shattered, every tree is smashed, and nothing that I have ever hated or loved can survive me . . .

I have had the courage to innovate and thus astonished my contemporaries, who remained in the groove of God, though He was abolished in the thought of the age. Like Madame de Staël who dared to defy Napoleon, I dared to break down the Bastille

27

of conventional Christian morals. Even Voltaire thought God was necessary to save the millions from despair. Before me philosophers waged *cabbage wars*[8] against Christianity: I engaged in an all-out assault against the slave-morality of the Judeo-Christian.

This left me without a friend, and I was hermited in my loneliness. Out of my loneliness sprang the spooks of insanity, and so what happened is this: In crying out against the madness of God I have gone mad myself!

Everything can be acquired in solitude — except sanity.

9

A person can live only so long as he is drunk — drunk on wine, woman, ideas or Messianic passion. And in my Dionysian thirst I have been intoxicated with everything — even with the monkeydom of Darwin and the positivists.

But try as I may I cannot go Buddhist and get drunk on death. The idea of sinking into nothing horrifies me; like Dostoyevsky I am overcome by the frozen horror of eternity; to sleep for a billion years and never again see the dawn rising above the mountains . . . never again . . . never again.

That is why men need the myth of God. We are but a conglomeration of particles, accidental and meaningless, and this knowledge is too terrible to bear. Hence God or the man who takes His place in our fantasy . . .

We shall approach truth in proportion as we remove ourselves from life, said Socrates, about to drink the hemlock. Everything is vanity and a chasing after wind, but this Solomonic wisdom is hard to swallow. Until the very end I shall dream of her who first taught me the possibilities of romantic love. Against her kisses, Socrates, Schopenhauer, Solomon and Sakya-Muni are but envious eunuchs who have lost the zest for life.

---

[8] The phrase is Stendhal's. — Editor

Death is never better than life, despite Buddha and the saints. I who am dying know that there is nothing more tragic than a dead man, whether he is under the ground or walks as a living corpse through a world without faith in life or in the future . . . I have loved life in my mother's womb, and I love life now when my pall-bearers gather about me and wait for the signal to carry me into eternity.

10

I have suffered in my refusal to accept the consolations of other men: God and Immortality. But as Xerxes was in love with a plane-tree, I have clung to the trunk of a Utopian future and in this manner tried to recall God and immortality from the petri-fied forest of modern thought.

It has become fashionable to admire me for my negation of God, but my Zarathustra-optimism is merely Jehovah in disguise. Robber of God, I unbound myself from my atheistic knots and refused to let Him go, demanding a blessing from Him who is certainly dead.

But is God dead? What if I find myself face to face with Him — *Nietzsche-Antichrist* who built my life on the rock of unbelief? Perhaps I will bleed for the first time, as Lou did when, she con-fessed to me, at fifteen she was still a virgin and trembled in the presence of a man.

CHAPTER THREE

1

An anatomical story, a joke, a jest, something filthy and slimy in the nature of a common observation of an uncommonly delicate matter, has been going the rounds of this evil house, and has finally caught up with me. I use the word *anatomical* to describe this outrageous caricature of a story not because I am afraid of calling a dirty joke a dirty joke, but because the action wound about the word Germans commonly use to describe the vagina, and the careless use of that word has thrown me into a tumultuous series of reflections on the seriousness of things of the flesh as symbols of uncharted trends in our hidden, mysterious lives.

2

The story did not originate in this house. It is probably older than this house or this country and may even belong to an entirely different age. Yet it is personal not only to the one who first told it within these walls, but to everyone who has heard it retold, and to everyone who may some day find somber, unwilling residence here.

3

Whoever it was to whom the evil idea of telling the story in this dwelling of the mentally and spiritually wayward first occurred, it was he who set aside in his mind those elements of the purposeful and the accidental which rumbled in the foul depths of his belly, and rudely, violently mixed them to produce the first outburst of guffaws with which it was greeted. But is there, really, anything fundamentally comic in the aboriginal conception of the vagina as Nature's primary laboratory?

4

I have dreamed of my own mother's death, though under the circumstances in which I find myself, it is altogether possible, even likely, that she will outlive me. My mother — but do I really have to try to put on paper all the imaginable and unimaginable nonsense which rises into the top-layer of the human mind on the mere recollection of this word? All I can think of in connection with my mother, so heaven help me, if heaven there is anywhere, is that upon my father's death, less than six years after her marriage to him, she closed the door of her womb to all men and fixed a hostile eye for every male who came along and pleaded wordlessly with hands and eyes. That mine was the only male form on which she could look with approbation (and, sometimes, I thought, longing) made for me a prison only one who grew up in such a house can understand.

5

At this point, the average burgher will have become purple in the face, and he will cry out to me, or what he can reach of me in lonely space: *What business can it be of yours what your mother did with her life, you miserable ingrate?* I understand his rage and honor it, but I must make answer: What my mother did with her life concerns me very much because of how it impinged on my own life, on the life of my sister, and on the lives of all who came in contact with us. If my mother had not shut love out of our house, forcing my sister and myself to find it between ourselves, at least two people who lived in utter misery might have found some happiness on earth, and at least one, I am certain, would not have committed suicide.

6

The loneliness of a deserted womb! I once saw a photograph of a street in an American city which grew up during a rush for gold in that part of western United States and was completely abandoned as soon as the mining possibilities of the terrain had been exhausted. The photograph I saw must have been taken quite a few years after the last of the street's inhabitants had vanished. The wild brush had conquered all paths leading into it and away from it, it reached in height the highest of its houses, the loftiest of its roofs. No window was left unbroken or unbent, no door secure on its hinges, no single beam was left with any of the pride with which it is first taught to uphold a house. Even those ruins did not create an image of loneliness comparable to that of a deserted vagina — about which the people in this evil house are still twisting and turning their miserable bowels.

7

My poor aunt Rosalie! I think I now understand what she meant when she once complained to my mother, when she thought no one was within hearing, that what she was doing was walking the streets for Jesus!

8

The havoc one can make in the world without lifting a finger, without opening the door of one's house! (It is said of Kant, for instance, that his whole wandering over the surface of the earth was between his house and the university classrooms a short distance from it!)

9

The loneliness of an old maid is something else entirely. The old maid has grown away from the plumbing system of nature. She has broken no vital connections because she never had any to begin with.

10

And as it is with the old maid so it is with the bachelor. A bachelor looks better, of course, but he is no less miserable, believe me.

11

How wonderful it might have been — and how different would have been the journey I made through the world — if my mother had been a little less pious and let herself get married to any one of the available bachelors around us. How many hours I have spent wondering what sort of man she would have chosen, and what effect he would have had on me and Elisabeth.

12

With any kind of a new man about the house, Elisabeth never could have grown into the fierce, perverse little animal she is! As for me, I would probably have followed his example, and held on to whatever place in the world first fell to me. At best I would have become a first rate philologist!

13

Maybe I myself am nothing. But what will go on in the world as a result of my having lived my few unhappy years in it!

14

I have read and heard many interesting definitions of culture. Not one of them has brought out quite clearly the one quality of culture by which it both functions and can be recognized, the existence in fact as well as in feeling, of a dominion of good nature.

15

How can I explain this better than by pointing out that whereas the first implement of war was probably made in the secrecy of some cave in Asia Minor, the first cooking pot was most likely rounded out in the open, in some village on the north coast of Africa with all the neighbors and children looking on in wonder?

16

The oldest things in the world everywhere are the tombs of the conquerors. The reign of good nature under them is inaugurated only with their death.

17

Look about you. All creation struggles for its existence but is in uninterrupted enjoyment of the faculties of living and growing. Man is the only organic phenomenon who consciously engages in the promotion of ill-will.

18

In its original impulse (among the prehistoric peoples) religion was meant to define a limited dominion of good nature. And the dominion was so limited by the priests (politicians of those days) that sometimes even the Conqueror himself was excluded from the magic circle.

19

The first of the poems were nothing more than placid records of domestic events. An event makes its own music when you are in perfect accord with it.

20

As the things which facilitate eating, drinking and sleeping were fashioned by human hands, more craft and charm went into them, and the dominion of good nature among the people who used and admired them grew deeper and deeper.

21

No one ever tried to make an engine of war look beautiful. A country's handsomest general was never half so good-looking as its homeliest blacksmith.

22

The tyranny of priest-craft began as a tyranny of exclusive knowledge. From the very beginning, life depended, for regulation, on the observations arrived at by those who took the leisure to map out carefully the movements of the heavenly bodies. Rich man or idler, a man was bound to capitalize on this advantage, to make his intellectual dependents as dependent on him as he was on those above him in the material world.

23

As long as the gods are left undisturbed in their temples we are left undisturbed in our homes.

24

When the Trojan War was being fought for her, Helen was no more than a woman. The chronicles of the war, which were written long after the war had fought itself out, promoted her to the status of goddess.

25

In his essay on Theseus, Plutarch declares that he finds in

those stories least like poetry the best guidance in the direction of what seems to him truth. Historic truth is naturally what Plutarch has in mind, for it is historic truth which occupied him throughout his entire life; and if truth, like man, needs a certain moist kind of atmosphere to thrive in, one could not think of a better atmosphere for her than is to be garnered out of the best recollections of the experiences of the race. But does Plutarch really abandon the guidance of the instincts, which is the essence of the purely poetic conception he appears to spurn, for an exclusive dependence on dry facts? The secret of his style, and his survival by virtue of it as the one great indisputable historian of antiquity, urge eloquently to the contrary. He says of Theseus, for instance, that he was born out of wedlock and of uncertain parentage; but the ensuing biography, following a happy middle course between these two extremes, becomes the portrait neither of a god nor a bastard, but of a man.

26

In ancient Greece a man was accounted rich according to the multitude of his children, which, in our time, only serves to make a poor man poorer.

27

The French Revolution had no patience with religion, but neither did it have any patience with science. Lavoisier, who managed to prove Joseph Priestley's early sallies into the realm of oxygen, was beheaded by the Revolution which "had no use for chemists." Science does not appear to be better off at the hands of the leaders of the state who demand of it only such researches as tend to strengthen their war machinery.

28

Montaigne records: "The Seigneur de Fragnet, lieutenant to

the Marshal de Chatillon's company, having by him been put in government of Fuentarabia, in the place of Monsieur de Lude, and having surrendered it to the Spaniard, he was for that condemned to be degraded from all nobility, and both himself and his posterity declared ignoble, taxable and forever incapable of bearing arms, which severe sentence was accordingly later executed at Lyons." Under feudalism an act of cowardice made a man taxable. In our democracy we degrade him to this level only when he has shown an inclination to earn more money than he can spend.

29

The love of wealth and the love of knowledge are the two moving forces of the earth, and what is given to one must always be taken away from the other.

30

Voltaire was France taking a long deep breath of the English air of intellectual freedom.

31

Voltaire never tired of telling his people how much he loved the boldness with which the English thought, leaving them to guess for themselves that they had only to dare to think to achieve the same distinction, for boldness is as natural an attribute of thought as thought is a natural attribute of freedom.

32

The Chinese who (in *The Book of Permutations* published about 1100 B.C.) divided numbers into even and odd, brought into arithmetic an element of sex which is yet to be elaborated on.

33

Stendhal wanted to know how a Frenchman would go about it in order not to think like anybody else. He would be somewhat hurt, if he were around, to see how little of what a Frenchman does involves thinking at all.

34

If France ever gets Bismarck's Germany in the spot Russia once got the Germany of Frederick, it will be well for it to remember the deal made in the seventeenth century between the English Parliament and the Scotch nobles for the head of Charles I. Bismarck's head won't be nearly so fine, but Europe will happily pay more for it.

35

All socialistically minded men fail to understand that the unequal distribution of wealth, power and learning are essential in a community, for the continued exercise in it of sentiments such as pity, compassion, generosity and protectiveness, which are the ingredients of the only civilization that has ever had any kind of permanence among men.

36

It is curious, but none the less true, that there is more sunlight in the pictures of the English landscape school (executed in a foggy, dreary country) than in all the paintings discoverable in sunny Italy. What has always kept the sun out of Italian paintings is probably responsible for keeping all reason out of its reasoning.

37

It is not wealth which draws a people down the abyss artistically, but rather the method by which it amasses wealth.

38

Perhaps the real tragedy in the history of man came about, not when man first found himself and his help-meet naked, but when he first realized that it was necessary for him to go outside of his own person to offer worship to a deity. He did not know that he had been ejected from the Garden of Eden until he found himself outside the gate.

39

One can only stare with awe at the feet of the Greek statues. It is difficult to believe that with such feet a people could ever have permitted itself even the interference of sandals, or dared to risk walking in too strong a sun. If we had such feet we would probably spoil them with manicuring!

40

Of all the dreams of the modern world that of the pacifist is the shallowest and as close as sincerity can come to viciousness. No nation, except that of the Jew, ever managed to maintain itself except by conquest, and no nation has ever remained one without continually watering its roots by additional conquest. A nation that has given up the dream of conquest has already given up the dream of living. A pacifist nation is a nation dying, if not already securely dead.

41

Now that the presence of force has been eliminated from the scheme of the physical universe, it may be simpler to discourage it as a means of international persuasion.

42

Most of the disputes of the world are about actual possessions. The popular belief that where there is much smoke there must be some sort of fire belongs distinctly to the intellectual age of mankind in which fire was one of the four elements into which the whole content of the universe was supposed to be resolved. Among the philosophers of our own day the disputes are almost all about words and the nature of words. But it would be risky to suggest that where there are so many words there must be some underlying basis of fact; so frequently, when a later-day controversy has been sifted, it is discovered to be almost virtually factless.

43

I can understand the impulse which led the author of *Genesis* to make a record of a date. The habit still retains a certain amount of the poetry of probable usefulness in *Leviticus* and *Deuteronomy*. But in *Chronicles* and *Kings*, for instance, it begins to appear downright fatuous. Is there not a warning to unthinking historians of the essential emptiness of their data in its gradual multiplication *ad infinitum* and *ad absurdum?*

44

Thus far, all personal differences in matters attending the public welfare have been either psychological, or physiological, the first based on personal limitation, the second on limitations purely social. There is only one kind of difference left for a public-spirited person to develop, if we are to head for a pleasanter state of life than that which is our outlook at present, and that is one grounded in the limitations inherent in the very universe which is our home. We are overdrawing on our accounts everywhere. The universe is not, to begin with, so big as we think it is.

The world as an organism is of tremendous importance to itself, but of only the puniest significance for the individual. And, with all his perfections credited, man is an extremely imperfect creature! That being so, we can stop being so spendthrift of what we haven't got. Pretty nearly everything mankind owns that is worth anything is contained in a few buildings in Rome, Paris and London, and I would not take all the rest of the universe in exchange for the contents of one of them. Yet at this writing it would appear that the armed forces of mankind are prepared to devastate these buildings to settle an argument between men whose real potentialities are such that if they were the only men left in the world the whole race would have to die without posterity.

45

To stop an animal from moving forward in the course laid out for it by its natural instincts you have at least to hit it on the head with something hard. To obtain the same result with a man you have only to talk to him.

46

It is becoming a crime in most civilized communities to spread financial misinformation that lead to people losing money. But there is not a city in the world in which you cannot so pervert the facts concerning the habits and motives of some of its inhabitants as effectually to rob them of their right to existence!

47

Even if a man could actually create the laws for his people his importance as compared with the laws themselves would be comparable only to one of the spokes of the wheel which moves into their strategic places the stones which do the grinding of the mill.

48

King Louis, who said, *I am the State*, would have been more truthful if he had said instead, *I have suspended in my state the working of all laws except those which do the bidding of my pleasure*. But did Louis really have a good time of it? If he did, he left a minimum of evidence to sustain the idea. Fancy, for instance, having the privilege of reigning over a natural king like Descartes, and being unable to keep him home for more than two years at a clip.

49

The greatest philosopher of his time (and always to be reckoned among the great of any time) Descartes made a religious habit of soldiering. He soldiered for Holland, for Italy, for Russia, even for Prussia. Why, then, did he never put on a French uniform? Probably because he did not think it would be as much fun fighting for a man as it would be fighting for a creative law!

50

As we understand its working, law is primarily of the state, and only by process of reflection, of the individual. If there is a law ruling the individual as such, it is a special law that has to do with man as an idea rather than as an animal, and it subjects the individual inwardly with the completeness with which the state holds and molds him outwardly.

51

It would appear, therefore, that the law appertains to the outward, the finite world. It belongs to a sphere of life which has no boundaries, no limit and no qualities; for all boundaries are of infinity, all limits are of things which have no end, and all qualities are of the utterly incomprehensible.

52

A law by itself is a positive fact, and the only moral phase of its being is the relationship it bears to a community during the process of its influence. If it is generally obeyed it is a good law; if it is not obeyed, it is safe to take it for granted that it swam into the statute books as the result of mistaken, misleading and stupid legislation.

53

A philosophy of law is at best a derivation from a number of known codes of law, all in the process of being either obeyed or disobeyed. Its use is at best of a mysterious nature; it is quite useless as a philosophy, because my hand is only of service to my other hand, and no one makes a life-habit of maintaining balance on one foot.

54

The element of universal consent in law is its very charm and coloring. It is the lungs and heart of the law, too; the rhythm in which it was conceived, the atmosphere in which it continues to flourish.

55

Every society grows its own cycle of laws; this cycle is the whole domain of those laws which should be given an age limit: ten, fifteen or fifty years, at the end of which every law should be required to come up for reconsideration and readoption. This would not only assure laws against outliving their usefulness, it would act as a natural restraint to legislatures from continuing to flood the world with so many more and useless laws!

56

A law that is successful and necessary within one cycle of laws may be altogether out of place, and possibly destructive, in another cycle.

57

If there were a school for legislators (as why should there not be?) it would be important to teach therein to eagerly manned classrooms of expensively uneducated politicians that words such as *law, right, duty, property* and *crime* are abstractions that in themselves have no particular value and wait to receive contents of color and meaning from the particular circumstances in which they happen to be brought up. What is a duty in one country is not unlikely to be a crime in another. And even such virtues as *right* and *property* are not everywhere *virtues*.

58

Law is a light which in different countries attracts to it different species of blind insects.

59

The whole science of analytical jurisprudence — which tries to work out by mathematical formulae that which in law can only be truly determined by factual and sensory examination — is so much humbug, to be discarded and forgotten.

60

The business of practical legislation is the building of moral and intellectual trade routes — treaties and alliances, dykes and dams — by which the streams of popular emotion and commercial activity are conducted with the utmost economy to the state and the greatest financial aggrandisement of the constituent citizenry. The relationships of nations abound with gaps that could have been filled with wise alliances.

61

There are two sources of authority in the state: the sovereign and his machine which is the government. The sovereign is the source of intelligence in the state which is the juridic body. A good sovereign can do more for the body of the state with a faulty machinery than a poor sovereign can do with a perfect one.

62

The sovereign of a state may be a man, or a parliament or a congress. It follows as a natural possibility that a parliament of men is capable of emphasizing the greatness of one of its members, but that is something which rarely comes about. The competition among legislators for power is not in the language of praise, and it breeds the power of brutality. And whereas brutality may be compelling it is hardly ever attractive — and never inspiring.

63

As Hobbes pointed out so shrewdly in *The Leviathan*, the sovereign functions best as a fountain of example for the citizenry of the state: if he is a good man the state is already twice as good as it might have been, by that much!

64

One of Hobbes' curious reasons for preferring to see the state sovereignty vested in a king (among so many sounder, better reasons) is that the very presence among men of one raised higher in rank above themselves suggests persuasively the presence of a much higher elevation from which the more permanent virtues might be expected to flow beyond time and measure,

Hobbes lived to become a stout-staffed atheist!

65

Peace in a state presupposes the existence of a relationship of good nature and understanding between the administrators of the fixed laws and the continually growing, expanding and sweetening limb of the state.

66

The law — even such law as we call divine — ceases to be of any honest service to the state when the mortal terms in which it was conceived have been outworn in the course of the factional struggles by which the state balances itself; outworn, I mean, either in speech, in the authority of incident, or in both. Words are only the fabrics of the garments of ideas, and, being the garments of the governing emotions rather than the selecting emotions themselves, the laws are limited accordingly. So may the most marvelous wording of a law be outmoded even as the greatest ideas themselves are outmoded in the process of our human adventure. A common law whose applicability to human nature remains fresh and pliable is a divine law of the highest order!

67

For the satisfaction of his profoundest needs, the peasant (lucky fellow!) has only to obey his immediate superior in the community, and plough on in the happy persuasion that even the functionary he obeys is several times removed in power from terms of intimacy with the king of his country. A weekly reminder that a superior of his own, removed, say three times above him, in terms of power, is as far from the sphere of the king as the king himself is from the sphere of God, is calculated to maintain in the peasant a neat balance between right and wrong, between his desire for the good and his separatedness from evil.

68

The so-called laws of nature are not commands. They are observed uniformities in all laws which resemble commands only insofar as they have been ordered by some intelligent being. Our moral and divine laws come to us the same way. We contribute both to the understanding and befuddlement of divine laws and to the understanding and befuddlement of the laws of nature.

69

The indiscriminate identification of everything to which common speech gives the name of law was, and still is, a source of confusion. Every time a jurist turns to science he abuses law. Every time a scientist turns legislator he virtually locks behind him the door to his laboratory.

70

As a result of the meddling of economists with purely scientific law, certain principles of economy appear to have acquired a double character — that of scientific generalizations and that of rules which may with impunity be disobeyed.

71

Now the greatest evil which may befall a state is that it find itself in a mood of dispute with regard to some law, which one faction of the state is in perfect agreement with, while another, perhaps a minority, feels this as a violation of its natural right.

72

The greatest evil in civil law is that its value is being estimated at the value of the word, and that the word has become the key to both its analyses and its applicability. One might call this the

Narcissistic mood of the law — only that, either way, there is very little love lost.

73

The most amazing thing within my experience is the unconscious way men and women take it for granted that they are the natural superiors of the flora and fauna about them. What, for instance, do we know about animals, plants and birds that can possibly justify such a conclusion? As a matter of sober fact, we don't even look better, and sometimes we look many fathoms worse. I once saw in a zoo an animal with a face so beautiful and benign that I had to think of St. Francis of Assisi to match it in grandeur. What an extraordinary piece of arrogance, I thought, looking at the face of that beast, it would be for me to calmly take it for granted that what transpired behind that furry brow was of less importance than what goes on behind my thin-skinned one.

74

Have you ever seen a young girl half as pretty as the most abandoned little alley-cat?

75

Of all the inhabitants of this planet trees seem to me to be the noblest. They surely display the most perfect sense of symmetry. They are continually striving upwards without abandoning their roots which they sink deeper and deeper into the earth which begot them.

76

If ever I get home again, I think I will take a deeper look into the Egyptian *Book of the Dead* whose pages I have always rifled through but never read with the attention such a book demands from a reader in a world so entirely different from the one in which it was written. As a people, and as a ruling class, the Egyptians had only the faintest interest in problems of morality; they were, therefore of all nations, best equipped to initiate and carry out a program of scientific culture. That is to be envied them — although, as well as we can tell, they did not do very much about it. As a master of his opportunities, the evolving Egyptian is even to be less admired than his lineal successor, the evolving European.

77

I have always wanted to enlarge on my original observations on the evolving European whose most important function should be the filling of the gap between man as he is today and *superman* whom we may hope — in good time, infinite patience, and a talented courage — to achieve. The evolving European's task is to retain the Christian passion for truth in science and sincerity in living, while he trains his conscience to smile as he sticks his tongue out every time he passes a church, a synagogue, or a mosque.

78

And what is the superman to be like? It is not enough to expect of him that he just be able to put his tongue out at the absurd remnants of a dead world. And it is too much to expect of him that he will learn how to fully enjoy his life on this planet. For we shall never be able to subtract from man's life man's organic need to decay and die.

79

The evolving European will have to cut his bone-structure out of the mixture of Anglo-Saxon, Scandinavian, Gall, Celt, and Teuton who today strive for intellectual and spiritual mastery of the continent. You notice, I have said nothing of the Jew, who certainly is part and parcel of this great struggle. Somehow the Jew is of this struggle and yet not in it. Perhaps he is a sort of director, unofficial master of ceremonies. I don't know.

80

I wish the Scandinavians had not so easily given up their bid for the physical mastery of Europe. Ever since the humiliation of Charles XII at the hands of a Polish woman, and not a very beautiful one at that, if I am to take the word of Voltaire —

81

I do not like Germans, and I am particularly unfond of German Germans. Yet I count myself exceedingly lucky to have been born in Germany, surrounded by Germans of greater and lower degrees of detestableness, allowing me the occasional exuberant sensation of a sort of embodiment of a dawn breaking over a particularly dark forest.

82

Let those who lead the people lead, and let the people — their movements unobstructed by demagogues — let themselves be led into the plenitudes of the scientific age. Let there be just a little less bickering among those who have such a capacity for receiving and so little to offer. No good comes of all the public debate which the Americans consider so important in deciding a public issue. Deciding communal destiny by common vote is a good deal like choosing a wife by lottery.

83

Nothing has ever been done in Europe to revive the Bacchic rites practised in the classical age. Is it possible that the European's appetite for food and drink is at fault? Or is his reluctance to sit down at table with his neighbor?

84

In my lifetime I have met at least four people who thought I would look good at the center of a new religion. Three of them were women. It has made me suspicious of religion and even of women.

85

I have loved Socrates with an affection I have given no other human being in recorded history. I have even forgiven him his one great sin — the turning of reason into a tyrannous force.

CHAPTER FOUR

1

There have been, in all, four women in my life. The only two who brought me an approximate amount of happiness were prostitutes. But the happiness they brought me was the happiness of a moment. If I were ever mad enough to wish to give a history of my happiness with one or both of them I would have to institute a search for them. And if I looked for them and had the bad luck to find them they would at the same time cease being the daughters of divine accident and the creators of my extraordinary contentment.

Elisabeth was beautiful enough, but she was my sister. Lou was intelligent enough (a little too intelligent sometimes), but she refused to marry me. There is no happiness in anything we do unless it is the beneficiary of the stamp of approval of the society we live in. That applies to the thoughts we think as well as the women we wrestle with for whatever be the honors of coition of the moment.

After Elisabeth and Lou, what kind of a woman would make me happy, in the humming twilight of this fearful forcing-house, I ask myself.

No matter what mood I happen to be in, one condition for sexual happiness, for me, is that the woman be young. Without the aura of youth a woman, for me, is not even a woman. She might be the ticket-taker in charge of the portal of paradise, but an item of the interior she cannot, for me, ever be.

But if a woman is young what else can matter? I go on asking myself. Ah yes, what else can *possibly* matter? Let her be black as night, golden as the sun, or as red as the sunset of a heavy August afternoon, her arms become as liquid fire to engulf me at the very thought of her. The psychologists would explain that as deriving from my middle-aged state, and, and usual, they would be wrong.

There never was a time when I could look at a middle-aged woman without laughing, and at an old woman without vast pity. As I show so amply in *The Dawn of Day* I was born into the youth of the world. I am youth itself, and youth cries out to youth no matter how wide the abysses and the styles of rhetoric which separate them.

On further thought, it appears to me that the leg-spread of a woman matters no little, not as much as youth matters, not nearly as much, but it matters. Those little ponies are delightful enough to look at, yes indeed. But is it possible for such a tiny organism to encompass, take in, all that is me? I wonder about that, and it troubles me.

A small woman is not enough — unless her sole usefulness is to inspire the lust to be poured into a larger frame.

But given all the wonders of women rolled into one (a radiant young woman with long, delightfully tapering legs) what attribute of hers could plot to spoil my appetite for her? Many, many things, alas. A wart at the base of her nose, or a peasant nose with wrinkles on the sides. Big red hands. Feet too wide and without ankles or graceful insteps. A very narrow forehead . . .

On the other hand, granted the perfect woman whom I desire perfectly, what assurance is there that I will give her the happiness needed to carve the moment of our meeting into something memorable in time and space?

Suddenly I am narrowed down to a very shaky faith, the belief that there being so many, many ways in which a man can satisfy even the most lustful of women, a man who loves a woman as passionately as I would love such a woman, could not possibly fail. Just bring her to me, and I will be the knife to carve out her uttermost in delight, never fear.

2

I think so often of Wagner, of Lou Salomé, even of that scamp Paul Rée, and almost never of that good old teacher of mine, Ritschel, the contriver of my first sensation of intellectual independence, the man to whom I must owe a good share of the scholarly virtues I have developed. In his way, Ritschel was a truer artist than Wagner. As for his validity as a human being, except for what may have existed behind the personal veil which I never violated, he was the most complete human being I ever knew.

3

I think what attracted me most (at the beginning) to Schopenhauer's writing was its unaffected simplicity and earnestness. What a relief I found after the untidiness of Kant, the pompousness of Fichte, the emotionless tyranny of Hegel. A thinker as great as any of his predecessors, Schopenhauer was unashamed of being first of all a writer.

4

How, by means of a set of personal experience so different from mine, did Schopenhauer manage to arrive at philosophical conclusions so close to my own heart? The one great difference between us is that Schopenhauer — I cannot understand how — managed to live at such enviable peace with his disillusionment.

5

In one respect Schopenhauer resembles the Hebrew author of *Ecclesiastes* who wrote so eloquently of the vanity of human wishes without branding men's small desires sinful or symptoms of the fundamental corruptness of human nature. In his estimation, human nature did not suffer degration because it failed to prove itself of a more than common origin.

6

In my worst moment I have never felt like a sinner, I have never sunk so low in my spirits that I felt as if I needed to make confession to anyone. To attain such a feeling it must be necessary to be the product of a Catholic upbringing and inbreeding.

7

The pain which accompanies loss of faith could be the birth-throes of art.

8

Schopenhauer grew out of Kant the way Kant grew out of Galileo and the way Galileo grew out of the enlightened gossip of the scholars of his day. I have already grown so far beyond Schopenhauer, and into such shallows, that I doubt if I myself shall ever have a spiritual or intellectual successor.

9

In many ways Kant was the creator of the modern world — and what an exclusive world — in which only those things can exist which can be conceived in terms of human sense and experience. In this world the human mind is the supreme dictator and only those things can enter the realm of existence which are prepared (and disposed) to be subject to its rule.

10

Schopenhauer drew a sharp line between himself and Kant, when he proclaimed that the world was his idea, and that human experience did not so much as enter into his calculations.

Schopenhauer reopened all the gates of existence closed by Kant, but took a hopelessly sour view of everything he saw. I ask myself, how can I love so much in a world he loved so little?

11

Why this constant reversion to the subject of salvation as if our life on earth were nothing more than an unremitting curse?

12

Things-in-themselves are not our proper concern, because if we grasped their meaning, if their strange qualities entered into our instinctive system of calculation, what would become of our simple organic needs and desires?

13

What has brought Schopenhauer to mind is this perfect Schopenhauer day that, with its heavy, cloud-brooding, deep-gray sky has been plucking at the rheumatism in my bones from the moment I opened my eyes. Schopenhauer days like this one visit Germany at least a hundred times a year. Luckily for us, Schopenhauers themselves come much less frequently.

Schopenhauer, not Goethe, is the true natural poet of this stubborn, frost-bitten country of ours, with the police our only true midwives and the stones our only prophets. We are doomed to defeat in our wars as well as in our philosophies. Military victory, if by mistake it stays with us, does not in the least suit our frowning dispositions.

14

I was able to induce my sister to put on a solemn face, but that was as far as I could get her to go along with me into the Schopenhauer mood. For a while my only two converts were my intellectual boon-companions, Mushacke and von Gersdorff, and by the time they were fully converted I was no longer quite certain how much of a Disciple I myself was.

15

I have asked of man that he make himself a bridge for Superman, in that way demanding sacrifices on the altars of unknown gods. In so doing I have not been a philosopher so much as a moralist. A little Schopenhauer can be a dangerous thing — if you don't happen to be Schopenhauer.

16

Why is it that I can catch thought after thought on paper, as they present themselves in my mind, yet if some one comes up to me and merely asks me for the time of day I grow confused, the knowledge that I am expected to produce a series of familiar sounds by way of answer to the man's question paralyzes my whole system and reduces me to intellectual impotence? Can things happen to the mechanism of our thoughts without hurting the thoughts themselves? Is the spiritual element in us entirely free of the material channels through which it flows?

17

Either that man occupying the chair facing the door through which I must pass for my daily constitutional is cock-eyed or I am. One of us had better learn how to keep out of the other's way. And why does he look at me as if I were about to make a flying leap for the window and freedom?

18

Schumann and Schopenhauer are the two poles of my existence. Between them I am borne up into wonder. Between them I am crushed as between millstones.

19

There is a little man here who often talks to me. He has told me all about himself, and his story is the most superbly uninteresting one I have ever heard in my life. If I listened to him at all it was because I could see him measuring out, as he talked to me, the full stature of the average citizen in any part of the world.

He was, until the nervous breakdown which brought him here, a dealer in stocks and bonds, using the merchant's bag of tricks to buy cheap and sell dear. His business brought him to his office about ten o'clock every weekday morning and let him go about half past four in the afternoon. Within those six hours, with the help of a staff of four or five more or less innocent employees, he manipulated into growing and diminishing groups the stocks of which he knew that the bigger crooks needed them to carry out their larger schemes of depredation.

Once back in his comfortable home, with his wife and children, he assumed the role every German burgher likes to play, the role of the righteous and religious citizen. When he tired his family with his self-justifying tales, he called in the neighbors. When the neighbors tired of him, he thought of prominent members of his church. And when they were exhausted he remembered the tax-lists. With all of these people he had but a single theme: his own profits were honest and God-fearing, the profits of his competitors, got at his expense, naturally, constituted blood-money of the lowest form of dishonesty and depravity. How do I know the substance of what he said to all those good people? It was to me he came after he had exhausted the tax-lists.

What happened when his inner conscience, that still, small voice, said to him: *You foul little liar, do you know of anyone with a deeper blood-greediness than yours?* I think I know his answer to that, too. He donates to a charity. All these scoundrels are devoted to some charity or other.

20

I am a man of genius. Therefore I can afford to smile or spit at you.

21

The rich say that money is of no real importance. They do not give it away only out of fear that those they might give it to could be injured in their sense of values. Myself, I never really wanted money. The only time I ever think of money is when I happen to need it.

22

I did a great deal of maturing in Leipzig, a vast amount of masturbating, and not nearly so much whoring as I should have done.

23

I would rather be a good psychologist than the God of Genesis.

24

I feel about Bismarck the way Moses must have felt about Amalek or Joshua about Og King of Bashan. Only, I am a citizen of Amalek, I break eggs every morning with Og.

25

The irony of my life is that I praise the strong, sympathize with the weak, and bear an unquenchable love for the utterly helpless. It is this impossible contradiction in my life which reconciles me to my present dwelling among the lesser gods.

26

As Germany is the negation of France, Russia is the negation of Germany. Russia has two important advantages over us. She has more room to fight in and more Jews to fight with.

27

I got the biggest scare of my life in 1866 when the cholera broke out all about me and I fled the city. I know now that one can do much worse than die the swift, violent, retching death of the cholera.

28

So many of the people I have known — relatives mostly — who I expected would outlive me, have died, God had better watch out for His one fading laurel.

When I remember the incident, I wonder what that lovely blonde singer, Fraulein Raabe, did with the songs I wrote for her especially and sent her by courier. I was so anxious to make some physical contact with her loveliness, and since the one uppermost in my mind was patently impossible, I chose to do it by way of her delightful little throat. But I probably wound up with — from the amative point of view, not the digestive — the most negligible of her orifices.

29

It's always a mistake to take me to a play. I laugh in the wrong places and when I cry during a performance it is never where a member of the audience is expected to shed a tear. At musicales I am always the soul of sobriety. That is because, knowing that nothing is expected of me, I take notice of nothing in particular and forgive everybody and everything. Perhaps that is the secret of the sudden aloofness of God towards the world which He has not presented with a prophet for such a long time. If that's so, shouldn't someone tell the Pope about it?

30

What I object to most in the doctors here is their conversation, the amount of empty, unconscionable, useless twaddle they make about them and to all sides of them. I remember a job of stitching and sewing perpetrated on my anatomy in my youth when, while mounting a horse, I was thrown against the pommel of the saddle and injured my breast and side. Only in such a contingency, where the flesh is torn and the bone is broken, is a doctor of any real use.

31

What I suffer most of, here, is loneliness, though it is hardly a new sensation to me. But there are many kinds of lonelinesses. There is the loneliness of places, the least damaging of lonelinesses because where a place is far from another human habitation, hope and desire set up consolations in the future for which the human spirit can wait happily. And there is the loneliness of a lofty aim, most blest of lonelinesses, involving as it does plans not for oneself but for mankind in general, and so needs have no care for possible disappointments to follow. And then there is, alas, the loneliness which is without any hope of compensations, the loneliness due to the individual's failure to reach some common understanding with the world. That is the bitterest loneliness of all, the loneliness which is eating away at the heart of my existence.

32

Every artist is the joyous inheritance of the few who understand him. The artist is born for his audience and his audience is born for him. In the eyes of heaven they are equal to each other. I do not include mob-worship which is as obnoxious and useless as the scorn of mobs affected by pseudo-artists and lovers.

33

The wrong people come to this house and the wrong people are permitted to depart from it.

34

I have been in love with only two women, maybe with only one, and I am as far removed from the angels as ever.

35

I remember with reverence the father I never really knew, and I can think only with loathing of my mother, knowing as I do that there is nothing she would not do to bring me consolation and comfort. God does well to hide behind His peak on Mount Sinai.

36

To keep a clear digestive tract, eat prunes and study philology. As long as I reserved my energies for the contemplation of the trifling goddess of arranged sounds I was always in good health and cheerful spirits. It was only when I deserted philology for philosophy that Pandora's evil brood attacked me. Poor Rhode thought I was going up in the world when the first chair in philosophy was offered me at Basel.

37

None of the things I love are good for me. Even beer. A single glass of it and I become drowsy enough to prefer sleep to conversation.

38

Owls and moles I used to call my fellow teachers at the university who were happy in their work. I should have followed this up by characterizing the rebellious ones as rats. Is it not they who continually undermine the house of philosophy?

39

A quarrel between philosophers should be taken as seriously as a philosophical argument between two bricklayers.

40

I had one more of those trying conversations with my sister today. Mother had come along with her, as usual, and, as usual, remained in the doctor's office instead of visiting with me.

Why all this sudden kindness? I asked Elisabeth.

It's your own fault, Fritz, she told me. *You take too much out of her when she exposes herself to your conversation. You don't imagine she enjoys being here without seeing you?*

You can take solace in the thought that you torture me enough for the two of you.

How do we torture you?

By prying. Mother pries in the office while you pry here. Why don't both of you start letting me alone?

Don't you want us to come here any more?

There my heart failed me. The truth is I don't really know.

Suddenly she looked sharply at me and that dangerous look came into her eyes.

Do you do any writing here? she asked me.

I've written enough about the world, I said to her. *Let the world now write about me.*

But that is already happening, she assured me. *Brandes and Strindberg are no longer the only ones to proclaim your genius. There are others, many others. Even I have been asked to write my impressions of you.*

I could hardly believe my ears.

You!

Yes, and I am offered money, too.

But you won't do it!

Why not?

You don't know anything about me or my ideas.

Who can possibly know you better than your own sister?

Yes, and who can possibly know me less? Promise me, Elisabeth, you won't do it.

She hesitated, and for a moment it seemed as if she might yield.

I can't, she finally said.

And why can't you? I demanded.

She laughed quickly.

Simply because I haven't yet made up my mind, Fritz!

And in a minute she was gone.

41

I have been trying to imagine what my sister is capable of telling the world about me.

Would she tell how early in childhood she made a practice of crawling into my bed Saturday mornings to play with my genitalia, and, after a while, got into the habit of treating them as if they were special toys of hers?

Would she tell the world how for many years she haunted the world of my senses with those marvelous fingers of hers, driving me to a premature and hopeless awakening? So that for a whole spasm of my life I was unable to think of beauty or pleasure except in terms of her eyes and her damnably wonderful fingers? So refurbishing my life that in place of the strange goddess who visits the imagination of every normal adolescent I could only look forward to headaches and a sister?

But those are not the things Elisabeth would tell the world about me — if someone could be found who was foolish enough to encourage her to write about me. Then what *would* Elisabeth write about in the articles they are threatening to buy from her? I can't for the life of me guess.

Would she tell how eagerly she joined me in every hope but always fell back when it was sorrow which struck at me?

Would she tell how, whenever it appeared as if I were about to make a real friend of a man or woman, she would find some reason for my not having anything to do with him or her — usually a moral reason?

Would she tell how she instigated my mother to join her in blackmailing the reputation of Lou Salomé so that eventually even I joined in the abuse which they both heaped upon her?

Would she tell how, to spite me, she went off with Förster to breed Jew-hatred in South America, that it was mostly to hide from me that she let herself take unto her this unripe plum of a man?

But no, the truth is not for poor Elisabeth.

42

I once spent two days of a week reading Hesiod's *Works and Days* to one group of students, and two more days reading *Oedipus Rex* to another. One could read Hesiod to young people often enough to kill them, though if it were girls to whom I read *Oedipus Rex* they might all wind up great with child.

43

So much in the intellectual world has been fenced off and graded by Darwin's theory of evolution that I wonder why so little of it enters into the calculations of contemporary thinkers. We are so afraid of the English, we are even scared to share philosophic truth with them.

44

But it is not better in England where, I understand, Darwin's disciples have so much trouble sustaining the most elementary of Darwinisms that the attempts to go on from his fundamental premises are few and far between. As a matter of record, the English have always been more interested in facts than in ideas. That is why it will never be possible to stampede an English mob into an unreasonable (or bloody) course of action. No one will ever talk them into partaking of any social broth but one of which they have first sipped slowly and carefully, blowing on every spoonful of reform.

45

One of the new inmates of this house is a convert to Catholicism. He wears his cross conspicuously, and I heard him tell the doctor that he will not join in any services that have not first been approved of by his priest. Listening to him reminds me of the time my friend and comrade Romundt, a teacher of Schopenhauer and a disbeliever if I ever met one, publicly announced his intention of joining the Church of Rome. On me and on many others of his university associates it made the same impression as if he had told us that he was tired of being a man and that at some future date he would enter a cage in the local zoo and become a monkey. *What has made you so tired of the adventure of thinking?* we asked, and, of course, he would not answer. I have the same queer feeling every time that I hear of someone — almost anyone — being instructed in *the faith*. No one ever becomes a Catholic by inspiration; you must be instructed on how to live in a religion fully eighty percent of whose adherents are semi-literates.

46

In whatever ways I have been right about Wagner, I was certainly wrong when I confused the need of understanding him and his work with the needs of the struggling culture of our time. What has music to do with culture, anyway? Not only is the best of music a refinement of the instinct which bids us bellow when we are in pain, it remains, under all our attempts to refine its appeal, a purely primitive expression of the animal which underlies every human being. I have met almost every kind of musician, but never one of whom I could feel that he was a thoroughly civilized human being.

47

I once tried to reconcile gods and artists by suggesting that gods are only men posing as artists. By what conceit, then, do we arrogate to the gods the right to love without also partaking of the less seemly of our organic functions? It was not until the Renaissance that it occurred to us that the more distant of our creators might find it necessary to move their bowels, and we finally got, in the pictures of the Ascension, the spectacle of one tier of angels urinating over another.

48

There is nothing scientific in our mortality, and there is even less of morality in our science. To reconcile these two a new set of gods will have to be conceived and ordained and popularized.

CHAPTER FIVE

1

Ah, Orestes, the blood of your mother is on your conscience and at your heels the avenging furies are tracking you down into doom! I am filled with remorse, mother; I know I have killed you with my vast hatred, huge and strong enough to destroy all the mothers in the world![1]

But Iphigenie[2] will expiate my foul crime, she knows the agony of Tantalus, the water that mocks the lips, the fruit that eludes the gasp till hunger and thirst drive the balked soul into matricidal madness! She will expiate my guilt and her own, for the priestess of virtue sank with me to the lowest pit of Tartarus, to the bottomless wickedness of the Egyptians who defied the barriers of blood! Ah, this Dionysian frenzy, this joy in life that turns the underworld into Paradise where all earthly hates and evils dissolve in the rapture of the eternal moment, and dark sins burn with the flames of comets shooting through the whirling abysses of space!

The fort has fallen and my body lies by the ruined walls. But Iphigenie defies the thunderbolts of Zeus; she gathers the frag-

---

[1] Nietzsche's guilt-feeling plunged him through the labyrinth of remorse and delirium. The mad passages are omitted from this farrago of sense and nonsense. — Editor

---

[2] Nietzsche's sister. — Editor

ments of Orestes together, every bleeding fragment, and calls upon the gods to perform the great miracle, to make me whole again in body, mind and spirit! This is my star-destiny, to be restored to the wholeness of a planet where every dead blade of grass sings with the green of resurrected life . . .

Iphigenie, Iphigenie, thy brother Orestes awaits the miracle of thy healing hands! Fear not the thunderbolts of Zeus: there is nothing in heaven or earth that can stop our will to wholeness and holiness but our cowardice, our own wild despair! Arise, demons, blow the trumpets, march round and round the terror of the soul till its walls go tumbling down! Arise, Satan, arise, storm heaven, scatter the angels of darkness and cast thy fierce light upon the empty throne of Christ . . .

Who is he? Yes it is Nietzsche, the son of Odin with his Thor-hammer pounding the planets to dust! I am the great Destroyer, the great Builder; I build a new heaven and earth to make room for the spirit of Prometheus, the boundless soul of Zarathustra! . . . Alas, alas, the Builder himself is demolished: how can dust become a god, the God of gods? In the thunder of the will all graves tremble and gape open. Arise, Dust, and march to your manhood, to your Godmanhood, upon the holy mountain where the serpent and the eagle await the homecoming of Zarathustra! In a burst of Mozart-music the gates of joy open and man marches into his inheritance . . .

Finally be of one mind, united in feeling.[3] Iphigenie, Iphigenie, are we not united in body, mind and spirit? Is not thy destiny my preordained fate, do we not vibrate together to the winds of love and hatred like an Æolian harp throbbing to the fingers of the storm? Iphigenie, Iphigenie, dread not the gods who know no sin but weakness, not even the dark Pharonic lust of the blood that seeks its own image in the stews of a lighthouse at Pharos for the

---

[3] Quotation from Saint Paul. — Editor

guidance of seamen — and I am smashed on the rocks! . . .

Ah. Iphigenie, Iphigenie, fear not the gods, for the gods are in us: we are the gods we dread and out of our self-dread comes madness! This tragic discord; it is ourselves divided against ourselves. Do not pray to the gods, do not pray:

> Rettet mich
> Und rettet euer Bild in meiner Seele![4]

Do not pray to the gods, for the gods are in us; the mirror reflects their image; we are the gods and all the strength of heaven! Pray rather to yourself, grasp the earth like Antaeus, and be strong with the might of the almighty Earth! We are the guardians of our own destiny; I am your fate and you are mine . . .

Iphigenie, Iphigenie, Orestes has fallen into the pit; the earth crumbles over his head, the good earth that he trusted to the last! Rescue me, my lover, rescue the lover of life! . . . Help! Help! I am buried alive, my sister! Help, help, Iphigenie! Help! —

2

If I had cracked safes and smashed heads instead of chasing phantoms with my philosophical hammer, I would still be enjoying the company of my Russian Calypso who filled her cave with Khornyakov, Leontyev, Aksakov, Fedorov, Solovev, Bakunin, Kropotkin, Mikhailovsky, Kreevsky, Belinsky, Dostoyevsky, Herzen and Tolstoy. All these religionists and God-intoxicated atheists, the whole regiment of Russian Messiahs, were paraded before me and I had to defend my views against theirs, or I was deprived of my nightly allotment of kisses. Because I was a philosopher she posed as one too, and even while she was dress-

---

[4] "Save me, and save your image in my soul!" Nietzsche is quoting from Goethe's Christianized version of *Iphigenie*. — Editor

ing in her boudoir I had to keep my mind off her voluptuous body and defend myself against the charge that I had stolen my ideas from Leontyev!

Leontyev — his name and his thoughts were as unknown to me as a black philosopher in the heart of the Congo! This philosopher who turned monk tried to defend the obscene tyranny of the Czar by saying that the phenomenon of Pushkin justified all the sufferings of the Russian people. If all the Russians have to offer is Pushkin, then they deserve their sufferings! It is true that Leontyev was opposed to the Russian Messianic idea of equality which destroys culture, but the collapse of culture may be a fortunate event if a new race of barbarians will arise — Rousseau's savages — who will annihilate a culture rooted in the lies and hypocrisies of our conventional civilization! Rather than be a Czarist apologist for pogrom-made culture, I am ready to join the Socialists in their war upon the pseudo-culture of the Philistines and the anti-Semites!

My attitude to culture is the polar opposite of Leontyevism, and my Russian charmer knew it, but she penalized me for desecrating our love-nest by dragging in the cuckoos of Socrates, Kant and Hegel. Venus is jealous of Minerva, and if the goddess of wisdom tries to display the brilliance of her mind while the goddess of love is removing her girdle, the war between the two deities drives all heaven and earth into mortal combat. The naked thighs of Venus flash across the universe like the Sword of the Last Judgment, and any philosopher who dares to swear loyalty to the virginal Minerva is cut to pieces!

I sensed as much, when, following the example of Plato, Boethius, Boehme, Goethe and Solovev, I tried to personalize philosophy in the virgin-Sophia, the integral concept of the Eternal Feminine that comes before our dividedness and fall through the disruptive serpent of sex. On the wings of a Kabbalist's imagination I flew to the unitive heaven of bliss where

Minerva and Venus are fused in the torrid heat of passion which welds our androgynous nature in the simple body of Plato's lovers. But the dream of the virgin-Sophia violates the rigid law of biologic truth. The mystical Eros demands the complete abandonment of the mind to the welter of turning thighs and heaving breasts. Despite Saint Augustine, who wrote his *Confession* as an exhausted, Tolstoyan rake, sex-union involves the animal in us more than the angel, and since a philosopher cannot condescend to the beast in him, a passionate woman like Lou has no use for him — except as a target for her arrogance.

Stendhal — the only man in Europe who was my intellectual equal — was in the same predicament when he wrote *Lamiel*. Despite all the books he read on the art of love, which he incorporated in his novels and essays, he could not, as an objective philosopher and psychologist, bow to the hairy animal in him and counter the naked passion of a mistress with the violence of the beast. He therefore dreamt himself into his fictional character of a philosophical burglar full of bestial lust and apt quotations from Molière and Corneille. This philosophical burglar, making war upon society which makes war upon him — as he says — has the choice of cutting the heroine's throat or ravishing her. The heroine makes up his mind for him by submitting ecstatically to the rape.

This was Stendhal's judgment upon himself and it is his judgment upon me as well. My worship of the Lady Philosophy, the virgin-Sophia, was an heretical abandonment of the shrine of Aphrodite where Lou lay on her damask couch, like a sacred harlot, demanding complete surrender to the divine ecstasy of the flesh. I ascended her couch not as a devotee of Aphrodite but as a fugitive from Pallas Athene: I could never reconcile myself to my own *blond beast* — Stendhal's burglar, rapist and wholesale assassin — and Lou punished me for my incorrigible virtue, my preference for the Puritanism of my sister which I abandoned in

MY SISTER AND I

thought but not in action . . .

Every woman is a harlot at heart and unless a man under-
stands this he cannot enter into the virgin purity of her being. If I
ever break out of my paralysis I shall begin life again by leaving
the riddle of the Sphinx to eunuches and philosophers and
becoming a second-story man. Then when I surprise a semi-
naked beauty in her boudoir I shall put my knife to her throat
and let her make her great Decision. Like Stendhal's *Lamiel* she
will be delighted by my bestiality, my unmasked energy which
meets the furious drive of her own female nature.

And if she seeks to lure me into a discussion of philosophy
merely to test the genuineness of my beasthood, I shall without
ceremony slice her throat from ear to ear, dismember her body
with a butcher's saw and cast the pieces into a blazing furnace! . . .

Ah, my dear Russian lady, you shall yet enjoy a demonstra-
tion of my frightfulness! I shall *act* my philosophy: the skull of
Caesar shall rattle in the storm, making a noise like the death of
empires!

3

This was my tragedy: I became an apostle to the Christians,
preaching Antichrist with the same fanatical zeal that Saint Paul
preached redemption through the blood of Jesus. I who believed
that all is fated, that we must love Man's fate with true Stoic
hardihood, I, the stern promulgator of *Amor fati*, put on the
mantle of Elijah, and with the cosmic frenzy of a Jeremiah
pronounced doom upon our age, the age of the triumphant
Philistines.[5]

What I hated in Carlyle, his smug, canting, Pecksniffian

---

[5] Nietzsche, like Matthew Arnold, identifies *the Philistines* with the middle-class,
thus joining Carlyle, Ruskin and other Victorian critics of bourgeois democracy —
the Tory phalanx. — Editor

assumption of the Messiah's role — this curse of the Christ-smitten Jew — entered my very vitals until I began to prophesy through my wounds instead of letting them heal with Stoic resignation.

What a pathos of distance between Heraclitus and his disciple Nietzsche, who despite his revolt against the slave-morality of Jesus is barred from his Heraclitean ideal by nineteen Christian centuries of love and pity! Heraclitus, the Ephesian, did not have any Naumburg to contend with, no hypocritical townspeople who saturated the atmosphere with Christian feeling and poisoned the mind with thoughts of the Crucifixion. This Christian poison has remained in my blood, so that the proud eagle and the wise serpent — the common possession of Heraclitus and Zarathustra — have fused in the shameful image of the Cross.

Like the Ephesian I still retain an aristocratic scorn for morals, for comfort and ease, and, like him, I glorify strife, but *unlike* the ancient philosopher, I have allowed this strife to enter my soul, so that my spirit has become a battlefield between two world-views, the Judeo-Christian and the Græco-Roman, the moral and the unmoral. This conflict, which was already present in Plato, the augur of Christ's disease of love and compassion, split my mind in two, so that my friends received mad, fantastic letters from Turin signed "the Crucified" and "Dionysos."

Heraclitus wrote no such squibs and libels generated by a distraught mind sundered by the conflicts of our age. He had a faith in eternal Reason, the only part of his creed which I did not adopt, because, deluded by Schopenhauer, I confused time with eternity, and placed the Philistine on the empty throne of God, the Philistine whose mindlessness and irrational aimlessness became for me the qualities of Godhead. Fighting the Philistines, I became a Philistine myself, abandoning the Heraclitean will to reason for the blind will to power, the will that destroys itself in impotence if it is not guided by a cosmic Mind, as Pascal so clearly realized.

Now in the grip of this creeping paralysis which makes every paragraph I write a Calvary of the soul, an Apocalyptic anguish, I realize more than ever that my crusade against Socrates was really a war upon myself, I mean that part of my rational being which I possessed in common with Heraclitus, my will to reason, my passion for absolute Truth, which forced me, despite myself, to renounce Wagner and Wagnerism — the cesspools of irrational treacle which the ignorant still mistake for the organ-pipes of divine music.

I do not agree with Shakespeare that the gods torment and mutilate us as schoolboys torture and pull off the wings of flies. On the contrary, the gods have been kind to me, and through the lesson of paralysis and brain disease they have taught me to value physical and mental health all the more, crushing my Dionysian frenzy into a better appreciation of Apollonian calm and Socratic reason. I enjoy the invincible optimism of Goethe who said: *We stand in the protection of loving gods who care for us better than we care for ourselves.*

4

Not only gods but goddesses protect us from ourselves. My Russian Venus, by demonstrating the destructiveness and futility of Dionysian madness, brought me back to my Spinozistic conviction that man's divinity is expressed in the love of truth, that the Greek orgy is a wild, corybantic effort to stamp out the fear and ignorance of life in erotic hysteria and shameless sexual practices. Lou Salomé became a drug to me, like the chloral and Javanese narcotic which I stopped using during our frenzied bouts together, a drug which swept me through all the terrible abysses of agony and bliss described by the English opium-eater De Quincey.

Having cured myself of Lou Salomé I felt like a reformed

drug-addict who could once again enjoy Spinoza's intellectual love of God and revel once more in the kingdom of the human spirit. How deep Zarathustra had fallen; this eagle and his snake looking down upon him with scorn from the great height of cosmic awareness!

But such is the dialectical paradox of life — a paradox which Heraclitus was first to discover — that Lou's Judas-treachery was really a blessed display of divine grace: having taught me the meaninglessness of her sterile kisses, she forced me to remove the Dionysian foundations of my philosophy — foundations built on a cloud — and place it in the firm bedrock of scientific knowledge. I wove into my power-thought the findings of the Social Darwinists, and if the Socialists spin me on my head and turn me into an advocate of People's Power, I am ready to stand on my head for their benefit. I do not dread the democratic triumph of the People, if history has decreed the triumph of the many over the few. What matters is the virile strength of Life itself which always decrees that victory must go to the strong — strong in body, mind and spirit. Mere brute force, I am now convinced, is not in harmony with the cosmic scheme of things.

This, of course, was known by Pascal long ago. Force must be compatible with rational justice, otherwise it breaks into barbarism. This was the pivotal idea of Paul Rée, the Jew, who together with Lou Salomé (is she a crypto-Jewess from the house of Herod?) worked on me with the fanaticism of Saint Paul pounding his Christ-message into the iron skulls of the Romans. She depreciated her Cleopatra role, insisting that she had more respect for the serpent of Zarathustra than the serpent of the Nile. Just as Paul[6] denied Jehovah with his head and affirmed him with his heart, Lou affirmed Venus with her heart but denied her with her head.

---

[6] Nietzsche means Paul Rée, of course, not Saint Paul. — Editor

She convinced me that we could no longer play the role of Ovidian lovers, since the centuries that intervened between Augustus and Tolstoy were hurdles which we, in our Christian consciousness of sin, could not leap. The idylls of Theocritus and the love-songs of Catullus celebrated a classic age that had not heard of original sin, and a woman's body was not transformed by conscience-stricken poets into the body of Deity itself. The "little pastor" in me rebelled against her Cyprian nakedness and the ghost of her murdered conscience haunted her into an acceptance of the Tolstoyan creed that sexual expression was somehow the work of the Devil.

And so we both put on fig-leaves and banished ourselves from the Garden, while my sister Elisabeth gave us a strong push from the rear to make sure that we did not follow the example of Lot's wife and look back with longing on the flaming city of our sins . . .

Who but a woman can give a man integration in a world shattered to bleeding bits by the Caesars of industrialism? Only the womb knows the agony of man's mutilated life, divided against itself, and only the womb can recall man back to the cosmos of Heraclitus who in a world of tumultuous change could yet eye the unchanging Absolute, the divine Reason riding the chaos of the ages and holding aloft the banners of harmony and peace.

5

For nature there is renovation, for man there is none. Dear Horace, how well you have spoken! In my rustic retreat, as in yours, nature renews itself constantly; the buds burst into sunflowers, worshiping Helios like Julian the Apostate who yearned to return man to nature and thus assure his immortality. But we can still escape the cosmic cattle-yard of the Philistines where courage and hardihood are measured by Carlyle's *cash-nexus* and every human sentiment reduces itself to Iago's advice: *Put money in thy purse.*

We can still turn from Plato's Thrasymachus with his obscene lust for the power of the Philistine drowning himself in sybaritic enjoyments, to the Stoic discipline of Zarathustra who commands the future, breathes mountain air and takes no nourishment from newspapers, politics, beer and Wagnerian music. We can still train our wills to seek their best sky-haunted selves — the Superman ideal!

Why do we find racks and thumbscrews for our own minds, twisting our misery to the breaking-point of madness? The Medusa-glare of paralysis is turning me into stone, but I can still turn my face towards the garden and watch the roses straining towards their incense, smitten by their own delightful fragrance. There is a luxury in being alive, without goal or purpose, sucking the sun like a garden flower, forgetting the anguish of being in the mere lust for life.

That is the wisdom of cattle which are not cursed by the mortal malady of the Ideal and, lowing knee-deep in clover, resign themselves to their finite nature, refusing to challenge the heavens with Satanic scorn. Alas, alas, I have sought to rise above my cattledom and bleed like one of Virgil's bulls, turning the green grass red with my bellowing death. Yet my bellows are silent and the Lama does not suspect that my broken skies are aflame with lightning and rock with thunder when I smile pleasantly as the guests are introduced — like Homer's catalogue of ships . . .

As the twilight descends upon the garden and the last rays of sun depart forever, I am filled with a holy resignation and repeat with the Stoic Emperor:[7] *Whatever is expedient unto thee, O world, is expedient unto me; nothing can either be unseasonable unto me or out*

---

[7] Marcus Aurelius. — Editor

of date which unto thee is seasonable. O Nature, from thee are all things, in thee all things subsist and to thee all things tend. Could he say of Athens thou lovely city of Cecrops; shalt not thou say of the world thou lovely city of God?

Thus spake Zarathustra, who is the incarnation of every man who has said Yea to Life in the midst of death, thus transcending his mortality, and in his divine Godmanhood wishing himself into a dancing star!

6

When I proposed to the Dutch girl in Geneva, after a few hours' acquaintanceship, I was terrified at the thought that she might accept my rash proposal, which came in a sudden fit of Wagnerian romanticism. But the stars favored me that day, and the pretty Dutch girl flatly turned me down.

I should have followed my colleague Burckhardt's example. His copy of Schopenhauer was annotated entirely with question marks, and I should have tagged question marks to all the women who fascinated me, including Fräulein Salomé. Belief in women is a form of idolatry, and in an age when principles no longer command the loyalty of men we bow down before idols in Prussian uniforms or silken petticoats.

The idea of idolatry, whether it refers to a government or a girl, is not a lapse into paganism but into stupidity. Frederick the Great said: "If I had more than one life I would sacrifice them to the Fatherland. I do not think of fame, but of the State alone." Of course Frederick, with his Machiavellian cunning, lied like Baron Munchausen, but even if he meant it he would still be a royal idiot, despite his apotheosis in the pages of Carlyle. But it is a healthy instinct to give flesh and blood to ideas and theories, otherwise they wander about like the shades in the Hades of Homer, mere phantoms of the damned.

It was a healthy instinct on my part to seek the concrete

reality of love in the body of the Dutch girl, but I should have remembered that she was merely a fleeting embodiment of the Platonic Form, the absolute Beauty that the artist can only grasp in the creative imagination. Although a belief in Plato is not a part of my creed, any philosopher can be seized upon in an emergency when the Lorelei sings her wild song on the rock and lures the fisherman to destruction . . .

At least the blonde Dutch girl introduced me to Longfellow and his poem *Excelsior* which I at first thought was a plagiarism of my Superman idea, until I discovered that the masterpiece was as old as myself. Ever since then I have had a sincere respect for the New England poet, even though I am told that every brothel-harlot in America can recite his poetry, especially *The Village Blacksmith*.

7

Like Titania she forgot my face in the moonlight and bestowed her kisses on an ass. But this is inevitable when a lion lives among jackasses and the braying of a donkey sounds like a love-song in feline ears.

I live in my own elemental universe where Goethean sense and sensibility combine to create the atmosphere of enjoyment. I with my mountain-vision — what have I to do with the cattle in the valley or with the stallions that mount their mares at the command of nature?

Only Aspasia could understand my love-passion, because she lived in a Periclean age when mind was flesh and flesh was mind, the two fusing in the bright flame of nuptial love. But Athens has given way to the Rousseau-rage for equality, and I stand, a giant among pygmies who know no sound but the bray of the flesh and have brothered the ass like Saint Francis . . .

Some day I shall go to the house where Rousseau was born and smash all the windows. Meanwhile I shall live for cultural duties and awaken the philosopher, the artist and the saint in me and in others. Must I mope over Titania and her ass and exile myself from the vast community of European culture?

8

Pascal, the keen huntsman, pursued every phenomenon to its lair, the infinitesimally small and the mammoth dinosaurs of the mud. But could he explain the love-at-first-sight of Candide and the beautiful Cunegonde "after dinner as they were leaving the table"?

Does a full stomach have a direct relation to the sentiment of romantic love which is unknown among jungle savages, many of whom have ruled the word "love" out of their language and have substituted the word *appetite* instead? Christian missionaries have found it difficult to preach love to aborigines, just as they cannot saddle them with the idea of God because their highest idea in life is not God but elephant steaks or wild boar meat.

I touch upon this bit of philology — which was my speciality at Basel — because, like the unfortunate Candide, I have been expelled from the magic castle of love *with a volley of kicks in the rear.*

I fell in love at first sight after having dinner with my Russian Helen: too bad I do not suffer from Carlyle's dyspepsia; if the food had turned sour in my stomach my love-affair might have died with the first belch!

9

I am a hybrid of Socrates and shade, a thinking phantom among the damned. The world is weary of philosophers; I am weary of my Socratic self. What Socrates assumed to be a remedy was only another manifestation of the disease — the disease of *thought!* My spirit has dared the ultimate truth, the absolute certainty, and this certainty has made me mad. My wisdom, at last, is disenchanted; I know less than Hamlet, less than Socrates, *less than nothing!* This is the final truth: *there is no truth*, there is only the dying spirit hanging in agony on the Cross . . .

O rat-catcher of Athens, O Crito, I too owe Æsculapius a cock. I too was sick for a time with the disease of life, rejecting Death, the doctor, dodging him with my reason, with my instincts, with my masks of illusion, with my disguises of sky-towering thoughts. Now the masquerade is over, the farce ends. *Der Vorhang fällt, das Stück ist aus!* The last light of all sputters into darkness — *das arme Licht war meine Seele.*[8]

Like the Danaides I was compelled to pour water into a vessel full of holes. Now the sieve is sinking, the galleys of Socrates are devoured by the waves, and all the galley-slaves drown with their ships, while the skies roar with the flames of the world's madness. O Antichrist, O "third man" of Aristotle, O impotent mediator between earth and sky: where is your Hellenic wisdom at this Apocalyptic hour, this moment of final doom? Answer me, Mathilde,[9] watching your poet on his mattress-grave! . . . But can a cow answer when Socrates himself cannot solve the riddle? Even the rock of Goethe melts away in the blazing sun of the Nazarene!

Thou hast conquered, O Galilean; Julian the Apostate lies crushed beneath your heels. Thou hast conquered me, O Heine, thy meek Nazarene has crushed the proud Hellene who has defied him, and even now, in his dying moment, defies him forever! The vine wreaths of Dionysos trail in the dust; he is torn to pieces and flung to the wolves, but the winds lift their trum-

---

[8] "The curtain falls, the piece is over. The poor light was my soul." Nietzsche is quoting from the dying Heine in whom he found a close spiritual kinship. — Editor

---

[9] Heine's ignorant peasant-wife who knew him only through his suffering. Nietzsche's irony reaches the height of pathos. — Editor

pets and blow life through the world's funeral! . . .

I am no longer a plump Hellene filled with the joy of life, look-ing with smiling condescension on the lowly Nazarenes; I am nothing but a poor Jew, sick unto death, an emaciated image of misery, an unhappy wretch! I am an unhappy wretch, too, dear Heine, but shall Nazareth or Jehovah claim me because the grave yawns open? Nay, nay: *where there are graves there are also resurrections!*

Those do not betray Life, Life never betrays!

10

God hath made foolish the wisdom of the world, said Saint Paul. Not God but our own idiocy has turned culture into anti-culture so that the modern sophists — the humanists, the empiricists, the relativists, the utilitarians and the individualists — find themselves in the same twilight of the mind whose vapors are seething in my brain, a purple fog that threatens to plunge into total darkness.

I cannot reconcile myself to the Epicurean thought: *Learn betimes to die, or, if you like it better, to pass over to the gods.* It is not for me to choose to become a god or a corpse, a superman or a handful of bitter dust: such sophistic reasoning is possible for Epicurus sunning himself in his luxuriant garden, but not for me, sweating blood and torment in the garden of Gethsemane, feeling my mind and body rot as the rood is prepared for my crucifixion.

Tranquility of mind, peace of soul while the love of my heart is gone and I am mocked by an epileptic Jew who stands in the center of my brain and laughs hilariously like a riotous Philistine, while Samson, blinded and chained to a pillar, bellows his wrath at his tormentors. *God hath made foolish the wisdom of the world!* . . . Enough, enough, this Philistine laughter must cease! I shall crash the pillars of sanity and plunge headlong into the ruins! . . .

God hath made foolish the wisdom of the world. Ah, Jew, thou knowest how to mock the warrior of culture since he can fight no longer, having lost faith in his cause. But death puts an end to all mockery; laughter must stop this side of the grave!

11

Since I am dying, I Gaius Caesar,[10] called also Caligula, order the death of Tiberius, grandson of Emperor Tiberius, who has assumed the *toga virilis* and whose vicarious death may alleviate the sufferings of my last hours on earth.

I order the death of Potitus, the plebeian, who promised to die in the event I recovered from my illness; since I may still recover I decree that he make good his oath and suffer the penalty of crucifixion.

I order the deification of my sister Drusilla Elisabeth, that a golden effigy of her shall be set up in the Senate house, and that in the temple of Venus in the Forum a statue of her shall be dedicated of the same size as that of the Goddess and honored by the same rites.

I decree also that a shrine in her honor shall be built, a temple with twenty priests, women as well as men, and on her birthday a festival shall be celebrated equal in rank to the Ludi Megaleures.

Signed, Gaius Caesar, Imperator.

12

When Hegel was finishing his *Phenomenology*, he looked out the window and saw Napoleon's troops enter Jena. I look out this madhouse window in Jena and see the phantoms at Napoleon's

---

[10] Nietzsche at this point is obviously mad, though he is sane enough to weave his sister into his pattern of lunacy which leads to the suspicion that his "obvious" madness may be a subterfuge — one of the many masks he used to hide his terrible thoughts. Nietzsche's mother is said to have confiscated many of these "mad" effusions — the products of a broken mind. — Editor

army marching past me, laughing at the philosopher with the hammer as they must have laughed at Hegel with his *world-historical character*, the man who embodies an era and creates it.

What Napoleon, the self-appointed aristocrat, created is the *delusion* of power, the same delusion of grandeur that obsessed me when I appointed myself the intellectual despot of Europe. It is forever true that the genius, in his warfare against the Philistines, puffs himself up to heroic stature, and, like Goethe, chooses an unkempt, nauseating boor like Frederick the Great as his *alter ego*, the man who incarnates his secret will to power. In the same manner I thought myself into Napoleon, and in worshiping him I, Professor Nietzsche, with my spectacled eyes and scholar's stoop, mounted a white charger and rode furiously into battle — "the greatest man who has come into the world since Caesar," as Stendhal called Bonaparte.

This madhouse has cured me of such nonsense, for every other man looks upon himself as Napoleon, and if I were permitted to enter the women's quarters I would find female Bonapartes and Caesars as opinionated, tyrannical and remorseless as the Lama or Mama herself. Now that I have met my Waterloo and am caged up here in Saint Helena, I can be anti-Nietzschean enough to realize that the masses, whom I called *manure*, are really the triumphant force in history, while the Caesars and Napoleons are merely sparks struck from the iron boots of the People which grind into the dust every manifestation of genius and Caesarism that fails to carry out the People's will.

The Rousseauan democrats and Socialists will greet this confession with triumphant exaltation: it is the first time in my thinking career that I have admitted the heroic role of the anonymous crowd which romantics like Hugo, Scott, Delacroix, Michelet and Berlioz have made the keystone of their aesthetic creed. The aristocratic Hellenes, on the other hand, will accuse me of betraying the cause of culture by entering the Jewish camp of the

Nazarenes where Heine retreated when he was dying. They will attribute my renegade Hebraism to my madness, which is the truth. Having stripped myself of all illusions, I have gone mad; the last veil had dropped from the dancing Salomé, and the tray is brought in, bearing the head of John the Baptist — my system of aristocratic thought.

Nietzsche contra Nietzsche: I will astound the world with my self-treason. But am I not mounting the horse of Napoleon again and riding back into the battlefield of aristocratic thought which I have just abandoned? . . . The Caesarism of the genius is congenital: having nothing but his mind to fight with, he abstracts himself from the mindless masses and barricades himself behind his false thesis of anti-democratic thought. But his will to power is really a will to powerlessness, a will to exile himself from his humanity. But once we have embarked on the adventure of the human, as Pascal suggested, we cannot plunge back to the subhuman or drive forward towards the Superhuman.

We are limited by our humanity; to break out of the walls of our bodies and challenge the gods with Promethean defiance: that is the path I have followed, a path I sought to retreat from when I wrote *Human All-Too Human* and *The Joyful Wisdom.* But if we remain within the barriers of the human we come to the conclusion with Macbeth that life is *a tale told by an idiot;* life, as dictated by the Philistines, becomes a mockery of life and we are forced to call upon the imaginary gods within us to transcend life and live in the rare atmosphere of the Superman — the pure air of Messianic madness. And so atheists like Delacroix, Berlioz and myself become God-intoxicated artists, and through the medium of art seduce ourselves into the roles of frenzied Messiahs, warriors of the Ideal which we reject as religious superstition.

What do I know? asked Montaigne. Renaissance man took pride in knowing, but we, in the savage indignation of our hearts, are bogged in the confusion of modern thought and feeling, which despite the shallow optimism of our age, forces us to say as Berlioz said: *What's the use? Thought and feeling have negated themselves; we are in the very vortex of nihilism; that is why I have predicted an age of chaos and delirium when men drink from the cup of trembling and collapse in the slaughter of universal war.*

An Aristophanes of the twentieth century will pillory me as Democritus was once lampooned: *Long live King Vortex who has dethroned Zeus!* Or I shall be raised aloft in a basket with Socrates and Zarathustra sniffing the mountain air of pure intelligence while the groundlings laugh, biting into their sausages and draining their beer mugs to demonstrate their mundane superiority over the sky-scraping philosophers.

The truth is that modern thought is like the frightened Andromeda chained to the sea-girt rock while the hell-breathing Chimæra of nihilism spits fire and brimstone upon her beautiful nakedness. Like a conquering Perseus I rushed to the rescue of that divine captive, holding her chaste nakedness in my arms. But since I am a creature of my age I found myself spitting flame upon her thighs and bosom: I was myself the Chimæra, a part of our time's madness which I had fought in the role of the timeless Perseus, the Socratic thinker whose mind ticks with the mind of the Absolute.

Damned by faith and unfaith, by reason and instinct, by flesh and by the spirit, I see the Chimæra devouring Andromeda in a burst of flaming madness. And this flaming madness is in my brain: I am the Devoured and the Devourer, the killer and the slain.

But outside the madhouse window I look in and see Nietzsche, the philosopher, foaming at the mouth, gazing at Socrates in the mirror and smashing the treacherous image of himself. I join Napoleon's army, the army of the people, for there is nothing left but the mindless masses that shall generate minds of their own . . .

If I cannot be Napoleon Bonaparte, *I can at least be Peter Schlemihl!*

13

Rousseau was the greatest high priest of those who kiss and tell, but in enrolling Madame de Warens into the communion of the saints he was not adding to history but merely feeding his own egregious vanity. I could not do the same for Cosima, Lou or the Lama for I have too much respect for truth to shape it into the image of a romantic or religious ideal.

If I have been cruel in my revelations with regard to the fair sex, I could not match the audacity of George Sand, who turned all her lovers into printer's ink and coined her kisses into ready cash to take care of herself and her family.

If I have used a metaphorical knife to slice off a female head or two, I have not been as ferocious as Claudius's Agrippina who slew Lollia Paulina because she feared her as a rival for the Emperor's affections. As she did not recognize the woman's head when it was brought to her, Dio Cassius tells us, she opened the mouth with her own hand and inspected the teeth which had certain dental peculiarities.

I have never been guilty of such frightfulness, especially in relation to women, and though I have cautioned others to be hard and ruthless, I have borne the yoke of pity all my life and when I saw a horse in Turin beaten by his master I rushed out of the house and embraced the animal, shedding bitter tears over his fate.

This has been the cause of my ruin: the split between my preachment and practice, and this has been a part of the great sundering in the mind of the West, which, like mine, is going mad.

Like Dicaepolis[11] the sturdy peasant, I want peace at any price, and as I am the only one who wants it, I have concluded a solemn treaty with myself. But the charcoal burners[12] of Acharnae hasten to attack me as a traitor to the cause of war, a cause that I have glorified in my writings.

But have I? How clever of the Nietzscheans to turn Nietzsche against himself! When I praised war I did not mean the butchery of populations towards which modern wars are tending. In such wars only the soldiers of the Bismarcks reap any benefits: they coin the blood of men, women and children into gold and silver. Ever since Waterloo war has become an antiquated and wasteful way of settling disputes, and we need another Aristophanes to drown our warriors in waves of laughter! When mass butchery becomes ridiculous and is stripped of all nobility, the Philistines will cease to advocate it, fearing to make themselves the objects of public derision.

But in saying this I fear I am acting like the ancient Greek who set fire to the school of Socrates in order to free Athens of Socratic rhetoric which hides unreason in the dialectical veils of reason. The cult of war is too deeply rooted in the consciousness of Europeans to be uprooted by the hands of laughter and even when it will become a bloody farce threatening the existence of humanity itself, men will rush to their beer-gardens,[13] drinking the bitter brew of death and destruction!

---

[11] Hero of Aristophanes' play *The Acharnians*. — Editor

---

[12] Asylum guards? — Editor

---

[13] Nietzsche's hatred of beer — a shocking heresy to a true German — is here associated with the deadly poison of world suicide! — Translator

But the laughter is a precious thing in itself — as the maniacs in this madhouse realize — and though it can not stop war, it can at least make the demagogues look foolish as they are pursued by the hounds of irony in their metaphorical underwear. In *The Knights* Aristophanes makes the slave Demosthenes cross-examine a sausage-seller to discover whether he is ignorant enough to become a statesman and a war-maker. Our Bismarcks should not be allowed to rule and ruin nations until they are interviewed by a madman like myself: being a perfect idiot I can recognize political morons without asking too many questions.

Plato tells us that the Graces, seeking a temple which should not perish, chose the soul of Aristophanes. The spirit of laughter is imperishable, and I am so imbued with the spirit that I laugh at my own madness. Contemporary man, seeking a hiding-place from the furies of mass warfare, can barricade himself in my brain: here Laughter reigns supreme, and those who cling to this clown's garments can contemplate the Abyss with a smile.

14

My sister has read me an article[14] by an   writer who has perhaps shown a greater understanding of my historic significance than I have myself. He writes:

I have revolted against the leveling effect of such philosophies as Hegelianism and Socialism and such religions as Christianity which must inevitably remove the pathos of distance

---

[14] The copy is here so bad that the nationality of the writer and the quotation Nietzsche gives from him could not be made out with any certainty. It was at first conjectured that the reference might have been to an article by John G. Robertson, but the date of its appearance, 1898, ruled it out. — Editor

between the strong-minded few and the weak-minded many, thus grinding human culture into a common mold of sterile mediocrity. The modern sophists, by forcing philosophy to "bake bread" for the masses, have, like Protagoras, shaved the mind itself into the Heraclitean flux, leaving no standard for judgment except the whim and fancy of the individual. We have reached the ultimate nihilism of the sophist Gorgias: *Nothing is; knowledge cannot be communicated because nothing actually exists.*

I realize, as Parmenides did long ago, that the pivotal problem of philosophy was to rediscover *that which permanently is,* the ideal of the Superman towards which all human striving must be directed. The paradox of life lies in the fact that if we abandon the ideal for the real, the Absolute for the Relative, eternity for time, we do not retain our humanity but lose it in the whirling vortex of ceaseless change. Not man but *Superman* is the measure; Protagoras must give way to Nietzsche, and we must go star-gazing again like Thales, even though, like him, some of us may fall into a well.

Of course I thought it advisable to have a Thracian maid accompany me on my star-gazing walks through the fields, but instead of guarding me against a fatal misstep she actually put her pretty leg out so that I stumbled over it and fell. I therefore advise philosophers to do their star-gazing alone, and when they spy a dancing star to make sure it is not a figment of their imaginations, a trap to catch the gullible . . .

I am thankful to the English writer especially because I am completely neglected in England or denounced as Antichrist. On the contrary, if Christianity means the substitution of the Cross for humbug and opportunism, then surely I must be accepted as a disciple of Jesus. If, as Justin Martyr said, Socrates was the only Christian *before* the coming of Christ, I have been the only Christian *after* the coming of Christ.

This is the factual truth which the next century will discover when it builds on my hypothesis of power-thought a world-structure without humbug, a building as lie-proof as the Parthenon itself.

15

Like George Sand, Lou Salomé had only two idols — her art and her body — and her art was usually expressed through her Venus-body. George Sand's fiction was merely confession of her erotic being; she studied every boudoir gesture, measured every sigh of her numerous lovers and with infinite detail recorded them in her books. But this Napoleon of the bedroom, this strategist of many a campaign in the naked battles of the sexes, was a mere corporal in comparison to Lou, whose dress of studied simplicity merely accentuated the voluptuous contours of her body, and whose pungent perfume, as provocative as the naked loveliness of Helen, was a summons to ardor, to the mystic ritual of Aphrodite.

Like George Sand, too, she was a law unto herself, but only a woman can defy the laws of man and nature without suffering the vengeance of the gods. Women, like Jews, have never been allowed the status of mortality: they are either angels or demons, or both, thronging the Jacob's ladder between heaven and hell. They do not will to exist because they are existence itself, embodying the eternal principle of good and evil. Since woman is an elemental force it is as ridiculous to accuse a woman of bad morals as it is to indict the lightning for striking a church and thus making a mockery of God.

Aristides was ostracized because people were tired of having him called the Just, and men exile themselves from human decency by seeking to justify themselves at the expense of the Eternal Feminine, the riddle of the ages. And contemplating humanity as a whole, in the sober light of realism, I agree with Lessing's exclamation:

Der Mensch, wo ist er her?
Zu schlecht für einen Gott, zu gut fürs Ungefähr.[15]

The desire to be good is an illusion — a fantasy that few women indulge in. Their virtue was once man's greatest achievement — the triumph of art over feminine nature. But Lou Salomé, trained in the school of Russian nihilism, has chosen female emancipation and cast off the straitjacket of Philistine morals. This is what attracted me to her, her fierce Aspasia-like rejection of those middle-class values which I only dared deny in my books.

If I had lost faith in her it is because I lost faith in myself, in my life's star. But now my Zarathustra-prayer has been answered: *Give me, ye Powers, madness, that I may believe in myself.* Being stark mad, I believe firmly in myself and cling to Lou with the cosmic certainty of Job. To paraphrase the distraught Jew who dared to force God to justify his ways to man, I can truthfully say: *Though she slay me, yet shall I trust in her.*

16

I have tried to turn philosophy into an art — the art of living. With this goal in mind I followed the example of Empedocles of Agrigentum and sought to organize all knowledge into a single whole, to harmonize with the symphony of the planets. Music, poetry, science, philosophy, ethics, politics and literature — I studied them all to establish man's hegemony over nature, so that he could pass beyond man to Godmanhood, reaching the goal of the Superman.

But since there was no love in my age or in my private life, I could not conceive of any cosmic Love rooted in man's members, as Empedocles put it, and the cosmic conflict between love and

---

[15] "Oh man, what path is thine?
Too good art thou for chance, too base to be divine."

strife which harmonized itself in the process of dynamic living, became for me strife alone, the sheer brutality of social Darwinism. It was Lou Salomé who pounded away at her Tolstoyan thesis of love's hegemony over hate, a thesis that Empedocles himself expounded and in which I lost faith when I was exposed as a child to the frost-bitten Puritanism of Naumburg with its chilling atmosphere of prudery and decorum.

In her arms I could well believe with Empedocles that cosmic love was rooted in my own members and vouched for itself. And if I acted like Goethe's Werther when she was taken from me through the despicable tactics of the Lama, it was because I was hysterical with dread that I would lose my grip on the love which had become for me life itself, life naked and triumphant!

The legend-makers saw Empedocles plunging into the belching flames of Aetna, but this fate was reserved not for the great pre-Socratic but for me alone. Having been separated from the love of my life, the love that made me human, I made my desperate plunge into the fires of madness, hoping like Zarathustra to snatch faith in myself by going out of my mind and entering a higher region of sanity — the sanity of the raving lunatic, the normal madness of the damned!

CHAPTER SIX

1

A woman passed by the window yesterday morning and when the last glimpse of her died out in my eyes, she had taken almost all of my tenderness away with her.

I would like to describe this in detail because I believe it is one of the few vital experiences possible to a sick man or a prisoner.

(May it not at least be conjectured that the sick and the imprisoned in our midst form the top-soil out of which grows all that is beautiful and desirable in the backyard of this ugly mill?)

I saw the faint outline of her long-distance-veiled face, but the face itself — the thing one might live and dream with — I did not catch a glimpse of. A long brown cloak which fell carelessly from her shoulders all but covered her tall, lingering form. It was the most desperate guess-work to imagine her breasts, her waist-line, her thighs and her feet.

Nowhere, nohow could I get even the echo of a hint of what her eyes might be like.

As she moved into my vision she became everything I had of hope. While she remained in my eyes she was all I knew of beauty. I was outside the pale of sweetness when she finally faded out of the landscape.

I once thought that a bird which passed this same window might be God on an inspection tour. But what God ever brought as much into a human life as did this anonymous woman?

2

I have learned too little from too many teachers. Reading in the classics — and dreaming of the throat of Fräulein Raabe — have brought me the only pure happiness I can mention without humiliation.

3

I speak of my own joyful wisdom as contrasted with the sad wisdom which is that of Arthur Schopenhauer. Schopenhauer had this much more to offer the world: sadness only lets down into deeper sadness, whereas the letdown from joy is to what I am living through now.

4

If freaks are what children delight in seeing, and it is desirable to humor the little ones in this strange whim of theirs, they need not necessarily be sent to the circus, where sadness is always accompanied by a strain of brutality. We have only to extend their schooling into the high schools and colleges of our great country. There they meet, in their instructors, the utmost of what can be expected in human freaks.

5

All these tragic interruptions in the solemn journey from one hole to another!

6

I seem to have paused in my career of violence after the first blood-letting. Did I undergo a change of mind about the glory of waging the good fight? A good doctor should be able to find out. But first one would have to find a good doctor.

7

As I grow older I am more and more fascinated by ideas and less and less attracted by people.

8

With my poor eyesight it is easier for me to recognize a good idea than an old friend. With my eyesight what it is, how is a new friend of mine ever to become an old friend?

9

If I had the choice of how to be brought up in a second childhood, I think I would prefer a brothel to a pious home such as I was actually brought up in. Unless I happen to be in love with her, the sight of a woman usually strikes me as an anomaly. It is I, of course, who am out of place.

10

No, it is not the world that is out of joint, but I, its great lover, I the lover of the natural — who never did a natural thing unless I could find an artificial act that would do just as well. Witness: I do not live, I write.

11

As a Dionysian I am a reveler who does not revel, a bohemian who does not enjoy drinking, an exponent of the universal whirl who is even too sick to put his arm around the waist-line of a woman and dance.

12

I have every confidence in my future until I remember Schopenhauer, with whom I break every morning and become reconciled all over again every twilight. With all his faults, he was fuller, purer, more understanding than I can ever be. He was even a little madder. I can forgive him almost anything but that.

13

An artist is a man who disciplines himself as if he were a god and, for the rest, behaves as if his own chance of pleasure is to act like a human being.

14

Apollonian art and Dionysian living — two vaporous dreams — form an ideal for a community, not for any individual. It is a mistake to try to go too deeply into their comparative values because none of their values are of a comparable nature and they are each of equal importance in the development of any race or nation. This Dionysian — who is capable only of an Apollonian expression of his energies — would have been able to settle down into a much more peaceful mode of life if this bit of understanding had come to him a little earlier.

15

Modern life suffers of one radical departure from the ways of the Greeks. Greek artists thought of themselves as not only artists in their own lights, but as artisans of the Greek state. We live only as individuals, our aims are individual aims, our achievements are limited to personal glories. We measure our powers not along the rising line of communal greatness but as we compare in growth and stature with other individuals more or less like ourselves. We write poems to women, carve out statues to politicians and entertain hopes which apply to tiny spasms of action.

16

As a matter of sober fact, individuals have no more value in themselves than they do when they form hastily into violent mobs. They are nothing while they live and they are less than nothing after they are securely dead.

17

I could speak forever about the army without ever approaching an understanding of it — in Prussian life or in my own. When a fit of patriotism brought me into it, I was inconsiderately shoved into the cavalry — where a horse always stood between me and any military objective I contemplated. It is a matter of record that no horse was ever broken in by me, but that one of them bent and almost broke me.

18

The state of personal grace, human excellency — chief attributes of the citizen of the Greek state — how do they level against the cold iron of Bismarck?

19

The wall of a city divided the Greeks from barbarism. It usually left out more than it let in.

20

The faculties of destruction had to be kept alive in Athens whose citizens were always so heavily outnumbered by their slaves. But it would be a mistake to try to discover in this the secret of their cultural predominance. In approximately the same situation, what have we received from the American state of Alabama?

21

Waters in which whales may swim in search of ocean small fry are deep waters. Germany is such a sea for the Jew-baiting Prussians.

22

The saddest possible reflection on Greek culture is that while it is a record of the triumph of Athens over the primitive peoples surrounding her, it is, above all things, a record of spiritual failure. You see in it life not building upward but peering down into its own roots, fiercely resolved that it is the shell of a void containing sufficient explosives to effect its own complete annihilation.

23

I don't expect anyone in my time to think like me or to find a home in my particular style of writing and thinking. But as sure as I am that the doctor will reach out his hand for my pulse as he passes by, and smile that meaningless, idiotic smile of his, I am sure that all the savants of today and tomorrow will come to the same end — my end.

24

How do you get along with the other people in this house? Elisabeth asked me the other day.

I told her that I get along very well with the inmates but that is hardly true of my relations with the doctors, who make all the trouble here not only for me but for the rest of the inmates.

But you have to have doctors, Elisabeth said.

That's so. You have to have doctors and you have to have notaries and lawyers, and God help us all.

25

After Elisabeth left yesterday a man walked in who was so charming and intelligent that I shuddered to think he might be another doctor. He did not come up to me with the usual doctorial boldness, but asked to be introduced to me, and when we were alone he asked me if I still thought I was justified in making goodness and power interchangeable words. When I answered that I was still of the same mind he asked me if I did not think my understanding of the word was a corruption of what is meant by goodness in the Christian gospels. *Jesus and his disciples were good-hearted men*, I said to him, *but they were bad economists. Goodness should be encouraged among men, among the rich as well as among the poor, but the fact remains that the means of being good are only to be found among the rich.*

26

In the world of ideas the philosophers do quite nobly, thank you. It is the paradoxes which bring that early gray to their thinning hair. Yet what are paradoxes but the tests of durability to which all ideas must be exposed if they are to have any future or any meaning? I have entertained all ideas and fought all paradoxes. I would have done better to give music lessons and find myself a wife with whom to have a household full of children.

27

To long for an ideal, knowing the price in blood people will have to pay in order to usher it into a practical existence; to invoke power knowing the price which power demands for the most trifling of favors; to want good, knowing that good comes of evil and it may, within itself, without any further notice, revert to its original nature; these are only some of the costs a man must bear for wanting to be a philosopher, instead of a grocer or an apothecary.

28

I have tried to breathe like Schumann, think like Schopenhauer and write like Plato. Never has the blessed tranquility of Schumann entered my soul for as much as a moment.

Schopenhauer is a fortress easier to fly over than to conquer. One might learn to write like Plato, but, this accomplished, could one bear the thought that Plato himself might some day, by the divine accident of returns in time, find himself reading it?

29

Somewhere in my soul there is a secret altar, hidden away among the thorny bushes of my personal vanity. With the help of red autumn leaves, plucked from the surrounding forest, I have spelled out on it the name Wilamowitz. Every once in a while I come to this altar and offer on it a sacrifice of gratitude. It is my debt not only to a sincere if somewhat unfortunate scholar, but, mostly, to the man who brought an ignominious end to my career as a philologist.

30

If I have one talent it is to make people angry. I make a rainbow of urine over the world and, in such matters, the world is never slow to reciprocate.

31

The first historian was the world's first great cheat and murderer. What carnage upon carnage must we give ourselves over to, in order to keep up with his extraordinary pretensions, his matchless lies, his unconscionable slanders? I once divided historians into monumental, antiquarian and critical. The only monumental historians I can now think of are the monumental liars.

32

Let us have no more great men. Let the little men settle back quietly into their inalienable dungheaps.

33

We can no more free ourselves from history than we can liberate ourselves from our fundamental animalism. It has become as natural for a man to remember Alexander as to pass water. It is as sequential to think of Napoleon as to head for the nearest lavatory after a heavy meal.

34

If I had my way I would not only burn all of the history books, I would pluck all the famous paintings off the walls of all the museums, I would take all the books off the shelves of the libraries, and store all of them in air-tight cellars for approximately a hundred years. Perhaps that way the little world of our time would get another big start. I would leave the statues where they are. Without them we might accidentally slip back again to our position on all fours.

35

If the world was as bad as Schopenhauer left it, I, Friedrich Nietzsche, did very little to improve it.

36

I once described the evil principle in Nature as our eternal inability to find what we seek. But when did Nature ever agree to make us a partner to her secrets? And how much more dreadful things might be if we found half the things we look for!

37

When I first heard Wagner I was quite young and altogether innocent of any knowledge of life's darker meanings. When I began to take Wagnerianism seriously, his music had to plough its way to my more sensitive regions through floods of dysentery, diphtheria and migraine headaches. I ask myself: What did I really hear, those days?

38

I loved Wagner part of the time. I never stopped loving Cosima. From Tribschen to Bayreuth the voyage as from Cosima to Wagner to Cosima. The first time Wagner invited me to Bayreuth, I decided to decline, and I did not go. I would never have gone there at all if I did not, suddenly, remember that Cosima was there too. That made quite a difference.

39

The first schism between Wagner and myself was the result of Wagner's unconscious impatience with me during my first Bayreuth visit. I came to talk about Greek tragedy and all he had in mind was Wagner and the world's failure to fall upon its knees before him.

40

If Wagner had not been a bad musician he would undoubtedly have made his mark as a great actor. As an actor Wagner would never have condescended to accept any of the roles he himself created.

41

Wagner's music would, nevertheless, have reached its objective, so terrifying was the frenzy with which he promoted it, if he had had some idea of how much of the abnormal, extravagant splendor, intoxicating sensuous dreaming go into the making of the average concert-goer. As it was, all the fire in Wagner's *dramatis personae* was low and weed-choked, all of his furies died in a fog of fardling.

42

Do we exist for the enlightenment of the mob, or is the mob the manure of which we, the giants of the earth, emerge, making possible our appearance, and conditioning our development?

43

As my faith in Wagner ebbs so does my confidence in myself as a citizen in the world of music. That opera which Wagner thought I should write — and with which he taunted me so frequently — it will never stop haunting me.

44

I have gone beyond Wagner, beyond music, into the music of my own prose. Woden wears wooden shoes whose clatter threatens to drown out the soft footsteps of Zarathustra. It will be a war to the death.

45

I could have been married off — in spite of Malwida's stupidity, Wagner's cajoling and my own unbreakable shyness — if only one of these meddlers had understood that I am not at all interested in middle-aged women with ancient yellowing virginities in good cloistral standing. Was it such a leap of the imagination to conjecture that the author of *The Dawn of Day* would have to have a young girl — even if she were only a little street-walker? They would make Zarathustra a boarder in an old ladies' home!

46

I was born into the wrong climate and into the wrong age. For a while I was so completely disarmed that I had to divide my time between gardening and my Greeks — the Greeks yielding me as much sustenance as my garden. My only salvation is to retreat as far south from this northern fastness as my slender means will take me.

47

I am so much like Leopardi, and yet so unlike him, too. Leopardi was proud, oversensitive, and chronically miserable, one of those who plot vengeance on the world for their own bad digestions. I suffer but I do not think of inflicting suffering on others. I would bring happiness to people if I thought it could possibly do them any good.

48

No, art does not justify life, it does not even justify itself. Neither art nor life stand in any crying need of justification.

49

The needs of my sexual nature grow, they do not diminish. I used to think, *Soon, soon, I will be through with it, I will be able to give over all of my passionate nature to the needs of philosophy*. Nothing of the sort is happening, and now I do not think it is ever likely to happen. Philosophy will always have to play second fiddle to the needs of my organic nature. It's like dying by fire.

50

The quietest, the deepest, the most rib-shattering jokes are played by life itself. I began my friendship with Paul Rée as the result of reading his *Psychological Observations*, a pitifully dull book in which he set out to prove the supremacy of self-love — and what did my years of association with Rée prove? That to understand his thesis you had to know Rée himself.

51

True understanding is not in the kernel of the atom, or in the kernel of the golden rule, but in what we happen to be digesting for the moment and finding it good.

52

Pity of others is a ghoulish species of self-gratification. Pity of ourselves is the lowest sort of self-degradation. If God really pities us, he is playing with loaded dice.

53

After my departure from Basel I tried working by night and sleeping by day. It was a comfort to know that while those dreadful little beasts were scurrying about their nasty little plots of mischief, I was released from the upper layer of consciousness which I inhabit with them only when I, too, am awake. And it was wonderful to work in the loneliness of the night — the only true loneliness possible to those of us who do not share the dreams of the armies of the little. I could play with myself at being a prince of darkness (a sort of Mephistopheles of the lower regions) but always I could feel the morning creep in on me, and it became more and more trying . . .

54

In all this talk of personal freedom, will you tell me what it is that we are free to do that would not be best left undone? We must think our way through the stumbling blocks of the material world. We must brace ourselves for every gradation of the surface of the earth. We must eat or perish. Where are the great alternatives?

55

Death is the X of all problems in metaphysics. Its role in life is not likely to be ascertained in our time or in the ways in which we think. Death is not cessation of consciousness or even of immediate personality, we are so haunted by the forms and figures and feelings of people who have passed away . . . What *is* death? No one really knows.

56

Kant's moral formula — *Act as if by your will the maxim of your act were about to become a universal law of nature* — is a piece of typically German hypocrisy. I do not remember that I felt that I had such a choice in anything I found it necessary to do. Nor can I imagine any sane person adopting this attitude in any situation conceivable to me. Kant has in mind what he thinks is the common good of the community? But what is the common good? and was Kant the man best qualified to perceive it for us?

57

I did not know when I wrote in *The Dawn of Day* that the only way for an artist to resist society's stupid pressure on him was to assume *the dance of darkness* which I am now making before the world. Am I following my own advice or is it my advice that is now following me inexorably, like a shadow?

58

In *Zarathustra* I opened out arms wide enough to embrace the whole world. If only he had come to me in the days of my towering love — so that she might have succumbed to me in the regular stream of incoming humanity. Without *Zarathustra* under my belt, I can afford to look into the eyes of the Old Man himself — and wink.

59

Eternity, our great compassionate contemporary, who gives us our comrades and enemies, who endows us with the most bearable of our children, so darkly and swiftly moves these familiar images that sometimes we get the illusion of running into our very selves in the vast corridors of his house.

60

The world continues to call to me as brightly and as eagerly as it appeared to call to me from all the corners of the world during the writing of the fourth part of *Zarathustra*. Does it not seem overstrange that this Zarathustra should now sit about so lamely among these decrepit men and women!

61

Every occupation of man requires of him the wearing of a mask symbolizing his peculiar trade. These masks are in no way assumed, they grow out of people as they live, the way skin grows, the way fur develops over skin. There are masks for the merchants as well as for the professors, there are masks that fit thieves and there are masks that look natural only on saints. The greatest of all the masks is nakedness. If I believed in God, this would be the mask I would conceive him in.

CHAPTER SEVEN

1

I am paying dearly for the enchanting dreams of my youth: the currency in which one pays such debts certainly shrinks as one grows older; we pay in gold for what was received in dross. I say nothing of those intervals in this house when the whole world seems suddenly to break loose in delirious screams and wild cackles punctuated by the blowing of a bugle by a Bavarian lunatic who thinks he is the angel Gabriel summoning the dead to judgment. I am plunged into the Walpurgis Night of the soul streaked with lightning and made hideous with the yells of witches whose countenances merge into two female faces — one light and one dark.

Like De Quincey's opium vision of the Malay, the Dark Face terrifies me, while the Light Face reminds me that Lust wears an angelic mask behind which the demon of primitive desire smiles at the illusions of youth bent on the high adventure of romance.

Lust has taught me more than literature ever can, and all the libraries I have swallowed are so much paper compared to the perjured kisses of the Countess, the Circe who turned her lovers into swine. Unlike the dark flower of India I first encountered in a Cologne brothel, this fair beauty of Bonn looked as distant and chaste as the illuminated peaks of the Siebengebirge, and her blonde hair sparked like the lights of the vintagers that dazzled my eyes as I walked back, as a student, from the enchanted Rhine.

The outward façade of a being or a building has little relation to what is contained within the four walls of the body or the architectural structure. It was from the Countess that I first learned that thoughts are merely masks to hide our true ideas of ourselves and the world: we do not speak our thoughts because we often do not dare to admit them to ourselves.

It was at Pforta that I first met the Countess and it was our mutual interest in Humboldt that first brought us together. At least I thought she shared my passion for Humboldt, but at fifteen I did not realize yet that women think through the womb, and that they seize upon anything — even Humboldt — to quench the flame of their uterine passion.

The Countess, who was thirty, endured the anguish of adultery with considerable calm, looking upon my youthful inexperience with a certain voluptuous horror, dreading the inelegant, clumsy approaches of her *Martin* (she preferred to identify me with Luther, thus adding a fillip to her lust), and at the same time goading me on to greater and greater outbursts of erotic exuberance. I was a satyr in pursuit of a graceful, aristocratic faun, and she enjoyed the refinement of her sin, the vulgar debauchery of my embraces made pure in the cold sunlight of her snobbery.

She had a habit of standing outside my dormitory, hidden in the dark shadows cast by an elm tree, and whistling gently like a finch — a strange bird-call that somehow divorced her from the human and made her a disembodied voice, a single note in the great Handel-music of the universe. Or should I say Schumann's Faust-music? For, having discovered that I loved Humboldt, Schumann and solitary walks through the country-side, the Countess added Schumann and walking to her hobbies, taking solitary walks but always managing to discover me beside some forest-stream or looking down from a mountain peak into the broad green valleys below. There was a bloodhound in her being that tracked me down wherever I went, and I could hide nothing from her; my body, mind and soul were irretrievably in the possession of this siren who sought to hold me and at the same time dash me against the rocks.

I do not wish to detail my erotic intimacies with the Countess in the manner of *Manon Lescaut*, which, as Napoleon said, was a novel written for servants. Besides, I cannot compete with Abbé Prévost, Stendhal and Zola. Modern novels banish everything from their pages — including common sense — and I would be committing a rape upon art if I endeavored to imitate the modern novelist and describe in minute detail the bedroom behavior of the Countess for the mere purpose of shocking the reader into a sense of vicarious depravity.

The Countess to me is the secret spring of my intellectual and emotional life; she is more than a dead love affair: *she is my living Fate.* For, like De Quincey's Malay, she has appeared in my own nightmarish dreams when I was forced to take opium to dull the agonies of my physical sufferings. She is *the obscure Venus of the Hollow Hill*, the Baudelairean Venus grown diabolic and destructive among ages that would not accept her as divine. I see her huge thighs twining about me in naked, voluptuous shudders, her hard, white breasts pressing against the fortress of my being until it collapses like a house of cards in the tangled ruins of body, mind and soul. When she comes to me like a recurrent nightmare (my idea of *eternal recurrence* was suggested by the Countess), I am reminded of Stendhal's prophecy: *We must abandon all paradise. This age is destined to bring everything to confusion. We are marching towards chaos.*

This Prussian Countess, this diabolic Venus, contrived to find pleasure in the most fantastic follies, making me a part of her impromptu, experimental passion that would have driven me out of my senses in early youth had not my intellectual arrogance, my lust for culture, acted as a counterpoise to her incessant need for fornication. Imagining herself to be another Catherine de'Medici or Lucrezia Borgia, she strove to invent new criminal delights,

new amazing variations of the love-bout — and at the same time
tormented me for having seduced her from her chaste marriage
bed. I, a boy of fifteen, was the cruel hawk that had snatched the
mate from the chaste turtle-dove, as in Mérimée's parable,[1] I was
the buzzard that hovered over the dry bones of her marital bliss.

I was like a mouse at the bottom of an empty beer-keg,
unable to get out except at the thought of her naked body which
melted into electric waves and shot through me like a force of
gravity, pulling me up instead of down, up into her high bed,
properly curtained to hide the prying eyes of her conscience from
herself. Though a timid mouse — as shy and terrified as Kant
prodded by the glance of a dowager in a drawing-room — she
puffed me up to the size of an elephant and shrank in a sort of
cold agony as I threatened to strangle her for humiliating me to
the point of blotting out my manhood. Like the harassed and
insulted servant of Dostoyevsky, I cried out in my torment, *I too
am a man*, and to retrieve my human dignity I flogged her with
the riding-whip which she kept in her boudoir together with her
riding boots.

Unaware of the strange perversities of this Baudelairean
Venus, I merely fed her lust for self-torment and cruelty, driving
her into ecstasies of delight as the whip flicked across her bare
back arched like a frightened cat to receive the delicious terror of
my young fury awaking in the dawn of her bestial desires.

2

It was the Countess who taught me the difference between
love and sexual desire, the fierce impersonal passion shooting
hostile darts into the naked adversary and leaping upon the
enemy in a sudden encircling movement of legs and thighs.
Remembering the Countess, I have said that women should be

[1] In *Colomba*. — Editor

approached with a whip, but such is the perversity of feminine nature that cruelty does not quiet down the lust of woman, but on the contrary intensifies it to a fever pitch. The will to death is as strong as the will to life, and woman, who bears life in her womb, will turn death itself into a display of fireworks, cracking and shooting white, red, green, yellow and orange into the dark Cimmerian night and ricocheting upon the naked body of life.

Death cancels life and life cancels death in a constant spasm of resurrections. When she first made me undress her, as she blew out the lamp-light, I felt life seize me in an iron grip as her petticoats fell from her body, one by one like the petals of a great sunflower that was suddenly plunged into darkness. The Countess gleamed white and naked in my arms like the moon-eyes of a night owl that is wrapped in an amber haze, a yellow that has the hint of death in its dull effulgence. But she had bared her lily-white body to me with such bravado and abandon that she could not bribe her Lutheran conscience until she forced me to crawl at her feet, for daring to undress her rotten soul as well as her beautiful body.

I remember her last effort to break away from the perilous promiscuity that made love a mockery of life and twisted it into a Baudelairean flower of evil whose roots are sunk deep in the pit of death. The school at Pforta was formerly a monastery, and the dormitory rooms had a monkish odor about them, a mortuary flower of decay. One night, while my roommate was away on a visit to his parents in Leipzig, she managed to get into my "cell" in the guise of a young man, and while I was half-asleep she began to pummel me with a blunt instrument of whose nature I am ignorant even to this day.

Just as I was losing consciousness she suddenly changed her tactics, and her passion to destroy me recoiled upon itself, becoming a terrible desire to absorb my young body into her-self. The greatest tyrant over woman is woman, as the English novelist Meredith[2] said; her womb is a spider-web draining her mind and will and making her a slave to her irresistible sex-urge which pulls her with cosmic compulsion towards the defeat of her high moral purpose. Washing my wounds with her tears, she for the first time displayed the love that Saint Augustine discovered when he abandoned women for God and found in the re-virgined Mary the highest consummation of the flesh.

She left me like a flushed monk who had wrestled with the devil in the desert and gained the garland of victory; her love seemed welded to power, the power of Venus who had cast off the Serpent and who felt the fluids of the divine spirit in her breasts and thighs. During my last few months in Pforta I saw her as the unsullied Greek Venus emerging naked and white-breasted from the sea of Man's hunger for the delight of the world, but at the end the bat-wings of lust cast their shadows over our paradisiacal love, bringing back all the evil spirits that had turned our heaven of bliss into a hell of torment.

She insisted on being the man and striking me where it hurt most — in my virility — as Abelard was smitten by the ruffians who emasculated him and cut him off forever from the body of Heloise, from the body of all women, the source of the world's delight and the world's despair. In her constant shock of the senses, the astonishment of her perverse desires, she sought to emasculate me not only physically but mentally and spiritually as well, to make me a helpless eunuch squatting in the lap of her will to dominance. It was the Countess who taught me that the female must submit to the male or reverse the order of nature, pressing down upon him not only in the carnal sex-act but in the daily routine of individual and social living.

---

[2] Nietzsche is mistaken; it was Thackeray who made the remark in *Vanity Fair.* — Editor

3

My education in amour was continued at Leipzig where my passion for knowledge was combined with prodigious fancies about women whom I classified into sacred and profane, thus preserving the Pauline dualism of my Lutheran ancestors that reflected the split in society itself. In the greenhouse of the Countess at Pforta I had watched the tropical plants stretch out creepers like the arms and legs of lovers forever twining and embracing in a vast copulation of nature, a cosmic mating of earth and sky caught in the spasm of the great lust that drives the wheels of creation. It was in the greenhouse that the Countess first lured me to my fall, behind the back of her husband, for the lush, multi-colored plants had aroused in me a desire to gather all the scattered delights of nature and fuse them in the single divine passion for the body of woman which contained all the ecstasies of heaven and hell and the green earth between. At the greenhouse I had a vision of all life caught in a common orgasm, a spasm of delight, but in Leipzig I learned that the daughters of the poor and of the rich belonged to two different categories, and that it is proper to seduce servant-girls but not their high-born mistresses.

4

At fifteen I wrote in my diary: *Great is the domain of knowledge, eternal is the search for truth.* At Leipzig I discovered that college students confined their search for truth to beer-halls and brothels, and that it was more important to practice the art of fornication than to study the aesthetic systems of Aristotle or Schopenhauer. Thanks to the Countess's instruction I was a more experienced devotee to Priapus than most of my fellow-students, who had learned little in the arms of servant-girls except the platitudinous embraces that are derived from the artifice of the boudoir where the erotic nuances of Indian and Japanese courtesans are studied as punctiliously as the pious scan every paragraph and line of the Holy Bible.

It was in a Leipzig brothel that I first met the dark Counterpoise to the Countess, the semi-Indian girl, the Eurasian with the breath of the Far East in her oiled, perfumed body which was trained by centuries to go through the gamut of passion until lust itself became a gesture of the soul, knowing no desire but erotic fulfillment. Like the Countess, the dark flower of the Orient made her flesh the center of the world's delight, but the rapture was untainted by the pain of a guilty conscience and she gave herself freely and without sin as the daughters of Edom gave themselves to the Israelites in a ritual of self-abandon to the rhythms of nature.

But alas for the daughters of Canaan who were infected with the diseases of civilization and communicated its rottenness to the sons of Abraham, causing havoc and destruction in their midst. I blame my bone-rot and brain-rot on the beautiful Eurasian in the Leipzig brothel, whose large thighs enclosed the poison that killed Heine and me. For I look upon myself as already dead, indulging in a post-mortem on my body, mind and soul to frustrate the coroners of the future who will judge me by their own prejudices and extract homilies and parables out of my entrails. Heine on his mattress-grave and I in my asylum-tomb could both appreciate that cosmic Irony called Jehovah who throws us into the arms of a dark, sultry Venus and then blasts us with the lightning of syphilis, shattering us in body, mind and soul for daring to commit the greatest crime of all — the crime of love.

Many of my college *Franconians* were smitten with the same disease, but they cured it in time. But I, through my Promethean pride and fatal neglect, allowed the poisons to accumulate within me till I am like a sewer filled with the festering waste of a slum district where the girls walk the streets and wreak vengeance upon a city that condemns the poor to poverty and filth. Syphilis is the weapon of the poor against the rich, and I probably infected the Countess with my taint, for her second child was a Mongolian idiot and no doubt the evil fruit of our liaison.

Though I had fled Pforta for Leipzig with a sense of relief, as if Richter's *angel of our last hour* had at last abandoned her effort to bear me away on her black wings, I could not drive the Countess and the Eurasian from my blood. They were an integral part of the world of light and shadow, and when I see a white bird flash through the darkness outside the asylum window I think of the Countess and the Eurasian who divided my universe into white and black until they fused together in the inarticulate grey of our dead, dissolving age.

Jeder Mensch hat seine Narrheit,[3] as Tieck wrote to Kopke. Tieck, with his sense of cosmic irony could have appreciated my life's dilemma, my fear of love which combined with a love of fear to plant a taste of horror in my mind, forcing me out of the terror of incestuous delights into the arms of syphilitic harlots and aristocratic prostitutes. The varnished cadavers, the musk-scented skeletons, the perfumed skulls rattling with madness on my asylum window — these are the ghastly images that my sick brain conjures up, solid phantoms whirling about the nude, white body of the Countess, terrified of her nakedness and turning her dread into a cult of erotic brutality. And then as a foil to the Countess, the dark, cinnamon body of the Eurasian, unabashed in its nakedness, delighted in the fact that men could be drawn to the nude flesh as flies to a jar of honey.

My Achilles heel, flaw, or *folly* (as Tieck preferred to call it) was the Countess, who symbolizes in my mind the frailty of human nature which forced me later to abolish man altogether

---

[3] "Every human being has his folly." — Editor

and to place my imperiled faith in the Superman of the future. Her graveyard charm, like the disintegrating beauty of Venus, had an irresistible lure for me, which I later sought to overcome by plunging into Wagner's music and into the arms of his mistress Cosima, the Brunhilde of my dreams. But I discovered, to my deep sorrow, that both Wagner and Cosima were part of that very decadent, Philistine world I sought to escape, that Wagnerism was merely another symptom of the decay of the West. Wagner, like Baudelaire, had merely created *a new shudder*, as Hugo put it, a shudder I felt was trapped in the icy embrace of the blonde Countess.

The Countess came from the world of imagination, which is the world of Eternity, and therefore remains with me to the very end. She will probably haunt me beyond the grave — if we accept the Platonic thesis that the mind of man is immortal. I sometimes wonder whether she was a creature of the visible world or a phantasm created by my inner need to embody in flesh the perversities of our brute nature. But I remember distinctly the day when I was marching with the *Franconians*, flushed with the orgy of the previous night, shouting and singing, but becoming painfully aware of the fact that the trousers of my parade uniform were ripped at the seat, revealing a slice of my woolen underwear. Then her gay, impudent laughter broke in upon my discomfort and I knew that the Countess had followed her quarry forever determined to hunt me down into submission to her will.

In an Italian café frequented by students she revealed the fact that she was a widow: the Count, tired of her debaucheries, had locked himself up in his stable, and burned it over his head, putting a bullet through his skull. I remember her husband well: bearded and well-groomed, he looked like an Oriental pasha who sat with dignity on his canopied chair on a dais and discussed with me philosophy, philology, theology, political and military science — subjects I was delving in but of which he knew

119

absolutely nothing. When he discovered that the beautiful young
wife he adored was a Messalina who mixed her queenly blood
with common riff-raff like me, his aristocratic arrogance received
a fatal jolt and he could revenge the insult only by committing
suicide — as Orientals do when they stab themselves on the door-
steps of their mortal enemies.

She used a rare perfume and I breathed it in, had my being
in the fragrance of her white body which was sheathed in white
silk and ended in a chignon from which floated a white feather as
the symbol of my spiritual defeat. I was drowned in her, drowned
in a cry of white while the world about me was growing grey in
the twilight of the gods. While stretched nude on her bed she
made me step over her body and made the sign of the cross, at
which enigmatic gesture she burst into hilarious laughter. Then
she told me that one of her lovers was a bishop, and he always
made the sign of the cross when he stumbled over her on the bed.
In her perverted mind I was a Lutheran pastor whom she could
enjoy only by mixing her desire with the sense of the forbidden,
like the Madame Montespans who engaged in the blasphemous
rites of the Black Mass, enjoying the naked raptures, the voluptuous shudders of the damned.

5

My contempt for religion was fostered to a great extent by
the male and female Tartuffes — the Countess and her bishop —
who both testified to the fact that Christianity, by denying the
body, leads to a morbid absorption in its possibilities, that piety
leads to prudery and prudery to perversion. The Christian God is
actually a mask for Satan; hence the Devil finds his most ardent
worshipers in the churches.

Although I had reached the ripe age of eighteen, she still
found fault with my love-making, but I was mature enough to
humor her and exclaim: *Es kann nicht immer alles über alle Begriffe*

sein.[4] This is so in the field of letters or of love. I parried the Countess's dagger thrusts by ideas rather than insults, and she became more attached to me than ever, finding in me a new erotic dimension, the passion of the intellect which can be as carnal and ecstatic as the rapture of the flesh.

I discussed theology, philosophy and music with the Countess, and she seemed to grasp my ideas with a sort of intuitive understanding which has often made me feel that woman has a better mind than man because she is mindless and closer to the cosmic wisdom of nature. I took her to concerts and theaters (or rather, she took me, for she paid for the tickets), and once when we heard Patti in *Les Huguenots* she aroused my anger when she called the music *Jewish and obscene* because Meyerbeer had composed it. This was my first experience with the cultural snob who tries to confine art within national boundaries, as if the products of the creative imagination, the eternal emanations of the soul, could be choked into the four greasy walls of time and space. Later, when Wagner pointed to *the Jewish menace* of Meyerbeer and other Hebraic artists and composers I set him down as a barbarian and a Philistine, especially since Meyerbeer had helped him in his headlong drive to achieve public recognition for his decadent music which echoed the barbarism of a *cash-dollar*[5] century whose cultural triumph is the Stock Exchange.

The Countess's dislike for Jewish art did not extend to Jewish money (which is international), and she did not hesitate to contract a liaison with one of the Paris Rothschilds who was visiting friends in Leipzig. I found myself in the unenviable position of playing second fiddle to a Jewish multi-millionaire who was a true aristocrat, by blood and breeding, and made me feel my own

---

[4] "You can't always have everything better than any concept."

---

[5] Nietzsche uses the English — or rather, American — phrase. — Editor

inferior status as a son of poor, middle-class parents. It was then that I made the convenient discovery that I was descended from a Polish count who had stables full of thoroughbreds and rode wild horses with greater skill than the Countess's husband himself. This delusion persisted with me when I became a cavalry officer and undertook to ride a wild charger with calamitous results, for my injury went to the very depths of my being: I was a beggar on horseback who was riding towards a disastrous fall, towards a complete collapse of body, mind and spirit.

Once I took the Countess to a music festival at Cologne where the orchestra played Handel's *Israel in Egypt*. What has always struck me at these open-air concerts is the stark contrast between the bejeweled and bedizened audience sitting smug in its seats while getting the full impact of the music, while at the outer edges of the field are the riff-raff — the beggars, teamsters, drudges and retired prostitutes who stretch out their arms as stray bits of music float over them, as if they were prayers just beyond reach, prayers that speed on symphonic wings towards the Blessed Isles of man's hopes.

As Fate would have it, the Paris Rothschild showed up at the concert, and his money talked louder than my eloquent disquisition on the beauties of Handel, for he was soon ensconced on my seat, while I found myself edging my way to the outer circle of the ragged, the aged and the damned catching stray chords of broken music in a broken, disintegrating world. I felt all the anguish of Israel sweating blood in Egypt, without the help of Handel, but instead of hatred for the Paris Rothschild who had deprived me of my beloved Countess, I was filled with a sense of admiration for the rich Jew who, like a sorcerer, could tame the wild tides of the world's hatred and contempt by casting over them the yellow spell of his gold pieces.

6

While the Paris Rothschild was in the Promised Land with the Countess, I caught sight of a Eurasian in the ragged circle, listening to Handel, who looked like the twin sister of the dark-skinned harlot in the Pforta brothel. Unlike some prostitutes who retire loaded with prestige and honors — like Du Barry in her English retreat — all she had to show for her life-long devotion to Venus was burning circles around her eyes, a suppurating mouth, a purulent cheek whose running pus horrified and intrigued me at the same time, for here was Venus disintegrating into disease and death, Baudelaire's Aphrodite, the bourgeois whore, triumphant in her decay, whom Zola depicted in *Nana*.

That night, in a spasm of self-contempt and humiliation, I slept with this bag of virulent disease, and now the physicians at the asylum are computing the pathological results in their daily reports to the head doctor who is like Jehovah weighing me in the dread balance of good and evil. As I have written, *There is no such thing as moral phenomena, but only a moral interpretation of phenomena,*[6] and the medical Pharisees who see me as a horrible example of genius gone mad through my defiance of the Ten Commandments are taking the usual revenge of mediocrities on men of talent and brilliance who can only be judged by their own standards and not by the yard-sticks set up for the mob.

7

Fate has punished me not for my vices but for my virtues, my moral inhibitions which prevented me from living my philosophy fully as Goethe and George Sand turned their romances into printer's ink and bridged the chasm between art and life. Like Flaubert I sought to place life and the creative imagination

---

[6] In *Beyond Good and Evil.*

in separate categories, to annihilate the philosopher for the sake of his philosophy, forgetting that there is a living link between existence and thought and that when this link is broken the artist or philosopher is hurled into morbidity and madness. This is something which the brain specialists do not understand: they are as naïve as my sister who raised her hands in holy horror when she discovered that I was living my philosophy in Tautenburg, where Lou Salomé, the Russian Jewess, whose wisdom and erotic passion matched George Sand's, offered her body as a sacrifice to my will to wholeness and sanity. Unlike the Countess, whose love was a form of barbarous revenge, a sensuality that uprooted my being, Lou Salomé erased the shame[7] of my immortality and thus restored my pride in my manhood, which was being undermined by my Pauline dread of the flesh.

This is something for the brain specialists to ponder on: not my vices but my virtue has been the cause of my physical, moral and spiritual breakdown. An incident of my college days has been recorded which sheds more light on my condition than my doctors and friends realize. While in Cologne, after my experience with the Countess and the Eurasian, I asked a gentleman to direct me to a certain restaurant, but instead he steered me to a notorious house of ill fame. The brothel girls in all stages of undress flaunted their studied nakedness in my face, attempting to arouse me by lewd posturings, lascivious glances and ribald jokes. I broke away from the tight circle of naked and semi-naked flesh oozing with the hot, obscene breath of the brothel, and dashed to the dusty piano in a far-off corner where I struck a single wild chord — a cry of rage against a brothelized universe whose oppressive odor lay like a coffin-lid upon our business civilization.

---

[7] Compare Nietzsche's aphorism: *To be ashamed of one's immortality is a step on the ladder at the end of which one is ashamed also of one's morality.* — Editor

It was my dread of the social bawdy-house that made me listen to my sister's plea to give up Lou Salomé, for she knew of my adolescent obsession for the Countess and the Eurasian, and she forced me to believe that Lou was a combination of the frigid, perverse blonde and the dark, sultry brunette. I am crucified erotically between the two thieves of Black and White, and the Lama removed me from the cross only to nail me to a more terrible fate — the road of incestuous longings that demanded a dark consummation at the very core of my tormented being.

8

The impotence of Christian love led my sister into a desperate effort to fulfill herself in a dark and forbidden area of erotic expression. Trained by my mother to repress her natural sex-emotions, she discovered too late that her effort to dam up her erotic desires merely unleashed a torrent of dark, abnormal passions that rushed through her being in full flood till she became a destructive force of nature that broke through all barriers of morals and civilization. She began to love what she desired least, and I was flung into the treacherous undertow of her outlawed passions which sucked us into their tidal will.

The Goethean German who complains that *two souls, alas, dwell in my breast*, is merely deluding himself, for we are *das tückische Volk* (the deceptive people) who imagine that we veer between barbarism and culture when we are savages by instinct — such unregenerate barbarians as the Lama and myself. But I do not hate Germans enough to be blinded to the fact that Saint Augustine was nearer to the truth than the Pelagians and the followers of Rousseau: human nature has been marked from the beginning with the brand of the beast — Darwin merely confirms the Bishop of Hippo in his belief that we are all cursed by our *original sin*, the sin of our pre-Adamic bestial beginnings. The savagery of the German, his Teutonic fury, is merely an intensification of Man's inhuman nature.

When Europe, intoxicated by the dream of Rousseau, danced around the Tree of Liberty of the Revolution, it did not realize that its glowing romanticism would be shattered against the rock of Napoleon, just as today our Pelagian belief in the perfectibility of human nature is smashed against the stone wall of our simian heredity. Poetry, as I have said, is the highest metaphysical task of men, but our poetic passion has obscured the hard fact that we are just a little removed from the tiger and the gorilla and that the "angelic" female is so close to the beast of the jungle that I doubt whether the human race can ever become human, much less superhuman.

9

My youthful Goethean belief that the Eternal Feminine can lift man up into the heaven of wholeness and wholesomeness was merely a perverse effort to let God in through the back door of my being after I had flung Him out the window: atheism is a bitter brew that requires a strong stomach to contain. But my experience with the Countess, the Eurasian, my sister, and many other females of their type, leads me to the sad conclusion that women are not higher beings than men, but our need for gods and semi-gods leads us to deify the Eternal Feminine as we glorify the Promethean Superman or bend the knee to genius, as I have bowed in reverence before my own greatness.

In my college days I and the other *Franconians* cheered Hedwig Raabe, the actress, or fell madly in love with the gay, impish humor of Frederike Grossmann, whose songs we sang and whom we toasted over the beer-table, but these beautiful women of the stage were merely figments of our erotic or aesthetic imagination. It is the tragedy of man that he confuses the stage of the theater with the stage of life and that women are better actresses in the drawing-room and bedroom than they are before the footlights. They dress their naked bodies in glamour, and, like Esther, perfume their skins macerated in aromatics, steeped in oil of palms for six months, and six months in cinnamon before presenting themselves before the deluded eyes of the monarch. If Ahasuerus was fooled — he who had traffic with hundreds of women — the reader may forgive poor Fritz Nietzsche, *the little parson*, if he confused the Countess and the Eurasian with God Himself and thought that their bodies were the doorways to Paradise, the gates to eternal bliss.

10

Each man is his own chimæra, as Baudelaire says; we are crushed by the monstrous delusion which is ourselves. But women especially are betrayed by their sex-nature into the belief that they are immortal goddesses who can lift their lovers out of their private hells into the heaven of erotic delights. Women like the Countess, Cosima Wagner, or even Lou Salomé, are nothing but voluptuous, cajoling cats, whose supple bodies and velvety paws are forever creeping into the souls of men, causing moral and spiritual havoc in the innermost depths of our beings. If Goethe could have probed a little deeper into feminine nature he would have described a second Werther who was driven to suicide not by frustrated love but by love carnally fulfilled. A thousand Werthers commit spiritual suicide, broken on the wheel of lust, to one who knocks his brains out because some idiotic servant-girl refuses to spread her thighs to his erotic passions.

Like Schoreel[8] I shall live for my art (if I can live at all); the fair sex has lost all claim on me. The life of a people lies in its artists, men with creative vision. Kill the artist and you kill the

---

[8] Johannes Schoreel, Madame Pichler's romantic lover. Madame Pichler, celebrated literary lady of Germany, died in 1843 at the age of seventy-four. Nietzsche must have read her in his youth. — Editor

life of a country. I have always considered myself an artist rather than a thinker, looking upon poetry as the highest consummation of metaphysics. But if women have contributed to my physical and moral downfall, they have been mere blind instruments in the hands of an ironic Jehovah who smites us into agony that we may know the true meaning of life.

With Dostoyevsky I can truly say: *I have loved; I have also suffered, but, above all, I can truly say I have lived!*

CHAPTER EIGHT

1

The questions which confront us in our waking hours — that shock and surprise us, and reveal to us how little of our unconscious nature ever makes the return journey into consciousness! One morning last week it was: What happened to a little silver knife my father left, after he died, which the whole family agreed was to be mine? This morning: Why do I recollect so little of the days and nights of Basel, where Elisabeth and I set up house after the surrender of my precious professorship, and upon my return from my cure at Steinabad in the Black Forest? No clouds beset the scene in my mind. Of all my recollections of that period it is certainly among the clearest. Yet I give the incident so little attention. Just another of the intangible mysteries which surround my relationship with my sister.

2

It did not occur to me to suspect that the intimacy between Elisabeth and myself might have become known to any member of the family (or any of the major figures in our lives, not related to us by ties of blood) until the day Aunt Rosalie called me into the chamber of the house where she lay dying. I was not surprised when she brusquely asked mother to leave me alone with her. Aunt Rosalie had always elected herself my protagonist, the link between my life at home and the broader horizons that beckoned me. I can only do justice to the conversation which followed between her and me by reproducing it in full.

You know I'm dying, Fritz, she sighed.

I hope not, Aunt Rosalie, I said fervently.

Hope don't help, Fritz. The fact is I'm dying, and you'll only hasten my death if you make me go through all this rubbish about what might be and cannot be. It's important to recognize that I'm dying, that you're going to go on living. Do we understand each other?

Yes, Aunt Rosalie.

I want you to know that I'm leaving you a pretty big share of my money. That should help you over a lot of rough spots.

Thank you, Aunt Rosalie.

You're welcome, Fritz. With your father dead, you're the only brain left in the family. I'm sure he'd have wanted me to do exactly what I'm doing. But that's not what I called you in for.

There was something in her voice of such an ominous quality that I could only lean forward and stare at her.

You'll need all your courage to sit quietly through what I have to tell you, she resumed. *And it'll do you good to listen and keep quiet. There'll be no point in denials or arguments, Fritz, because what I have to tell you is the simple truth, and there would be no sense in making me argue it. I'm not very strong, and you wouldn't want me to waste the little energy left to me. So listen carefully, Fritz. I have known for quite a long time of what has been going on between you and Elisabeth.*

In spite of being warned I almost fell out of the chair I was sitting in, as she coolly pronounced the last sentence.

The knowledge came to me accidentally, Fritz, she continued. *I didn't spy on you. And you don't have to flare up, because I'm not going to lecture you. I have wanted to speak to you about it a number of times, as I felt some older person should, but I didn't know how. In a way I did spy on you, because once I knew what both of you were up to I couldn't help, for any number of reasons, trying to determine whether or not you'd got out of the habit. You've had long stretches of separation, but somehow you get back to it as soon as either of you finds the opportunity.*

I said I was not going to lecture you. But how can I help telling you that it's no good for both of you?

I made no move to interrupt her.

You're wise to keep quiet, Fritz, she continued. *There's really nothing you can add to or subtract from what I've seen with my own eyes. There's a horrible word for such goings-on between brother and sister, and a host of other words not much better. I shan't utter one of them. I still love you, Fritz, and I have high hopes for you. Only I must tell you this. If you continue your misconduct with your sister you'll slowly gamble away your immortal soul. Stop it.*

By this time she was so completely exhausted that when she moved her hand in the direction of the door I knew that she meant for me to leave, and I did.

3

That was how I learned that Aunt Rosalie knew everything. How about my mother? My grandparents? And how about those schoolfellows of mine who constantly noticed how Elisabeth hung on every word I uttered in her presence? And what about Förster, her husband? Was it her fear of his suspicions that finally decided Elisabeth on going along with him on that mad venture into South America? Was it his discovery of the truth that led to his committing suicide?

4

Aunt Rosalie had followed the intimacy between me and my sister thoroughly enough to understand that by the time I had to leave for Pforta, it was not her hands that sought out me, but mine that sought out her, and that the tears which bedewed my pillow were the result of the heartbreak with which I contemplated a long separation from her.

5

On the day I returned to Bayreuth from Clarens, where I had visited with my mother and sister, Wagner pretended to be astonished at my good spirits and asked me if being with my family always had this invigorating effect on me. I attributed all to Elisabeth, of course.[1] But now I wonder. How much did Wagner suspect?

6

And there was the time Cosima wrote to me, suggesting that I ask Elisabeth to come to Bayreuth to look after her children, so that we, Cosima and I, might go together on a business tour. Did she suspect what was going on between Elisabeth and me and try that way to force a spiritual separation between us?

7

Most of the time I think of myself as, in childhood, I used to think of the God of *Genesis* — a Rejected Bridegroom.

8

Where other philosophers write books I write little paragraphs. Where a book is really needed I find it necessary to keep utterly silent.

9

Somewhere in the middle of *The Antichrist* I lost my feeling of resentment. I can't say why, but suddenly I felt like quoting instead of castigating Scripture. I was in my teens again. After

---

[1] Nietzsche is quoted as saying to Wagner: "It is because of my sister's company, as she has something invigorating about her which reconciles a man to the world." — Editor

that I must have blundered on for at least fifty pages before I found again the thunderbolts with which I concluded this, the most lyric of my writings.

10

One point is still left undeveloped in my system: the dangerous belief that the truth of a statement stamps it as moral.

Is an untruth therefore immoral? And does that make all the undiscovered facts of science *amoral?*

A whole system of moral equations could be set up here. What a pity I myself am too tired to try it!

11

Human differences are mainly differences in language. Would, then, a single language, adopted by all races and nations, solve most of our difficulties? Hardly. We need all of our differences for those eternal and fierce struggles in which our ideas and passions are refined. If we could trace the origin of all our cultural wealth we should discover that at least eighty percent of it resides in those very differences of language that appear so troublesome.

12

We have developed only three systems of numbers — as against a thousand languages and ten thousand systems of thought.

13

Kant would have been a better philosopher if he had had at least ten years of teaching philology, which would have emphasized for him the importance of making oneself understand before one can be sure one is understood.

14

Democracy is of numbers and stems directly from the anonymous mathematician destroyed in the fires of the Alexandrian library. What a pity that human nature is not built along the simple lines of, say, Euclid's propositions!

15

Yes, for happiness, *No* for truth runs through human experience like the chorus of a ballad.

16

Regularity of thought and conduct is one thing, and must come of itself, out of a sequence of events: order is what some demagogue imposes on a sequence of events which would not, of themselves, yield to anything resembling order.

17

Being and becoming, night and day, black and white, continue to order and befuddle our limited understanding; it is in fact these simple differentiations which are responsible for most of our tragic misunderstandings in human conduct.

18

A featureless Parmenides with the fiery flux of Heraclitus is the most potent of the godheads formed for us by the legendry of the Philosophic Seas. There the sun sets finally on our most precious dreams.

19

Boscovitch and his silly Atom haunt me endlessly. Between the heavy sound the name makes in my ear and the false simplicity of his explanations of the origin of matter I do not know whether to laugh or cry.

20

Every man is born a prisoner of his own length, breadth and depth of consciousness. How long he lasts depends on how long it takes him to achieve a fourth dimension, or, in the language of the populace, the identity of his own soul. Perhaps the only way to achieve grace is to place oneself in front of a swiftly approaching train. It that were true, gunpowder would make a greater contribution than philosophy to the achievement of personal immortality.

21

I am the Minotaur of the philosophers of my time. I will never be conquered by any rash Theseus. To make certain of that, I have taken the precaution to make Ariadne[2] my private prisoner.

22

God seems to have made everything in the visible world except color — by which alone the world is rendered visible. Man has created good manners. But of what good is that, since God has failed to create good men?

23

No matter how limited his vision, every philosopher at least once in his life reaches the following crossroads: he has to decide between the plan by which he must live and the one by which he would like to interpret the world. It presents him with a set of extracurricular problems that haunt him all through his public life as a teacher.

---

[2] Reference to Cosima Wagner. — Editor

24

If you can't read Plato for the sheer fun of it, read him for the lesson which shouts to you between lines of every dialogue: *There is only one world, the world of human experience.*

25

We go through the pangs of hunger in order that we may find the after-pleasure of remaining as we are; we desire more than we can have or enjoy, only that it may become possible for us to approve at least part of what we see, and so hope to heaven that all our blunders are not in the past.

26

Passion is the identification of hope as a vehicle into the future. Passion is the only protection we have against the extraordinary vanity of our desires.

27

The world is as much mine as it is the world of that cross-eyed man who takes up such a firm position near the door that appears to block eternally my escape from these confines.

28

Knowledge first derives from living. Secondary knowledge comes from research into the conclusions of those who came before us. A thin shroud is all we finally take with us into our graves.

29

All knowledge is divided into acceptable and not acceptable. What are the priority rights of acceptable knowledge? That it can rain catfish as well as water is not acceptable knowledge however often it may be proved to have happened. Is it because this kind of knowledge is unclassifiable? It is possible, then, that classifying is one of the great sins of the world.

30

All our metaphysical calculations are conditioned by the fact that we are organic animals with definite animal needs and functions.

31

In the world of sensation everything depends on experience. Rain is one thing to a man, quite another to a tree, and still something else to a hill or mountain. And still different to the sky which is being relieved by the downfall.

32

I used to let myself believe that the mind is a by-product of the body. What do you get first, the harbor or the city, the city or the state, the state or the world, the world or God?

33

The will of one man is the command of another. Where there is no will there is anarchy. Anarchy precedes all acts of creation.

34

The Egyptians left behind them a true history of their national character in their *Book of the Dead*. To characterize our time one would have to write a *Book of Escaped Germans* — to include a few who wanted to escape but never managed to get away — like me. If — heaven forbid — I became the author of such a work I would place at the head of it an account of Heinrich Heine and I would terminate it with a commentary on

Karl Marx, with whom the ends of creation would have been served much better if he had remained in Germany, where he would either have been Prussianized or shot. As it is, Marx found sanctuary from Prussianism in England, where he is still firing theories at us across the English Channel. In such a scheme I would wish myself somewhere in the middle, where, approximately, I am.

35

What is one to say — good, bad or indifferent — about Heine which he has not already said infinitely better himself? One might just as well try to describe the sun, beyond saying that it shines and what we see we see only by its light.

36

As for Karl Marx, he writes not a bad German which he adorns with copious quotations from Latin and French — languages he does not seem to know too well — in order to impress the lowly and confuse those who could be expected to understand.

37

In Heine the Jews gave us too much, in Marx too little.

38

For Heine the world was the stage of a war in which people were constantly hurt, with compensation for this damage rising high in resultant benefits to the general spirit of man. Marx's world is divided between the many who are hungry and the few who are sated. Marx does not bewail the arrangement for its injustice to the many. He contents himself with advocating a similar injustice for the few.

39

Karl Marx is to the Law of Supply and Demand what Darwin is to the Law of the Survival of the Fittest. Both *laws* are the result of a new passion of the eighteenth century — research with a point of view.

40

Truth is still elusive. However, she is no longer a young girl but an old bitch with all of her front teeth missing.

41

Let me not be misunderstood: I avoid reading Marx as passionately as I pursue every new paragraph of Heine's.

42

Skeletally, Capitalism differs from Feudalism only in the means of over-lordship. But what could be called the *culture of communication*, education, almost evenly divided between science and letters, and universalized by popular schools, is gradually erasing old class distinctions between rulers and ruled. This culture recognizes neither nobleness of birth nor the advantages of superiority in wealth. Under its influence, the owners of the industrial machine and those who labor to turn its wheels shuffle up the broad steps of the temple of the future, hat in hand, in an equality of adoration in no need of the certification of force.

43

Most of the faults of Capitalism are known to me, as are also its virtues, and the prospect of some day having to pass out of it into a new system has no terrors for me. I know that the emergence of a people out of one form of tyranny into another is merely a conversion from one form to another of the ancient

hand-to-hand struggle for existence by which mankind continually balances itself. Socialist theorists distinguish between the life
we know and the one they think they can bring on by talking of
the possibility of mankind learning to live in a state of harmony.
But I know that people do not want to live in a state of harmony
with one another, and quite frankly, I do not think it is desirable
either as living or as harmony. Take away from people the com-
paratively joyous struggle of every-day barter, and you convert
them into a spying, lying, informing, mischief-mongering community in which a definite percentage of them has to be kept
under restraint to satisfy the innate smouldering lusts of power-
by-proxy.

44

There are many remedies still available for Capitalism —
which, I dare say, is not half as ill as our doctors would have us
believe. One of them might, I think, do the whole trick for
Europe: a moving up of the clock of currency, a sort of broad
transfusion of the power of purchase.

45

Marx's *Das Kapital* makes two discoveries in economics
which have been the cause of all the socialistic celebration: that
surplus value is created by forcing the laborer to produce in a
day's work more than he actually needs, and even more than is
needed by both laborer and employer combined; and that this has
led the capitalist to force the laborer into such a low standard of
living as not only to render it unnecessary for the employer to
work but to enrich him to a point where (even though he accom-
plishes it not by force but by legislation) he becomes as absolutely
the laborer's master as was the feudal lord before the Industrial
Revolution.

46

It never occurred to Marx to notice that whereas the feudal lord attained his overlordship by brutal physical conquest, the capitalist does so by an interest in the production of commodities as useful to the people as they are to himself.

47

The fact that the capitalist achieves his dominance by the process of legislation seems to me nothing to sneer at, in view of the fact that under this arrangement hundreds of laborers graduate into higher and still higher levels of the economic world, something that could not possibly have happened under feudalism.

48

The whole point of the Marxian ideology, that since surplus labor is a natural condition of mankind it should be surrendered to the state rather than to private capitalists, is being completely laughed out of consideration by what is happening in the world today. If it were not so difficult for the state to obtain funds for warfare by the process of taxation, if the wealth of America, say, were concentrated in Washington, instead of a hundred different great cities, Americans today would be building ten ships and twenty guns to the one ship and the one gun they must now limit themselves to, and the same thing would happen in all the other democratic countries.

49

A man's choice of an ideology for the conduct of his affairs on a new sociological scheme would be more proof against demagogues and their wiles if he could be got to understand that the first act of a new government in assuming power is to subtract

wealth from all of its constituents for the creation of a new
central authority and power; and that by the time it has brought
itself to the point where it has become stable enough, and sufficiently overwhelming as compared with any individual or group
of individuals, to be able to hand out favors, there is already in
existence, and firmly entrenched in the affections of the chiefs in
control, a party of favorites whose chances are so strong against
the chances of the average citizen even getting back his original
contribution, that it is almost axiomatic that he will be much
poorer under the new government than he was under the old.

50

Those who look to a Communist state as to a possible nur-
turer of science and art (which do so much to ameliorate the relationship of masters and people under Capitalism) should ask
themselves wherein the patronage of such a state could be expected to differ from the deadliness of any other form of government
in which the omnipotence of one man fathers the aridity of all
individual genius under his sway. Why can more be expected
from a dictatorship of the proletariat than we got from the
Mexican and Peruvian emperors or from what the French people
got under the benevolent despotism of Louis XIV in whose reign,
in spite of all his lying and coddling patronage, all the arts and
sciences came to a standstill, while to the north, in England, men
of independent thought and action were moving on, a full
century ahead of them . . .

51

The search for truth is still the greatest (and only sensible)
form of rebellion.

52

Property is sacred only when held safe against the encroachments of government.

53

More than anything else, civilization is a struggle between various styles of recollection.

CHAPTER NINE

1

What we cannot have by faith we will have by magical means: *Therefore I have given myself to magic!* With Faustian vehemence I have sought to storm the kingdom of riotous living and hold the naked Helen in my arms, crying out with Faust after his violent rape: *Feeling is all in all!*

Around this Faust-axis of unbounded lust I revolved at Tautenburg — to the horror of Elisabeth and her coterie of anti-Semites who cry for the blood of the Jew but look upon love outside the marriage-bond as the sin against the Holy Ghost for which there is no forgiveness in heaven or hell. My great sin was not in loving my Slavic Helen with the utmost abandon, but in surrendering to Goethe's fear of the flesh which intellectualized and spiritualized a woman's throbbing nakedness until there was nothing left but a symbol of Renaissance culture — *The Wanderer and his Shadow!* The dialectic doubt of Goethe's Mephistopheles seized me: *Where we are is hell, and where hell is there must we ever be* — even in the Eden of Tautenburg with my naked Eve.

2

I gave myself to the Devil for the sake of enlightenment after I achieved the final Socratic wisdom: I know that I know nothing. I had the choice between crucifixion with Christ and crucifixion on the body of my beloved disciple but I chose the latter alternative because it was a sweet agony — an agony of bliss. I countered my sister's Lutheran stupidity with a piece of Faustian cleverness; in the image I used in *Ecce Homo*, I swallowed a pot of jam in order to get rid of a sour taste.

And what did I gain by abandoning the throbbing body of Helen for Faustian ditch-digging, for my humanitarian effort which I disguised in my Superman philosophy, a philosophy which the Socialists have taken over to usher in the collective Superman, the Communist society, the triumph of the Mob? Having plumbed my tidal mind to its depths, I found, like Lucretius' plumb-line in the cosmos, a bottomless bottom, and I cried out, through Zarathustra:

Not the height, it is the declivity that is terrible!

The declivity, where the gaze shooteth downwards, and the hand graspeth upwards. There doth the heart grow giddy throughout its double will.

Ah, friends, do ye divine also my heart's double will?

This, this is my declivity and my danger, that my gaze shooteth towards the summit, and my hand would fain clutch and lean — on the depth!

3

With my Superman and my Blond Beast I sought to build a Babel's Tower, into the Absolute, but as Pascal warned his Renaissance contemporaries, a tower must be constructed on solid foundations or the groundwork will crack wide open, gaping to terrible abysses of nothingness, to plunging depths of maniacal despair. If my mind is cracking it is because I have felt the cracking of the foundations, the inner self-destruction of my whole intellectual being for which I sacrificed everything — even the friendship of Wagner which was more precious to me than Helen herself. Like Jesus I told my disciples: "Be not in anxiety," overcome the fragments of yourself by making of them a drawbridge to the Beyond-Man, but this drawbridge roared and thundered into the terrible Void, leaving me without God, without Man, and with only a flicker of evidence that I am still alive.

But with the terror of the Titan who dreads the cowardice of the human, I rushed to defend my fatality, my Godhead with "Anti-Christ," and thus protected myself against the Christian Circes whose vampirism, as practiced by the Lama and Mama was already sucking my blood. The Dionysian ogre called *Zarathustra* against St. Paul's blood-sucking Christ who reduces man to nothingness — *to utter exhaustion!*

4

Christianity and my anti-Christianity were both born out of the spirit of resentment, but the Christians resent life, while I resent death only, the pale kisses of the Crucified One. Therefore my mind recoils on itself, going back to the golden mean, without which, as Pascal confessed, we abandon our humanity and fall into the Pascalian pit of self-disgust.

Refusing the last Faustian evasion of humanitarianism, of ceaseless striving for a mirage, of Goethean subterfuge disguised as Promethean passion, for the Absolute, what is there left for me before my mind and body plunge into darkness and I cry out with the dying Goethe: *Mehr Licht! Mehr Licht!* Nothing but this — to reaffirm my love for the body of my Helen whose indwelling god shook to the drunken cries of Dionysos, the lust for being itself. In my dreams I hug her naked beauty like a fragment of a Lost Paradise that becomes whole and entire and cosmic with wonder in the act of passionate loving. She is my last idol construed from the spirit of magic out of the wrack and ruin and chaos of our shattered age. Her kisses draw me towards her.

5

The good doctor, with his English huckster's view of reality, will never understand my need for Helen, except in the gross sense of erotic satisfaction. Like that blockhead John Stuart Mill, he confuses the desirable, forgetting the Kantian *Ought*, the difference between the passions of the Mob and the refined hungers of the Superman dictated by cosmic principles which determine events. He reduces the interior world of the soul to an objective logic of pain and pleasure and seeks to cure sick minds on the basis of his pig-pleasure principle, the dogma of rational enjoyment.

The medics who hover over me like jackals over a dying lion can never understand my mortal sickness because truth is primarily of the spirit and they are only capable of rationalizing their own pig-worlds of outer sensation, never having entered the Aladdin's cave of interior dread alive with goblins, fairies, unicorns, centaurs, dragons and all the vital, active denizens of the human soul. All these transcendental creatures of the creative imagination they dismiss as mere pathology. To them the tree of Yggdrasil has its roots not in the sky but in a bourgeois pig's sty — a belief that aroused the just wrath of Carlyle.

6

The doctors here think I am mad because I pound the table and shout for more women, more wine and more song, with a Dionysian frenzy which they mistake for satyriasis and erotomania.

The doctors will never understand how, by a vast feat of imaginary strength, I shore up my life, combining Hercules and King Solomon: how, if I want to, I can clean the Augean stables of bourgeois industrialism and at the same time have time and energy left to sleep with a thousand women, satisfying them all. To the medics I am not the Napoleonic Center where God once was, not even at the mediocre periphery of existence, but cast out into the Void where the syphiloid exiles howl with maniacal glee in the Walpurgis Night of the soul.

How wrong they are — these culture-philistines, these savages in white uniforms, who cast their death pallor on the world of the beautiful — the Dionysian world of radiant energy and thundering joy! Their efforts in the mental hospital are devoted to a monkey-like imitation of the mad world, outside these walls; they have not yet undergone the process of de-intellectualization which Rousseau saw as the first requirement for the sane mind which seeks to escape the insanity of so-called civilization. These learned horses with their common horse-sense do not realize that I am trying *to live my knowledge*, and like Diogenes the Cynic am demonstrating by my wild horse-play my new gospel of *acting my beliefs*, plunging into the stream of experience even though the waters close over me and torrential madness shatters the timbers of my mind, crashing it into idiocy.

7

It was my Russian Helen who ushered me into the feminine principle of Sophia, of intuitive, mystical knowledge which the scientists and positivists cannot grasp because it lies *below* them and therefore *above* them. Their limited vision which sees life with the blinkers of common horse-sense without a superimposed metaphysic, subdues their hearts to their sensibility, reason and emotion, the power of knowledge and the knowledge of power. Until the moment I entered this madhouse I looked at life through a madhouse window — like a professional psychiatrist — but now that I have been clapped into this asylum I have become dangerously sane, trying to balance my masculine arrogance with Lou's feminine insight into the Unknown and Mysterious.

It was at Tautenburg that I was initiated into the rites of the priestess of Isis who in the orgy of erotic passion blots out the contradiction of male and female, of mind and emotion, of sense and sensibility, of upper and lower, of heaven and earth, fusing them all in Boehm's organic vision, like a Bach fugue or a

Beethoven symphony — the positive and negative energies in the soul.

Until I met Lou I could not escape from the scientific realm of statistics and quantity by rushing into the inward refuge of music with Wagner and the Wagnerians. But the Wagnerians, I discovered, were Cagliostros of music who dissolved the "I" and the "Thou," the polarity of male and female in the blood-cult of barbarism which expresses itself in the anti-Semitic history of Treitzschke and the Aryan blabberings of my brother-in-law Förster.

8

Was it because Elisabeth sensed my vigorous self-examination, following the example of La Rochefoucauld and Descartes, that she played the role of a female Iago and forced me to smother my Desdemona, the woman whose body was a sheet anchor; a buoy in the treacherous Wagnerian Seas that dashed romantic mariners like myself against the rocks of *Liebestod* and treacherous nihilism? I have said that the Germans were the swindlers of the intellect, that Fichte, Schelling, Schopenhauer, Hegel, Kant, Leibnitz and Schleiermacher were indeed *makers of veils*[1] and my sister sought to hide me behind the veil of Maya, of delusional Wagnerian nightmare so that I could not escape her blind, incestuous grip. Clinging to the body of my Russian Helen, I was able to retain my hold on the human and super-human. I was able to transcend myself in the miracle of her naked passion to re-weave my being in the warp and woof of "I" and "Thou," the paradoxical union of opposites so that her power of love and my love of power became one bright flame of ecstasy and delight.

---

[1] *Schleiermacher* literally translated.

9

What is there left for me now, cut off from the body of Life, but to make my death a furious protest against the dismemberment of my being? Therefore I cry for women — *more women!* — which is to me not a revolt from Reason, but a return to a sounder logic, to the Jaina life-principle of *anekantavada*, of many-sidedness, of the Within that slides into the Without, the Without into the Within, following the rhythm of erotics, the polar tension of male and female.

My love for Lou polarized me to invisible cosmic forces; I, the periphery, became the Center, my chaos became a dancing star. Now I am depolarized, depersonalized, dissolved — and death? Death? No, resurrection! *I am Dionysos!*

10

Those who love, but not wisely, despair of the power of love. When I was with my Russian Helen she pulled me with her subtle, Slavic ways into the magical circle of love, where Tolstoy and Dostoyevsky were ready with shears to prune my claws — a bird of prey cast among Christians and Christian Socialists interrogating the augurs for the millennium! Perhaps it was in my destiny that Elisabeth's treachery should be the means whereby I escaped Jerusalem and barricaded myself behind the seven hills of Rome. What an insult to my life's mission if it ended by my candidacy for sainthood — Saint Nietzsche, patron of culture-philistines like Wagner who kiss the big toe of papal lies and deceit!

Since I am a fatality, the goal towards which all civilization moves, it is obvious that Elisabeth's vicious behavior towards me is justified in the light of history where good becomes evil and evil good as in the idea-systems of Spinoza and Hegel, who is merely Spinoza geared to the tempo of our fast-moving industrial age. Elisabeth was fated to snarl her life up with mine, just as Byron was predestined to entangle his life with his elder sister Augusta.

11

This flash of illumination came to me when I strolled beyond the asylum grounds with Peter Gast, who told me that I have made a remarkable recovery, and at the same time hinted that I was perhaps shamming madness on the Baudelairean thesis that the only way to keep sane is to escape bourgeois civilization and lock yourself up in a madhouse. It was Gast who first mentioned the Ishmaelite Byrons, and I ripped the mask from my thoughts and exposed the Ishmaelite Nietzsches to his astounded view. It was then only that poor Gast thought I was mad, and I helped him to foster the delusion by kicking an innocent bystander in the shins. I have often expressed the view that Truth, the Salome-dancer, should never drop her seventh veil, for naked, unabashed Truth becomes a cannibalistic, blood-thirsty savage that demands the head of the Saint — and gets it served up to her on a platter.

It is best that the world should not know — at least in her lifetime — that Elisabeth played the same role in my life's drama as Augusta played in Byron's. Like Augusta, Elisabeth was a buffer and a shield against the maternal despot who smashed her lances of ridicule and stupidity against her counter-sarcasm until Elisabeth assumed the role of the maternal tyrant as soon as I began to show an interest in the fair sex. To maintain her dominance over me she seduced me into the sin of the Egyptians, thus making it possible for me to tear myself away from my sick Lutheran conscience, having matched Satan himself with my sin.

Byron too felt that he was the equal of Satan, his Calvinist conscience smashed on the rock of his certainty that he had passed beyond the greatest sinners — Manfred and Cain — and reached the ultimate in wickedness. Through Augusta he was enabled to sit next to the throne of His Satanic Majesty whom Schopenhauer ensconced in heaven. But Elisabeth puffed up my pride still more: I could not tolerate the Satanic compromise by allowing a Ruler to be above me and so I stood on my own head and became the Superman — the Monarch of the Universe. As I have written: "If there were Gods, how could I endure it to be not God! *Therefore* there are no Gods."

12

It was this Satanic pride of mine that Lou fought against, and she succeeded in cutting me down to her measure of love and passion which were human, all-too human. Lou was my good angel warring with the bad angel Elisabeth who aroused the demonic in me by the consciousness of the great sin we shared in common. She used all the stratagem of hell to tear me loose from my Slavic Helen, and since I am a Slav myself, a Pole of noble ancestry, Elisabeth's victory over us became a double defeat for Slavdom.

It grieves me to reveal all this because I still carry the yoke of pity with the rest of the Christian West, and there is grave danger, as I have said, *that man will bleed to death through the truth that he recognizes.* The knowledge of sorrow has softened into the sorrow of knowledge; we become aware of the Byronic complaint that "the Tree of Knowledge is not the Tree of Life." Since I do not expect this confession of mine to be made public until Mama, the Lama, Lou and myself are gathered into the bosom of Abraham (or Satan), I can hazard the shocking truth in the light of Spinoza's dictum that to forgive is to forget.

All accounts are settled in eternity, without malice and without regard to intellectual swindlers who dare not admit the truth, even to posterity. Fifty years after my death, when I shall have become a myth, my star will shine in the firmament as the

West is eclipsed in darkness, and by the light that I give, my power-philosophy will be re-examined not as power but as Providence.

13

A half-witted attendant here has caused considerable laughter by pretending he was St. Peter and telling his doctor that God has gone mad.

"What is his trouble?" asked the conniving medico.

"The Lord thinks he is Professor Nietzsche."

If God were alive this would not be a joke but an obvious fact.

14

I have been abused because I said in *Beyond Good and Evil* that we should think of women as property, as Orientals do. When Elisabeth read this statement she merely grinned, for she knows the bitter truth: women are the only private property that has complete control over its owner. Just as machinery in our industrial age has become human and uses a leather belt to flog the machine *hands* into slavery, woman is the Frankenstein's monster, built from the material of social graveyards, who hounds man to his doom. My advice to be hard towards them is as ludicrous as the advice of a Nietzschean mouse, at a convention of mice to be hard towards the despotic Cat.

And this feline analogy is a true one. As I have said in *Thus Spake Zarathustra*, women are not capable of friendship: they are still cats or birds, or at best can rise to the status of cows, although I do not agree with Schopenhauer that the erotic portions of woman, such as the breasts, are unaesthetic and cowlike and are mere traps set by nature to catch man through his mating instinct.

I once expressed the wish to have lived in the Athens of Pericles or in the Florence of the Medici because these were two golden ages when women were considered works of art and not candidates for a workshop or a pickle factory. Aspasia is my ideal woman, excelling in both the horizontal and vertical arts, in love and in wisdom, and for a time I thought Lou was my Aspasia-dream come true. My will to illusion has been the cause of my breakdown.

15

I have said that war is the only remedy against the deviating of the state ideal into a money-ideal. But the Bismarckian money-lords who have caused this deviation are claiming me as the apostle of war at any price. I have chanted a paean of war, I have heard Apollo, the great warrior, "horribly clanging his silver bow," but I have never identified Apollo with the beer-and-sausage soldiers of the Stock Exchange.

Therefore I resent the comfort of Mr. Moneybags who comes to visit me in this madhouse and assures me that he will take care of my future when I get out. It is because I fear that he will make good his threat that I prefer to remain here.

16

I have said somewhere,[2] that a good battle is worthy of a man's mettle but that real heroism consists in not fighting at all. I have also remarked that the greatest thoughts are the greatest events. But I do not look upon a Bismarckian war or a bloody pogrom as a great event. Prussians who raise the pirate's flag of war in the name of profit-and-grab, I have always despised, and Germans like my brother-in-law who whip up the blood-lust of the mob against their betters the Jews are beneath my contempt.

Yes, I must repeat: Germans give me acute indigestion, and if any more Germans visit me *I shall boot* them out of my sanctuary.

---

[2] *Human — All-Too Human.*

The English Civil War took place, said Hobbes, because power was divided among King, Lords and Commons. The Civil War in Naumburg occurred because power was divided among my mother, my sister and my aunts. A palace guard of petticoats kept watch over me; I was a monarch imprisoned in his own castle, and when I wrote *one must approach a woman with a whip* I struck panic in the Naumburg *ménage*. My aunts thought I meant it, and retreated hastily, but the Lama and Mama kept to their guns and shot volleys of abuse at me. As an old artilleryman I naturally fought back — not with cannon but with words. But they won out in the end, because I could not carry out in my private life the Hobbesian maxim I adopted: *Force and fraud are, in war, the two cardinal virtues.*

The more I contemplated Elisabeth the more I admired Caesar Borgia. He was too strong, clever and unscrupulous to be the victim of a petticoat's fury. At Tautenburg when I was with Lou and asserting the blond beast in me by defying the Lama and the gossip-mongers in town, I entertained the pleasant thought of giving my sister the Borgia treatment, and even experimented with a variety of poisons. But of course my homicidal plan never went beyond the experimental stage. My Lutheran conscience vetoed my will to be *as fierce as a lion and as cunning as a fox.* I tried to be Machiavelli's Prince but instead I was *the little pastor,* afraid of the God whom I buried in my youth.

17

An inmate here has a poodle which he calls Atma (the world-soul) after the poodle that Schopenhauer was so fond of. The dog has taken a fancy to me, as if he recognizes a fellow-philosopher confined to the dog-house. When one of the guards kicked the animal he yelped. *Stop,* I cried, *don't strike him! It's the soul of a friend of mine. I recognized his voice!*

One of the doctors solemnly made a note of my remark, as

further proof that I am out of my mind. The Philistine did not realize that I was merely aping Pythagoras and repeating his famous exclamation when he saw a dog being abused by a skunk in human form. But the idea of the transmigration of souls is not so foolish as it sounds, and my concept of *Eternal Recurrence* is merely a modern resurrection of the Pythagorean creed. We were once dogs and we slink back to our primal dogdom.

At least that is true of Schopenhauer, who recognized himself in his poodle; and his principal work, *The World as Will and Idea*, which he thought was dictated by the Holy Ghost, was really the product of his poodle-brain. Poodles are intelligent canines which learn tricks easily — and have a greater aptitude for trickery than the philosopher who despised life in his philosophy but lived like Petronius' bourgeois pig Trimalchio all the days of his swinish existence. This Dresden voluptuary who hated women in his books and loved them in his bed was once my idol, until I discovered that his ascetic Buddhism was merely a mask for Carlyle's Bitch Goddess — the Whore of Babylon herself.

18

I often wonder whether I would have been more fortunate if I had decided to let Schopenhauer's mother instead of my own give birth to me. My mother has settled down here in Weimar as Schopenhauer's mother did (she wants to be near her sunken son), but here the resemblance in their characters ends, except that they were both dominant females to whom mother-love was a convenient hammer with which to pound subservience and doggish servility into their sons.

Schopenhauer's mother was a bohemian blue-stocking who kept a literary salon and lovers who praised her books with their lips while they admired her body with their foppish eyes. She never assumed a Puritanic pose and therefore could not be accused of mental and moral double-dealing — the glaring vice of her famous offspring, who wrapped himself in the Buddhist veil of Maya, while he pulled the corsets off women with his brutish hands and threw an elderly seamstress down a flight of stairs to demonstrate his gospel of love and pity.

But for one thing I am thankful: when the old lady died after twenty years, he no longer had to pay her the fifteen thaler every quarter — as the result of a court judgment — and he noted in his account book: *Obit anus, abit onus.* (The old woman dies; the burden is gone.) When Mama finally departs from this veil of tears and receives her reward, I shall borrow Schopenhauer's prayers of relief — the only praiseworthy thought in all his philosophy.

Kant was bitten by the tarantula of mortality, Rousseau, but it was my mother who bit me, inflicting a fatal wound which Christians call conscience. Lou bit me too, but it was the bite of love which heals all wounds.

But now I am back in Kant's moral domain: the guards are strict and won't let me spit at the gibbering idiot who thumbs his nose at me all day and quotes: *Thus Spake Zarathustra, Professor Treitzschke.* He has me confused with the rabid Prussian militarist, and the idiots of the next century will make the same mistake, making me do a goose-step with imperialists like Bismarck whom I detest as the assassin of culture — a beer-guzzling, sausage-nibbling Philistine.

If I could conjure up the ghost of Diogenes I would be encouraged to spit into the face of respectable idiocy as the great Cynic did. But (alas!) the Greeks were civilized, despite their bad manners, while we are barbarians despite our good manners and the silk hats we place upon our bald pates.

19

Hegel dragged in a sixth sense — the historical sense — to overcome our scientific atheism and bind us to the divinity of existence. Yes, existence is divine — only the madmen can test the divinity of life with his sacred madness. An epileptic like Dostoyevsky turned his nervous ailment into a testimony of sublime faith in man, in the dignity of human existence. His Underman and my Overman are the same person clawing his way up out of the pit into the sunlight, bruised, battered and bloody like Joseph, but always eager to weld anguish into the hard steel of the Promethean soul.

If I collapse into total idiocy I will consider it a sacred state of being, and like a Trappist monk I will keep my lips tightly buttoned and confront the arrogant love of Mama and the Lama with absolute silence.

Madness has her victories no less great than sanity.

20

Zeno was honored with a golden crown and a monument in the Kerameikos. I expect no such beatification. I will be glad if no windows open and no chamber-pots will be emptied at my funeral as it crawls through the streets of Jena. This would be a sad end for the author of *Zarathustra*, the Promethean who sought to filch the fires from heaven and was chained to the rock of self-abnegation and torment.

The Koran says Saint Matthew was an honest man. Perhaps the worshipers of Allah will enshrine me in their memories as the only honest Christian in Europe — a Christian who was too proud to accept the slave-morality of Saint Paul and preferred, like Jesus himself, to roll in the thunder of the Old Testament.

21

The old maids of science are barren but honorable creatures who dare not create new tables of values for our age sick unto death. I as a philosopher had to seize a hammer and pound new values into the world. Now there are no new values, there are only new corpses and new graves. I lie here in the shadow of death while my Russian Helen is amusing herself in the stews of Paris — as all Helens do. And yet, and yet, who can give up the image of Helen — for that of the Virgin who puts into the mouths of her lovers the pale grapes of death?

Over my grave a lark sings, and I hear the sighing of a breeze in an evergreen. The air is stirring with new life: it must be the dawn of spring, though I have lost all sense of time, being already dead.

When, O Lost One, shall be my resurrection?

22

When I was in her arms, Lou asked, "Do you wish this to happen once more eternally?"[3]

Just like a woman to turn the sacred idea of Eternal Recurrence into a perpetual orgasm, the disruptive rapture of Dionysos. Not until I met my Russian Helen did I realize Solomon's grave predicament: he had not one but a thousand inexhaustible wombs to contend with. This was too much for any man, even for Solomon who was the only Jew with a passion for empire, a passion to extend the boundaries of his realm to the ends of the earth. In him the Jewish will to power reached its glorious apex: he sought to incorporate all heaven and all earth under the banner of Jehovah, imposing a *Pax Judaica* on the barbarian world.

Lou, like a female Solomon (Hypatia was her forerunner), had an equal lust to dominate the world of body, mind and spirit which she felt was incarnate in myself. By mastering me she could achieve world-mastery, but her anatomical destiny defeated her. Only great harlots like Pompadour and Montespan could rule the world from their bedrooms, but even they relied on the consent

---

[3] Quoting from Nietzsche's *Joyful Wisdom.*

of their royal lovers who were idiots. *But I am no idiot*, despite the psychiatrists' reports which deal only in lying statistics.

I shall communicate these thoughts to my friend Strindberg: the poor man suffers constantly from woman trouble, and he will be quite surprised to discover that Professor Nietzsche was a fellow-sufferer.

23

I lived my Eternal Return; I philosophized with my whole being and the wheel of Chaos whirled me into madness. But in her arms I felt the upward pull of the Eternal Feminine; she made me a Goethean and I was saved from damnation.

But now I am back on the terrible wheel.

The God of cosmic irony who judges over us passed a fitting judgment upon me: here in Weimar, in the intellectual kingdom of Goethe, I am confined in a madhouse: my belief in his Eternal Feminine — the belief of a moment — has recoiled against me, and I am eternally damned!

24

The people can be unwise, said Rousseau, *but they can never be wrong.* This is the fatal error of democracy — that mere numbers determine the justice or injustice of a cause. This error is demonstrated in this lunatic asylum. The madmen constitute a majority of the asylum community and hence look upon the minority of employees as their oppressors. What they do is right, even though they are punished by the asylum guards for doing the *right* things.

Their wrong reasoning is obvious to anyone who has read Machiavelli or has felt the end of a policeman's club, as I did in my student days at Bonn. What is right has always been determined by minorities who use clubs, codes or cannon to maintain their rule over the majorities. Of course psychological codes are more effective than cannon, and if the people in our democracies think they are in control of their own destinies it is because the slave-morality of the Christian binds both the master and the slave.

25

The millionaire and the pauper both go to the same church, they both listen to sermons on Christian love, Justice and benevolence; they both have the same right to go mad with fear of hunger and want, although few millionaires have been known to take advantage of this dubious privilege.

There is a millionaire in this mental hospital who calls himself Marc Antony and receives the favors of "Cleopatra" — the wife of an attendant. A madman with money can even make the beautiful and sane his willing slaves — despite Rousseau and his egalitarian humbug!

26

Everything goes by wager of battle in this world; strength, well-understood, is the measure of all worth. Give a thing time; if it can succeed it is the right thing. Lou thought that this Carlylean thought is the key to my philosophy, as if British Prussianism can be equated with the ideas of Zarathustra. Carlyle tried to prove that justice and force were synonymous and placed the face of Jehovah on the pirate's flag of British imperialism. I, on the contrary, have nothing to do with the word *justice*, which is merely honey to catch human flies.

In a power world the justice-mongers are merely barbarians dressed up as Christian reformists. *There are,* said Candillac, *two kinds of barbarians; the one precedes centuries of enlightenment, the other follows them.* The justice-mongers are Hectors, primitive power-men who live in a dying age of enlightenment and are afraid to display their clubs in public. When they are bold enough to show their bludgeons, they tell us they are wielding Wagnerian batons or papal scepters!

27

Moral idealism cannot override the economic compulsions of our Power Age: Ruskin, Carlyle and the other British blockheads, especially John Stuart Mill, have not learned the basic fact in modern living. If I were not Caesar I would be Christ, the Socialist, mount an ass and ride into Jerusalem with Karl Marx. The power-lust of the Marxists matches the power-lust of the Nietzscheans, but I prefer to ride to Jerusalem on an Arabian charger rather than a proletarian donkey.

Brandes calls me *an aristocratic radical* — and that is exactly what I am. *In my Father's house there are many Mansions,* and who but a Jew could unmask me, revealing the face of Disraeli, the Tory radical? The extreme reactionary and the extreme radical are brothers under the skin: both have a contempt for liberal, humanitarian humbug, and know but one road to success — the road to Power.

The people must be ruled by an iron hand, and I prophesy an age of proletarian Caesars who have turned Rousseau on his head as Marx has done and become heads of democratic dictatorships where the will of a sewer-digger and a pants-presser is identified with the will of God and is codified in Draconian laws written in letters of blood.

28

The Jews were the first people who refused to turn the culture values of the ancients into universals. They were my precursors who insisted on a complete Copernican revolution in the world of thought — the transvaluation of all values! But so powerful is the time-spirit, our age of crass commercialism and what Carlyle calls the cash-nexus, that even Jews (not all, I must admit) have confused Jehovah with the All-Mighty Banker. Bourgeois man turns God Himself into a bourgeois gentleman, and if the Swiss, as Pascal tells us, are insulted when they are called gentlemen, it is because they feel themselves superior to the bourgeois God who is nothing but a deified huckster.

29

Because I have substituted myself for the Lord I am accused of blasphemous egomania. But I am, in fact, extremely modest in my pretensions, my egomania being the obverse side of my sense of inferiority. A huckstering deity is too low a creature for my aristocratic taste, and for me to take the place of God is a *demotion*, not a promotion to the rare heights of Sinai — the Stock Exchange!

Having transvalued all values in the manner of the ancient Abraham, I should have left the God-idea severely alone and turned over this God-mongering business to the British imperialists, the hypocritical Carlyles who have discovered in God an Archimedean lever to lift London into the center of world power.

Thus Spake Zarathustra.

30

Ah, my beautiful disciple, you took my motto which I filched from the holy Assassins, the horror of the pious Crusaders: *Nothing is true; all things are lawful.* Like one of your Dostoyevsky heroes you did not hesitate to destroy me as an act of pure holiness dictated by your nihilistic gods.

The man of prey is an aristocrat; the woman of prey is a harlot, but the harlot is the ultimate in aristocracy: she has no pride of ownership, not even in her own body.

O Whore of Babylon, cover me with thy sins!

CHAPTER TEN

1

Of all the books in the Bible, *First Samuel*, especially in the opening passages, made the profoundest impression on me. In a way, it may be responsible for an important spiritual element in my life. It is where the Lord three times wakes the infant prophet in his sleep, and Samuel three times mistakes the heavenly voice for the voice of Eli asleep near him in the temple. Convinced, after the third time, that his prodigy is being called to higher services than those available to him in the house of sacrifices, Eli proceeds to instruct him in the ways of prophecy. I had no Eli (not even a Schopenhauer) when a similar visitation darkened the opening days of my adolescence. I was all of twelve when the Lord broke in on me in all His glory, a glaring fusion of the portraits of Abraham, Moses and the Young Jesus in our family Bible. In His second visitation He came to me not physically but in a shudder of consciousness in which good and evil both clamored before the gates of my soul for equal mastery. The third time He seized me in front of my house in the grasp of a terrible wind. I recognized the agency of a divine force because it was in that moment that I conceived of the Trinity as God the Father, God the Son, and God the Devil . . .

2

I replaced Samuel with Zarathustra, just as I was to replace the giant Wagner with little Peter Gast, who bore such a strong outward resemblance to the lord of Bayreuth. But what are resemblances? How big is big? And how little is little?

3

Without doubt, Peter is a definite personality who has a definite history with me, a history that does not in the least resemble the history Wagner has piled up on my frail nervous system. But what about the ghosts who haunt me — like the stranger who passed in front of me in a wood I was strolling leisurely through, looked steadfastly at me, smiled and walked on? What about all those gallant, mysterious, apparently purposeless ghosts who live with all us, follow us about, and then, without any warning, pass out of the range of our psyches into eternal anonymity?

4

There is sheer happiness in just riding on trains, eating at wayside stations, and planning new ventures into the future. It is to be uttered with sadness, but every city I have ever stopped at managed, after a while, to grow terribly tedious and without intellectual resources. This is more likely to be my fault than the fault of the places I live in and haunt. I guess the only place to go to, which is incapable of disappointing a fastidious traveler like me, is Nowhere . . .

5

Once I have decided on a journey, I want to get into the train as quickly as possible, if only to watch from one of its windows the eager faces of children following the people and the wheels, and listening to the dreadful, deliberate belching of the engine into a faultless sky. A train-ride is sometimes punctuated by the sound of church-bells suggesting that there are more mysterious, deadlier places one might go to. It doesn't make much difference to me whether, taking it for granted that the

165

church-bells have a true knowledge of destiny, one lands in heaven or hell. In either place, the tedium must be something devastating.

6

If only the Americans would work up a really healthy interest in my books, an interest strong enough to require a lecture course given by me in fascinating places like Detroit, Chicago, New York or San Francisco . . . I hear that Dickens did not like America because they refused to pay him the royalties his books earned him there. What an admirable people are these English! Even their artists are merchants to their fingertips.

7

A trip to America would mean trans-ocean travel, and I suspect that the Atlantic is even moodier than I am, and too cold to flatter my North-German concept of happiness. I love to climb mountains. I wonder what it would be like to climb one of those giant ocean waves one reads about in the travel stories. I wonder what would have happened if someone had induced Kant to take an ocean voyage.

8

What a wonderful thing it is to sweep back my recollections to those days in Genoa where I lived like a pauper among paupers, giving the peasants about me no more than my simple compassion for their fruitless lives. I lived literally on vegetables and water, but I must have looked to them like a prince in disguise.

9

Whenever I have to choose between being a public sinner and beating my breast privately in self-humiliation I always choose the humbler role. With Wagner, all his departures from the norm had to be shouted from the housetops . . . Whatever did Cosima see in the old blowhard?

10

I do not care much about the theater, or about any one of the lower forms of it which adorn the backyards of small towns. For better or worse, concerts draw me with a purely personal attraction. The whole entertainment world is one grand bonfire to which men, women and children are drawn to peer for glimpses of their individual destinies. They laugh and cry over the misfortunes of others, but when they are angry it is only with themselves . . .

11

State tyranny is almost a necessity for those incapable of self-tyranny.

12

My wants are so simple and so few: a warm climate for my bones, a clear atmosphere for my lungs, good vegetables for my stomach, and just a little intelligent conversation for the exercise of my mind . . .

13

I like children and children like me. But I must admit that I like children better who are complete strangers to me, and I like best those children I meet in a foreign country, whom I am not likely ever to meet again . . .

14

At Sils Maria in the Engadine I was of the age and mood in which Dante saw and transcribed his vision of the world.

But it is not my fault that Dante's Italy deserved *The Comedy* while my Germany is entitled to no better than these scribblings of mine . . .

15

It took one dazzling episode of the exquisite cruelty of *Carmen* to clear my brain forever of the cobwebs of the Wagnerian nightmare. What a single act of murder does for an individual it takes a whole war to do for a nation. But don't let it worry you. The Prussians will take care of this little thing for us in practically no time . . .

16

If I don't go to the United States I would like to visit the country to the south of it, Mexico, where, I hear, the climate is warmer and the people are infinitely more friendly. When all those queer people were milling about my poor sister with their plans for a purely Christian world to be started on the other side of the Atlantic, I met a world-wanderer who had been to Mexico. He gave me such a picture of Mexico that I wonder how I could let myself get so sick as to render almost hopeless the prospect of my ever getting there. According to that happy traveler, Mexico is a country where one sees nothing but peasant men, women and children because the bourgeois (whatever there is of this curious species) sleep through the days and venture out only at night when those who work and create the wealth of the country are fast asleep . . . It is the only country he ever saw, he said, in which the valleys were as high as the mountains, where the colors of earth, water and animal life blend so profoundly that one could conceive of the whole country as one physical unit. I would like to visit such a country even if I had to pay the penalty of watching one of its incongruous bull-fights . . .

17

Ah, my dark beloved! . . . Just to get you out of my
system I had to run away, and I am still escaping, from a
hundred people . . .

18

I dreamed last night that I stood before a throne of solid
black. On this condensed darkness sat a black-hooded figure in
whom I instinctively recognized my destiny.

What do you want of me? I asked.

There is only one thing left for you to do, said the voice of my
destiny. *I am your dragon, and you must find the axe sharp enough
to slay me.*

19

If the gods did not weep in floods of rain, how would the
soul of man have learned how to be sad?

20

One consolation I have, which no one can take away from
me. Had I married my Slavic Princess I might have been happy,
but the world would have had to wait another thousand years for
Zarathustra. On the other hand, if I had written Zarathustra
before meeting Lou, how could she have resisted me? If I could
have had my way it would have been this. But if I had to choose
between Lou and Zarathustra I think the woman would have
been my ultimate choice. The only potent sacrifices are those
which we are forced to make. Self-sacrifice is silly and pointless.

21

If you have never walked side by side with yourself on a
mountain-path while the sun rose slowly over the woods of

another horizon you have not yet found a scene fit for your rebirth as an individual soul.

22

Our culture is so threadbare, the mere sound of warfare tears it into bits.

23

Eternal recurrence underlies the whole sense of the dignity of man. If we had a better knowledge of the ways of animals, birds, insects and fish it is in the recurrence of certain phenomena that we should find understanding of their ways and lives. Without the conception of eternal recurrence what is a human being but an idle accident of time and place? Emphasized in countless millions of rebirths man becomes as conceptually existent as a spinning-wheel.

24

The common man would like to believe that he lives for one single aim — and that is as definite an expression as he can find of his ignorance of himself and of the ends for which he is destined. What is this grand aim he lives for? A woman? Children? The broadening of this slippery democracy there is so much talk of? To test the validity of these values of yours, my fine citizen, stand under any healthy tree, repeat these things to yourself, and see if the calm branches of the tree do not laugh you and your aim into eternal scorn.

25

There are people in this world who have been so completely milked of their precious illusions that they think there is left to them only one usefulness to which they can apply their remaining energies, and that is, to shrink out of the public eye in an act of moral suicide. Yet where is the chimney-sweep who, under the proper circumstances, would not make a first-rate prime minister? Or where is the king who, compelled by historic circumstances, would not become a first-rate bootblack?

26

I am only one voice in a chorus of millions of voices, one thought amidst thousands of thousands clamoring ponderously to be heard above me, a heart of flesh in a universe of flying comets and meteors . . .

27

What sets a man aside as a rich man, or puts him down as a poor one? His ability or inability to give up almost anything in his possessions without losing the sense of security.

28

The man who is to take these notes to my publisher is becoming particularly friendly. But I don't know whether he thinks I am a philosopher or just a lunatic.

This morning he found me near the window and asked me what I was searching for in the outside world.

You have only to follow my eyes, I told him. *If you see me looking into the sky you must know that it is an eagle I am looking for. But if my gaze goes downward the quarry I am hunting is a lion.*

But can you really expect to see a lion on a street in Jena? he asked.

If you have the eyes to see him with, why not? I replied.

29

During my last days at the Overbecks I experienced what any man must feel when he is told that the house to which he first brought his wife, and into which his children were born, has failed in its foundations and must be pulled down.

30

I remember Heinz, director of the University of Leipzig, arguing why it would be impossible for me to lecture there any longer. The best of all reasons for this he did not give because it was not within his knowing. A man cannot teach and whore under the same stars . . .

31

I talk best with myself. My thoughts are clearest when I myself consider them. I can feel my whole reaction to the world changing as another ken slips in on the scene . . .

32

I warm easily in the summer, but in winter, when most people look as if they are about to freeze up, I am entirely at my ease. Obviously my cloak of loneliness is proof against the heaviest of snows, the most stinging of frosts, the most penetrating of Arctic blasts . . .

33

What a difference it might have made in my life if the facts concerning Giordano Bruno had become clear to me a few years earlier, and discovery of Schopenhauer came to me now, when the walls of my castle are halfway down to the ground, and no self-respecting wind offers to blow over them . . .

34

If I am to believe a letter I have just received from Peter Gast, the word from Brandes has blown my name into many far places so that thousands of people who never heard my name before are now looking for my books, reading them wherever they can find them and talking about me. Suddenly this lonely soul finds itself in a sweathouse full of inquiring people. But I never wanted such a multitude. I don't need it. I need only the small readership which builds up the world or tears it down.

35

Was it just an accident that Förster was not only an anti-Semite but a follower of Wagner, an arch-anti-Semite of whom it is rumored that he was born of a Jewish father? Is it possible that some of my own strictures against the Jews proceed from the same mysterious influence?

36

Under the circumstances, Elisabeth could marry only an avowed anti-Semite like Förster — someone so completely unlike me that it would not multiply incest to go to bed with him.

37

If I can ever get out of this house of violence and talk someone into trusting me with paper and pencil, I will do even better with Empedocles than I ever did with Zarathustra. I'm surprised I did with Zarathustra as well as I did. He's so un-bearably pure!

38

If there were anything like justice in the physical world, Förster would have frozen in the waters which gave me so much warmth. When I finally came face to face with him I discovered that, as with his likeness in the dust, the human worm is at his best when he wriggles.

39

I am Lucifer-Dionysus. I am what I have always desperately

wanted to be, what I am not and what I never will be. Blessed be the dust which receives and covers and keeps us.

40

Germany is the only country in the world where I could have found it necessary to bring out the fourth part of Zarathustra at my own expense.

41

Cosima will outlive all of us. Where other children are baptized she was vaccinated.

42

English publishers are reputed for their bad judgment. French publishers are intelligent but unscrupulous. American publishers are notoriously dishonest. But German publishers are just downright stupid.

43

On one of our walks Lavizky asked me which of my books I liked the best. I told him I was not quite certain, but it must be one of the books I have not yet written. I have such a tenderness for everything in the world not yet born.

44

What a spectacle under the sun — Bismarck and I working for the same country in the same age, both with blood on our hands, mine not so easily seen because I wash so much more frequently.

45

I put everything I had into *The Genealogy of Morals*. It is now impossible for me ever to misunderstand myself.

CHAPTER ELEVEN

1

The ideal life is the lie of the ideal. I have been guilty of this lie despite the fact that I have ripped off the masks from fanatics who pose as the prophets of Jehovah and seek to ram their absolute truths down the throats of their victims in the name of science or religion. Like the English, whom I have castigated as peddlers of the Absolute, I have myself been a moral fanatic, seeking to retrieve the honor of a dead God by placing my Superman on his empty throne. And what is my theory of Eternal Recurrence but an heroic effort on my part to put method into the madness of the cosmos, to place an underlying reason behind all unreason, like a Buddhist who is terrified by his atheism and seeks to mask it by a thousand images of fear-born gods and godlets?

2

My *absolute* truths are like corpses which dissolve into dust at the mere touch of the wind; beneath my Elijah's mantle crawl the serpents of pride and deceit.

3

It was under the leading-strings of Cosima that I first learned to take the initial steps in the world of great lies which are called absolute truths. The betrayal of my best friend sickened my conscience to the point of death, but she *cured* me by convincing me that my conscience in itself was a sickness contracted in Naumburg in an atmosphere of Lutheran prudery and hypocrisy. She masked her brutish adultery behind the pious pretense of pure, self-denying love, and Tristan, in his amorous dalliance with Isolde, was made to feel like a brave knight of the Ideal, fighting the cant and idiocies of Philistine morals.

Of course Wagner deserved the horns I gave him, for a man who steals the wife of a friend with her eager connivance, cannot expect faithfulness on the part of his mistress; her only loyalty is to her flesh, and to indulge her flesh she will climb into strange beds as often as Faustine, the spouse of Marcus Aurelius.

But there was quite a difference between the Stoic Emperor and the Monarch of the Musical World. Aurelius not only forgave his wife's numerous adulteries, but after her death he erected temples in her honor, lifting her infidelities to divine status, as if she were a goddess on Olympus, engaged in cosmic orgies that made the stars shrink in shame behind a wall of clouds. Wagner, on the contrary, was too conceited to believe that his precious Cosima could ape Faustine, for he out-Caesared Caesar in his estimate of himself. In this estimate I shared, because, having cast off God, I had a fanatical need for God-worship, for the bright banner of the Ideal.

But no man is a hero to his wife — or his wife's lover! We all have a need for the independent life of the spirit, but we cannot kneel down before a god whose goddess we hold in our arms while his back is turned. And so my Superman was born, a synthetic Beyond-Man to make up for the loss of God, Schopenhauer, Wagner and every earthly genius that we are tempted to deify.

But my strongest defense against the malady of the Ideal was the cultivation of my own ego, which I puffed up to cosmic proportions: I substituted myself for the God whose funeral I announced to a shocked and outraged world. Since I was God, even Napoleon, who bestrides the nineteenth century like a Colossus, was reduced to a microbe in my mind and I was at peace. Like Beethoven I could not abide the worship of Napoleon, and I always remembered his *défi*: *If I knew as much about strategy as I do about counterpoint I'd make short shrift of that fellow.*

I made short shrift of Bonaparte by becoming a Napoleon of the intellect and following his example: I did not argue with my enemies but trampled them into the dust, demolishing and pulverizing them with the cannon of invective. But as an old artillery-man I realize that words are a feeble substitute for cannonballs, and my pulverized victims had a nasty habit of gathering their tiny pieces together and restoring themselves to total manhood.

It is only I who am utterly destroyed, trapped in the coffin of paralysis, while madness hammers the coffin whether I consider myself God, Superman, or have cured myself of the malady of the ideal by making myself the ideal that I have tried to follow, or if I cry with my beloved Emerson: *The seeds of Godlike power are in us still?* The coffin worms are making ready to devour all my pride, all my dreams and all my hopes. I am more miserable than the dying Jew on the cross, but I dare not cry aloud to God in my misery as the Jew did: shall Antichrist stoop to the craven weakness of Christ?

4

Shall it be said of great Yea-Sayer, the greatest Stoic since Zeno, that he has succumbed to the Buddhist-Christianity of Schopenhauer and grovels in self-pity, self-contempt, cowardice and abysmal remorse? Shall I ascend my pillar like Saint Simeon and expose my lean, crippled body to the mockery of the Philistines — those buzzards which are already flapping their wings, anxious for my carcass as hell is anxious for the souls of saints?

No, a thousand times no! In my youth, while still at Pforta, I became enamored of Emerson, whose spiritual beauty and nobility I tried to place upon the brows of Chopin and the composer of *Tristan*. But Emerson remains with me to the last, and his words I memorized in my youth are like Longfellow's banner with the strange device — *Excelsior* — a flag floating forever over my ruins. And so I repeat:

The seeds of godlike power are in us still;
Gods are we Bards, Saints, Heroes, if we will!

I am a god, and just as Virgil was called *deus* posterity will call me *deus* and enshrine my name among the immortals.

Thus Spake Zarathustra!

5

My house is full of Job's comforters, artists, writers, professors and bohemians, who hatch the bird's eggs of advice in their thick, bushy hair. Fortunately I am able to reject their silly suggestions on the ground of idiocy: my blank expression is sufficient proof to them that I do not understand their jabberings. Elisabeth wards them off with a painful gesture which says: *Leave the poor man alone; don't you see he has collapsed into total idiocy?*

6

The more I am in contact with the intelligentsia, the more I am delighted with the aptness of Napoleon's rebuke: *These intellectuals are like vermin in my clothes; I shall shake them off.* Napoleon's shot was directed especially at the conspiratorial Benjamin Constant and his blue-stocking mistress Madame de Staël.

It is Madame de Staël who intrigues me, because, despite physical ugliness, she reminds me so much of Fräulein Salomé. The brilliant mistress of Constant was the only woman in Europe who dared defy Napoleon. This petticoat fury, who was as amorous and rebellious as Byron, applied Goethe's maxim to herself: *Man should aim high . . . it is only man who can do the impossible.* She aimed high: she shot Napoleon out of the clouds of his glory and pinned him to the bourgeois earth, making him look like a little, henpecked husband badgered by a shrewish Katherine who knows the power of her female tongue and uses it to the utmost.

7

Fräulein Salomé likewise used the artillery of her tongue to hurl cannon-balls at my Napoleonic conceit, my delusion that I was called upon by some mysterious Destiny to set the world aright despite my Hamlet-like aversion to playing the role of Napoleon or Jesus which can only lead to St. Helena or the Cross. She called my attention to Turgenev's essay on Don Quixote and Hamlet and intimated that after I was exhausted by my quixotic effort to change the world, I would fall into a Hamlet-like despair, feigning madness like Hölderlin in order to avoid contact with so-called sane people — the unspeakable Philistines.

8

But my madness is not feigned: for weeks and months I lose all sense of time and space, fail to recognize anyone but my sister and try to recall myself out of the abyss by repeating over and over again: *I am Friedrich Nietzsche, the philosopher with the hammer.* In my dreams the hammer has turned into a spade and I find myself digging my own grave like a Trappist monk, burying myself under a pile of my books, doomed and desolated by the futility of all knowledge which philosophers mistake for God's wisdom . . .

9

Ah, when I held Lou in my arms I could think of humanity

in the block, because, possessing a woman's body, a philosopher possesses the throbbing body of humanity; he possesses the substance of existence, not the shadow, the lived experience, not the philosophical, moth-eaten abstraction.

10

This reminds me of Scarron's homily: a hundred years after Seneca's death a philosopher asked the reigning emperor for a small town in Calabria which was wholly ruined. He wanted to build a Utopia, after removing the rubbish, according to the blueprint of Plato's Republic. He wished to call the new city *Platonopolis*, but the emperor thought it would be more fitting to call it *The Asses' Paradise*. He had no faith in the divine reason of Plato or in the earthly reason of the Platonic philosopher. He had so little faith in the rationality of a philosopher that he was unwilling to risk to it the rule of a dump-heap.

11

All my life has been a combat between freedom and necessity, between my desire to be God and the necessity of remaining a worm, although a worm with shining wings. My romanticism has been my agony — which is the agony of my age, which seeks to transcend itself, and falls into the pit of doom and despair — the dusty anguish of Obermann and Amiel buried alive in the skepticism of the century.

12

But can I complain if I cannot make the leap from necessity to freedom? Even Engels, enamored of Feuerbach, says that is possible only in his Socialist Utopia — and we are a thousand miles away from that dubious Isle of the Blessed. Meanwhile I must seek comfort in Schelling, who says: *If there were no contradiction between freedom and necessity, not only philosophy but every higher spiritual aspiration would decay and perish.*

13

This is the fantastic paradox of life: we must dangle from the cross, crucified between the two thieves of freedom and necessity, as Jesus is eternally crucified (Pascal) for the life of the spirit hinges on an agonizing contradiction that drives the sanest mind into madness!

14

The thought of Power, not the power of thought, is the key to the enigma of Western culture. My failure to think in terms of political, economic and military power, in terms of institutions, as well as men and ideas, placed my whole system of thought in the Cloud-Cuckooland of Wagnerian aesthetics and Lutheran ethics. For despite my immoralism I was forever the moralist, forever pounding on the drums of moral value, of spiritual excellence when what matters is technology — the Machine that is grinding all men to the same level and makes democracy inevitable!

15

Under the influence of Paul Rée and Lou Salomé — two Jews[1] who filled me with the egalitarian ideas of Jerusalem — I wrote *The Dawn of Day*, which shows traces of my Jewish democratic poison which might have led me to study the role of machine power in the democratization of the West. I wrote: *The rule seems to me more interesting than the exception* — a statement which made me tremble when I found myself writing it, for it heralded the end of my aristocratic philosophy, and my acceptance of

---

[1] Nietzsche wrote *The Dawn of Day* in Venice, influenced by Rée's positivism, but he had not yet met Rée's friend Lou Salomé, who was introduced to him by the matchmaking spinster Malwida von Meysenbug, who probably was ignorant of Lou's origin. — Editor

democratic mediocrity as the norm for my thinking.

16

It was only my high estimate of myself, my megalomania, that saved me from the democratic insanity that places the mindless peasant on the same level with Napoleon and the author of Zarathustra, which, next to the Old Testament, is the greatest contribution to Western culture. In other words, my aristocratic madness saved me from the mob-madness of the Saint-Simonians and Marxists who have found in modern technology a powerful ally of the leveling spirit.

17

Had I remained under the thumb of that Jewess[2] I might have been haunting the British Museum like Marx, burying myself in the dry science of economics, gathering statistics instead of scanning the heavens for a dancing star! The pathos of distance between masters and slaves, exploiters and exploited, the élite and the half-wits, must be maintained at all cost, or culture will be a chaotic jumble of men, machinery, institutions, thoughts and ideas — like the bloody scene after a train wreck!

18

But the wreck is bound to come, for nothing can stop the democratic process begun by Martin Luther when, defying the hierarchical civilization of Rome, he nailed his theses to the Church door and cried out: *It is neither safe nor prudent to do aught against conscience. Here I stand; I cannot do otherwise!* Because Luther refused to bow to the necessary lie of the Church, the

---

[2] Nietzsche harps on the racial and religious origin of Lou Salomé. Despite his hatred of anti-Semitism, he was too much a child of his age not to recoil at the thought that a Jewess had contaminated him with the democratic heresy. — Editor

mindless peasants sought to take over state power, forcing him to agree to their slaughter to maintain the *status quo* of master and slave. Despite Luther's rejection of his own democratic philosophy, the democratic process cannot be stopped as long as thousands are herded together by factories and mines and feel the solidarity of men strong with their knowledge of machine-power.

19

I must insist again that as a man without money (my pension was cut in half while I was in the madhouse, because a mad philosopher is of no use to the wealthy élite at Basel), I do not care who wields power in the world, as long as the energy of the race is not exhausted and man is able to make a bridge of himself, a bridge to his Godmanhood, his Supermanhood, his moral and spiritual transfiguration. If Rousseau's savage is destined to abolish history and rise to power on the wreck of aristocratic culture, I shall not weep into my three-days' beard, but in my Oriental fatalism I shall mutter, *Kismet.* Perhaps Life has its reasons that I know not of and even my fatal paralysis is a warning to reject a civilization and a culture that find no place for the human, cutting itself off from all the vital energies of man who has become a mere appendage of Carlyle's "cash-nexus."

20

Perhaps mediocrity is more interesting than an effete aristocracy that has lost its will to power. Perhaps the "divine average" can actually assume Godhead, and, like Jesus the Carpenter, sit on the throne of Empire.

21

All things, even the most sublime, said Kant, *grow small under the hands of men when they turn the ideas thereof to their own use.* We thrust our hands into Plato's dovecote of the ideal and pull out —

not a pigeon but a mechanical cuckoo! What do the so-called Nietzscheans drag out of the lion's den of my philosophy? Not Daniel, the Superman, who defies the Monarchs of men and beasts, but the lion himself, the jungle king, seeking to reduce all civilization and culture to his jungle will. My system of thought is reduced to the brute naturalism against which I rebelled: if man is trapped in the static state of his beasthood then all culture is a fraud, and I will shoot down the first man who mentions Goethe or Shakespeare![3]

Man belongs to a different integrate level from the beast, he is forever ascending the ladder of being — and if there is an ape in us there is also an angel seeking release from our brutehood and our humanhood. The Superman is not my private fantasy: he is a reality of our biologic and spiritual nature, and if I have led people to believe otherwise I cry loud, *Mea culpa!*

Humanity is bogged deep in bestiality: must I see my philosophy used to drive the human spirit deeper into the swamp? But I shall go stark mad and die before this tragedy takes place!

22

Did God die by His own hand, disgusted with His pious worshipers who threw all their problems into His divine lap, being too cowardly and ignorant to handle them themselves? God the proud Stoic, killing Himself to retain His self-respect — that is bad news for Christians who were told by crackpots like Saint Paul and Luther that not good works but mere blind faith in Christ was enough for them to win eternal salvation!

---

[3] Compare the famous outburst of the Nazi: "When I hear the word 'culture' I cock my pistol." Thomas Mann points out that Spengler Nazi-fied and bestialized Nietzsche, reducing his Superman to a Storm Trooper Subman, a brute whose strength lies only in his muscles and machine-gun. — Editor

23

Not I but Saint Paul and Luther were the great immoralists who taught pious Christians how to murder, lie and steal and avoid the vengeance of Jehovah. It was Saint Paul and Luther who thrust *good* Christians beyond good and evil, beyond the moral law, and preached salvation through the hocus-pocus of Christ's sacrificial blood. Ever since then they have been redeeming themselves through the blood of the Jew Jesus and millions of his fellow-Jews. In the twentieth century, in a fit of nihilistic frenzy, they will turn all Europe into a butcher's slaughter-house and wash their sins white in the blood of Israel!

This is no mere fancy: Heine already has prophesied the coming debacle of Christian civilization, when the Germans dust off their old pagan gods and plunge the West into a terrible blood-bath! If God were actually alive He would not allow the twentieth century to happen. Therefore God must be dead. But how did he die? As a Stoic too proud to see His world botched up by so-called followers of Jesus? As a divine Pharisee in protest against the Christian slander of the Pharisees, noble Jews who believed in good works as the touchstone of moral character? God, the Pharisee, killing Himself in protest against such swine as Saint Peter, Saint Luke, Saint John and Saint Paul, who perverted the teachings of Moses by polluting them with the muddy waters of a decayed Hellenism and Oriental hogwash — *what a rebuke to fanatical Christians like my sister!*

Elisabeth could not stomach the fact that Lou Salomé was a Jewess, but God could not swallow the bitter truth that she was a Christian who worshiped the Prince of Peace by plotting pogroms with her wild-eyed anti-Semitic husband! So in a paroxysm of wrath and disgust He cut His throat with the jagged edge of a star and let His blood pour over the earth in a divine torment of remorse.

No, this version is too romantic — it smacks of Wagner and Wagnerism. Stendhal's explanation was more prosaic and more consistent with the truth. God, the mechanic, died a natural death — of heart disease! He left His world to His Son, who like me, knew nothing of mechanics, being a poet, a dreamer of wild dreams. The Son entered the cosmic workshop, scratched his head at the sight of the huge, complicated engine of existence, pulled the lever, and started the engine *in reverse*, causing mad havoc throughout the universe, filled with flying wheels and the debris of shattered machinery!

That is how it must have happened: not God but His Son is the cause of world chaos. God died of a heart attack and His Son got us into a cosmic fix.

Sometimes I think that His Son is Friedrich Nietzsche, who is now expiating his clumsy foolishness. He paralyzed the cosmos and now he himself is in the grip of paralysis!

24

After swallowing enough chloral hydrate to drown the agonies of the world, I said farewell to Lou Salomé in my Zarathustra *Grave Song*, bursting like a choral volcano in hot, flaming music of grief for my lost love driven away by those terrible hell-cats, Mama and the Lama, spawned out of the spitting malice of our homicidal age.

Fragments of the *Grave Song* float through my mind, and every fragment is like a dagger stabbing me into memory of my dear, dear love and the Lama's Great Betrayal:

Still am I the richest and most to be envied — I the loneliest one! For I *have possessed* you (*did I really possess my Russian Helen, the Jewess who set my world on fire?*), and ye possess me still. Tell me, to whom hath there ever fallen such rosy apples from the tree as have fallen unto me? . . .

Verily, too early did you die for me, ye fugitives. Yet ye did not flee from me, nor did I flee from you: innocent are we to each other in our faithlessness.

To kill *me*, did they strangle you, ye singing-birds of my hopes! Yea, at you ye dearest ones, did malice ever shoot its arrows — to hit my heart!

And they did it! Because ye were always my dearest, my possession and my possessedness: on *that account* had ye to die young, and far too early!

At my most vulnerable point did they shoot the arrow — namely at you whose skin is like down — or more like the smile that dieth at a glance! *(Ah, my Lou, my lost paradise, I die like Tasso in all the agonies of love-madness, and remembering your* Grave Song *I die again and again, forever tossed on the tidal death of our love!)*

But this word will I say to my enemies: What is all manslaughter in comparison with what ye have done to me! *(In killing my love you have slain the love of the world. O Mama and Lama! What is the world without love? A desert of broken gravestones, a wilderness of skulls from whose empty eye-sockets spring madness and delirium!)*

Worse evil did ye do unto me than all manslaughter; the irretrievable did ye take from me — thus do I speak unto you, mine enemies!

Slew ye not my youth's visions and dearest marvels! *(Answer me, Mama and Lama — answer the Crucified One, he who dangles from a thousand crosses of longing, frustration and regret!)* My playmates took you from me, the blessed spirits! To their memory do I deposit this wreath and this curse.

This curse upon you, mine enemies! . . . As a blind one did I once walk in blessed ways: then did you cast filth on the blind, on the blind one's course; and now is he disgruntled with the old footpath.

And when I performed my hardest task, and celebrated the triumph of my victories, then did ye make those who loved me call out that I then grieved them most. *Did you not play the role of a female Iago*, my Lama? Did you not pour poison into my ear, blasting the blossom of my love for Lou? And you, Mama, when you called my Redeemer a harlot, cast garbage into the sacred stream of my being, polluting my spirit, making my soul stink with the stench of Christianity — the odor of unburied corpses!

Verily, it was always your doing: ye embittered to me my best honey, and the diligence of my best bees . . . the incurably shameless. Thus have ye wounded the faith of my virtue.

And when I offered my holiest as a sacrifice, immediately did your "piety" put its fatter gifts beside it: so that my holiest suffocated in the fumes of your fat. *(Yes, my sister, in the fumes of your fat piety, of greasy incest and larded lust, my holiest love was choked to death.)*

And once did I want to dance as I had never yet danced; beyond all heavens did I want to dance. Then did ye seduce my favorite minstrel. (O Lou, my beloved, the harp and the harpstrings are gone; who shall play for me the Song of Life? Who shall awake in my feet the rhythm of the heavens so that I can dance to the bliss of a dancing star? O my lost minstrel — my lost paradise) . . .

Unspoken and unrealized hath my highest hope remained! And there have perished for me all the visions and consolations of my youth!

How did I ever bear it? How did I survive and surmount such wounds? How did my soul arise again out of those sepulchres?

Yea, something invulnerable, unburiable is with me, something that would rend rocks asunder: it is called *My Will* . . .

Yea, thou art still for me the demolisher of all graves. Hail to thee, My Will! And only where there are graves are there resurrections!

Thus sung Zarathustra!

Thus I sang, but in breaking out of my grave I succeeded only in preparing myself for a new burial, for as a post-feudal thinker I could only revolve on the Cartesian axis of doubt and learn only how to die. At times I fled from the conscious to the unconscious and like Saint Augustine argued from my existence to my thought, from being to thinking, but could not cast off the Socratic poison, which from Descartes to Hegel has cast the Western philosopher into a fever of pseudo-rationalism which is the death of the mind.

Like Zeno, the absolute rationalist, I went out of my way to avoid the dog-bite of illusion and Dionysian passion until Venus bit me into a frenzy of erotic excitement. Terrified, I let my sister dupe me into the idea that this bite was fatal, and so I "cured" myself with the "rationalism" of science, which is more irrational than Faust's magic because it gives no peace to the soul cast on the seas of unfaith of dark Cartesian doubt.

25

Skeletons of animals and bones of the dead! exclaimed Goethe, bored with the rationalistic web-spinning of the philosophers. Had I contented myself with my poetry and my Russian Helen, my cup of happiness would have been filled to overflowing. But I dreamt myself into the Theban Sphinx before which men stood and tried to solve the riddle of existence, fearing death if they failed.

26

Does the Sphinx know the riddle of life? No, the Sphinx has shattered itself in madness, and men know that life has no riddle which love cannot solve!

27

Woe unto them that call evil good and good evil! This was Paul Rée's favorite quotation from the Old Testament prophets from whom he could not break away because, like Isaiah and Jeremiah, he stood under the judgment of his God of Vengeance. Denying the Ideal, he was yet a fanatical idealist; despite his absolute skepticism, he still had absolute faith in the God of Righteousness who did not exist except in the minds of the ignorant. It was Paul Rée, the God-intoxicated atheist, who insisted that my power-philosophy was not new but was practiced by the ancient Aryans who flogged their captives into bondage and turned the forests of India into a vast slave-pen.

Has the Jewish God of Vengeance struck me down with paralysis because I called evil good and good evil? By deifying the Caesars, the Borgias and Napoleons, did I not strike out in the path of the ancient Pharaohs who achieved their private freedom at the expense of the rest of humanity? If freedom becomes the exclusive possession of a few bloody tyrants, then life is conquered by death, for without freedom men are mere living corpses, robbed of the privilege of decent burial. Moses knew this, hence his revolt against the bondage of Egypt, making his will the will of Israel.

28

I am my own property! cried Lou Salomé, *I won't bow to the orders of man, woman, God, Devil or the State.* These Jews and Jewesses — how they admire freedom, even going to the extent of inventing a God to help them in the war against slavery! When their God has served His purpose, they cast Him aside and seize upon Science to redeem them from the final bondage of property which has become the new Caesar of the Western world.

29

Why did Lou never give herself completely to me? Because her body was her own property; I could borrow it in our mutual need for erotic expression, but it always remained her own — her body and her soul! Men become little Caesars in the love-act;

they exert their will to power in the bedroom because they dare not mount the barricades or storm heaven with the fury of Napoleon, Bakunin, Proudhon, Marx — and the rest of the sky-stormers of the century. I have been a heaven-stormer myself, and what did a Jewess of twenty-four tell me when I became too arrogant in my demands? *Go visit a street-woman; you cannot have me except on the basis of mutual love and understanding!*

I understand her only too well. Every human being is God, not merely Jesus, Caesar or myself. Every person is an "unconquered being" in Feuerbach's sense, ready to smite Hegel's *absolute thinking* with the bludgeon of his Almighty Ego. But if every human being is God, what remains of my *pathos of distance*, the social space between the genius and the idiot? . . . Perhaps there is no social space between them: witness the case of Professor Nietzsche, the greatest genius of the nineteenth century, crumbling into the gibbering idiocy of a mindless paralytic . . .

To prove my philosophy false, was it necessary for Lou Salomé's God to smite me into madness? How hath the mighty fallen! I cannot even raise my right arm in defiance — for it is paralyzed!

30

Was Bach's *Concerto in D Minor* for two, three, or four violins? This odalisque by Ingres — was she not once in my harem at Tautenburg? Who am I? Of course I am Nero; I choked my mother with a thread of the girdle of the Paphian Venus, after ravishing a vestal virgin at the floating feast on the pond of Agrippa.[4] Poppaea knows my crime: she was present when the raft touched the shore and the Dionysian revelers rushed to the naked ladies of Rome awaiting them in the tented thickets and

---

[4] Nietzsche's mind has plunged deep into the mad labyrinth of guilt at the thought of his mother's death and his sister's "shame." — Editor

grottoes while the fountains splashed in the twilight, cooling the green air hot with the lust of the chaste wives and daughters of the first Roman houses . . .

31

Ah, the mad whirl of the satyrs, fauns, nymphs and dryads caught in the naked, Dionysian fury of a Roman twilight while the drunken shouts of the dryads pierced the purple-green air as the rowers slapped their nude thighs with their painted oars! It was then that I, Nero, first of the Augustinians, caught sight of the vestal Elisabeth who lured me into her tented grotto and then repelled me, joining the sirens on the terrace, whose bodies were covered in a green network that still reveals the most secret delights.

I seized the vestal and in the ecstasy of her ravishment she drew blood from my lips — the blood of a Caesar. Goaded into madness, I fell upon my mother Agrippina and strangled her with a string from the girdle of Venus. Her shade entered the Cimmerian regions and left me in peace at last.

32

Behold in me the tyrant of Turin! It is long since I felt the blood of a tyrant coursing through my veins, for I am a dead man at fifty, living on borrowed time — and my grandparents lived to an extreme old age! I who wished to become Jehovah and dictate my will to the world, cannot even write a sentence without suffering terrible pain in my cramped fingers! . . .

33

What I tried to do was to stand on my own shoulders, to superimpose nature upon nature, denying a Creator God, insisting that the world *lives on itself; feeds on its own excrement*, as I say somewhere among my notes. Where did Titanism of defiance lead me? To the same pit as Schopenhauer's Titanism of denial — to moral and spiritual exhaustion, to the nothingness of the Abyss!

My effort to leap over myself, to stand on my own head, has led me to the final declivity of being: I feel lower than the cockroach on the wall, which has a virile life and mocks my paralyzed body, my petrified arm which cannot swat its crawling insolence, its creeping defiance of my despair! Like Childe Roland I enter the Dark Tower of moral deadlock; my spirit is brought to bay and I must either embrace a dead God or a living hell . . . *But what if God lives, and I have doomed myself to destruction because I have separated myself from Him?*

This is a terrible thought, like Christ's on Golgotha — except in reverse! The Jew feared God had abandoned him, while I fear *myself* for having abandoned God! Must I bring myself to the altar as my own sacrifice, seeing my Promethean pride go up in smoke, finding salvation in my sacrificed being, in my ashes out of which the phoenix of my soul will arise in new, ineffable splendor? My *eternal recurrence* — is it the fundamental return to the Cross that towers above the Promethean rock and shatters the tomb of being into surrender to God's will? Jeremiah and Irenaeus look at apostasy as the signpost to redemption; in my final agony I may yet break through to the God of Life and leave the Dark Tower behind! . . .

But I am forever determined like Richard III to prove myself a villain; I cannot transcend my Satanism, the Titanic defiance of our Faustian age. The thought of me embracing a non-existent God is fantastic, and if I do so it is proof that my mind is eclipsed in total darkness! Nietzsche a God-believer; can a river run backward and choose another bed to flow through? Can a mountain sink to a valley and give its summit to cows to graze on?

34

I cannot let God transcend me; I can only transcend *myself* in infinite nothingness, in the eternal void of Not-Being, the ghost-land of shadows where the exiles from life float in the dark opacity of a blurred dream! As I wrote in *Zarathustra*, confessing the inner torment of my soul:

Have *I* still a goal? A haven towards which *my* sail is set?

A good wind? Ah, he only knoweth *whither* he saileth what wind is good, and a fair wind for him.

What still remaineth to me? A heart weary and flippant; an unstable will; fluttering wings; a broken backbone.

This seeking for my home: O Zarathustra, dost thou know that this seeking hath been my home-sickening, it eateth me up?

Where is *my* home? For it do I ask and seek, and have sought, but have not found it. O eternal everywhere, O eternal nowhere, O eternal *in vain!*

Thus spoke my shadow, the shadow of Zarathustra, the doomed shadow of my despair. I warned my shadow of my despair. I warned my shadow to avoid capture by a narrow faith, but there is more security in Plato's cave than in a boundless desert swept by the winds of doubt.

35

My self-worship has recoiled upon its own creed so that its infinite possibilities have become the possibility for — Nothing! That is why in my *Will to Power* I prophesied the impending catastrophe of world violence, of culture reduced to primal chaos, to Nothingness! *Nihilism stands before the door.* Destruction knocks at the door of my being, and in my own annihilation I see reflected the smashed face of the world reduced to a pulpy mass of confused Nothingness!

Nihilism stands before the door and knocks with the fist of

madness! Death has arrived — *and there is no escape!*

36

Jesus will be in agony until the end of the world, said Pascal. Humanity sleeps like Peter while I agonize — that is its sweet revenge for my contempt of humanity, the cornerstone of the new Socialist culture that I rejected with Promethean contempt. And so I must cling to the rock and be devoured by the vultures, suffering more torment than Jesus, because my faith in the Superman was merely a romantic delusion, while his faith in God was shaken but never in doubt.

Like the Romans trapped in the gorges at Caudium,[5] I am forced to surrender unconditionally to the enemy. But Christ, my eternal foe, shall never enjoy the spectacle of Nietzsche kneeling before the Cross: I have more pride than the Romans, more pride than Satan himself, who mourns his exile from heaven and forever plots to place himself on the vacant throne of God. Not Christ but Antichrist, myself is the Archimedean fulcrum of history: I am the leverage of the New Age of Power, and whether it swings in the direction of the people or Machiavelli's Prince is of little concern to me.

What is important is the might of the soul that decrees death to death and dedicates itself to eternal life.

God is dead, Christ is a myth, and man stands alone. But he stands alone in majesty!

37

There is nothing more loathsome, said Heine, than the ghosts, like the hobgoblins and kobolds of the German legends.

---

[5] The incident is referred to by Livy in his *History of Rome.* Nietzsche forgets that the Romans had the Hobson's choice of death or surrender — and chose surrender, throwing themselves on the mercy of the conqueror. Nietzsche invents a third alternative — to fight on! — Editor

Like Luther's, my mind has been infested with them from my early childhood. Trapped in a world haunted by the obscene demons of the German imagination, I came to the Lutheran conclusion that we have no moral freedom, no spiritual autonomy. Luther made an atheist out of me, for Luther, despite himself, was a demon-worshiping atheist. It was Luther who asked: "How can man prepare to do good since it is not even in his power to do evil? For it is God who is also responsible for bad works."

38

The *little parson*, prompted by Luther, began to look upon God as an impudent trickster who rewarded evil with good and good with evil, giving grace to the damned and damning those who are worthy of grace, acting not like a Jew but like Bismarck, the incarnation of Prussian falsehood and duplicity. As Michelet observed, Luther sank deeper and deeper into the swamp of sensuality and immorality as the result of his demonic conception of God. I had to proclaim myself an atheist in order to save God from His Lutheran worshipers — those obscene Satanists who hide their true instincts behind the pious masks of the Evangelical faith.

39

Justification by faith — what is this but a demonic invitation to break into a goat-song and substitute rape for revelation? While at Tautenburg in the arms of my Slavic Venus, I became a perfect Lutheran, that is to say a perfect immoralist, not only in thought but in action. I followed Luther's advice of eating and drinking and having a good time — the Lutheran cure for the Devil!

40

I drink a jug of beer under the Devil's nose and jeer at him, said

Luther. I am the only living German who despises beer as a bitter brew concocted in hell itself, but my Slavic Venus introduced me to her national drink, and so we drowned out the Devil in quarts of vodka! If we did not actually drown Beelzebub, we put him to flight by carrying on in such a devilish manner as to make him and the prudish Tautenburgers blush!

Imagining myself in Wittenberg instead of Tautenburg, I borrowed Luther's obscene mind and with his pious eyes saw the naked German witches flying on their broomsticks to the Brocken, where each witch approached the squatting Satan, taper in hand, and kissed him in the spot where his back ends. When the Devil threatened me, I repeated Luther's incantation: Kiss my ———, and the Devil, blushing to his tipped satyr's ears, dashed back to his infernal kingdom!

But only in Tautenburg could I believe with Luther that *God often acts like a madman (närrisch)*, preordaining the actions of His creatures and then plunging them into hell-fire if, like Adam or Eve, or Judas himself, they acted according to the predetermined wishes of the Lord. When I left Tautenburg I lost my Jewess, but I clung to the God of her fathers, the rational Jehovah, who rewards good and punishes evil and whose redeeming love rolls out of His vast anger, the divine wrath that cast havoc among the Philistines!

41

The crisis of our age has become my personal crisis, as in the case of Luther,[6] who was more logical than Erasmus because he was less of a logician and knew that the war between world-systems is won not by reason but by the fanatical zeal for a cause that the fanatic identifies with the cosmic process itself. We are now entering a new era of gigantic conflicts which shall usher in a

---

[6] Nietzsche is now "the little parson" defending Luther against — himself! — Editor

new kind of reality, a *spiritual* reality based on the needs of people, not crackpot philosophers like Hegel who rationalize their Prussian bias into a world-system of emerging truth.

42

Just as Saint Augustine abandoned pseudo-reason to fall back upon society, ravaged, smashed and awaiting his magic touch to organize it back into life and hope, our nineteenth century world, dissolving in blood and madness, awaits the great Augustinian organizers. They will put existence before thought, the body of life before the frail, thinking reed which Pascal identified as the mind, and build the twentieth century on the firm foundations of social need and necessity.

43

Of course these great strategists of human destiny will need a metaphysics to do their pioneering work of social engineering, and they will borrow their mental tools from my philosophy of power. But if they are not careful these social engineers may plunge the world back into nihilism, for the common people, having taken all power unto themselves, may, like a collective Samson, pull the temple of their civilization over their heads.

The masses need the myth of God to curb their Faustian will to self-destruction. But as early as 500 B.C., the pre-Socratic Xenophanes already discovered that we create God in our own image, according to our degree and form of understanding. Æthiopians make their gods black and snub-nosed, he said, while Thracians give their deities blue eyes and red hair, endowing them with their own peculiar characteristics. If lions and oxen could think and fashion images they would make their gods in their own likeness, just as Homer and Hesiod, observing the immoralities of the dominant classes, imagined that the gods were a pack of thieves, robbers and adulterers. Nothing, it seems can prevent the oppressed classes from turning their will to power into a God of Might, the divine Superman who will redeem them from the bondage of Egypt.

44

When all Humanity is leveled down to a common mass and there are no barriers of race, property or intellect to create moral and mental distinction between men — will the Utopia that Socialists dream about have arrived at last? I doubt it. When Society becomes an amorphous, shapeless pile — a democratic dungheap — we will be back to the prehistoric age of primitive tribalism when everything was held in common, including men's wives. But this seems inevitable, for humanity must revolve forever on the wheel of Eternal Recurrence. If my bootblack becomes my equal I shall not gnash my teeth in anger, but dream of the day when he will become a philosopher like myself — this will be sweet vengeance indeed! Let him spin metaphysical cobwebs: I shall be content with blacking boots and adding my bit to the amenities of life.

45

Luther realized the dangers and confusions of God-making when he wrote: "The temptations of the flesh are trifling; any woman can put an end to them. But God preserves us from the temptations bearing upon eternity. Then one ceases to know which is God and which is the Devil. *One even begins to wonder whether the Devil may not be God.*"

46

It was Schopenhauer who discovered that the blind, destructive Devil was God by the mere process of thinking his own brute nature into the cosmos in the manner previsioned by Xenophanes. If the Socialist believes that I have put a Prussian despot into the empty seat of the Lord, he is entitled to his belief. I have long ago insisted that a philosopher cannot separate himself from his philosophy and hide behind the screen of cosmic omniscience. Even Luther himself created his God in the image of the Devil he dreaded — an immoral prelogical Deity that had no more relation to Jesus's Jehovah, the God of absolute justice, than a Baal of Canaan which demanded the ravishment of virgins so that the seminal rain would descend from the heavens and the crops sprout out of the earth.

47

Did not Luther say: *The Devil, alas, has a stronghold from which to attack us; our flesh and blood belong to him*? If our flesh and blood belong to the Devil then we are in no better state of moral sanitation than the bishops at the Diet of Augsburg who Luther said were as full of devils as a dog is of fleas. And when Luther insisted that any woman can put an end to the trifling temptations of the flesh, he was contradicting himself, for it is through woman that the Devil extends his domain from the flesh and blood of man to his mind and soul! Luther should have known this, for he smashed all Christendom to a thousand sectarian fragments so that he could ravish a nun under the proper auspices of holy matrimony!

48

Ever since my childhood, when I was dubbed *the little parson* by my schoolmates, I have been under the fearful dominance of Luther's devil-ridden mind bequeathed to me by my Lutheran parents, uncles and aunts. The Lutheran will to ravish a nun was transferred to the nunnery here at Naumburg and the Lama, spotless and pure as any medieval prioress, encouraged the dark, demonic promptings of my Lutheran mind. When I sought a healthy erotic relationship with Lou Salomé she brought to my consciousness the anti-Semitic poison which every German drinks with his mother's milk. This too is our heritage from Luther, for, after giving the Germans the Jewish Bible as a substitute for the Pope, and rightly condemning Rome for its bloody persecution of Jewry, he poured the vials of his wrath upon the Jews because their democratic Bible, embraced by the revolting peasants, threatened Germany with wild anarchy and chaos! . . .

49

If I have been inconsistent in my attitude towards the Jews and the Jewess who caused such havoc in my life, it is because I am a child of Luther whose pathology is a part of the madness of our age. The Jew is the European symbol of democracy, of people's power which he identifies with the will of God but which Luther and I see as the Devil's handiwork, the Devil who plots to sow confusion and anarchy in the world. And yet the Jew, with his aristocratic pride and infinite demands, his cultural imperialism that has shaken the foundations of our Roman world order, also appealed to Luther, the destroyer of the Roman Antichrist, as he appeals to me who as Antichrist have also identified myself with Jesus, the Jew, the spiritual Superman who flung his gage of defiance against the Roman world.

50

While I was with Lou Salomé my center of awareness moved from my head to my heart, and all the Lutheran contradictions in my nature fused to a single passion of love for the Jewish people and all peoples. I removed my intellectual blinkers and saw life from the focus of the organic womb, the mystical realm that lies below Science and therefore is above it, dominating the complex demands of our total nature. This priestess of Isis interiorized my knowledge; I began to know life as a living experience, as the harmonious blending of the Seen and the Unseen, as an artistic activity in tune with cosmic forces that filled me with the splendor and desolation of godlike existence.

She was the female John the Baptist who heralded the coming faith of Simplicity which shall unite the Within and the Without, the Center and the Periphery, the body with the wind and Soul in the single matrix of the Womb. But having lost her I fell back upon my Lutheran devils, my divided being which can never reach out towards God, the Whole, and therefore assumes that God is dead . . .

So I am God's Widower! God is laughing up His cosmic sleeve at my foolish assumption.

51

Like Lord Kelvin, the English can understand nothing of which they could not make a mechanical model. Newton's mechanics, with its checks and balances, pistons, fly-wheels and pointers, has now become a part of the European mind — the vulgar mind of the Philistines.

There are English Nietzscheans who see me in their own mechanical mirrors and turn me into a tool wielded by money-grubbing monkeys. I refused to become a part of English monkeydom, just as Saint Athanasius fled from the pagan paradise of Emperor Julian. In this respect I am a Christian, for I do not make the pleasure of the flesh the basis of triumphant living.

Like the ancient Pythagoreans who indulged in futile number-fancies, the English mechanists and utilitarians seek to bolster up our confidence in the cosmos by presenting us with mathematical tables of pleasure and pain, forgetting that one man's joy is another man's grief. The hound that harries the fox does not share the same emotions as his victim, nor does the chicken in the fox's mouth share the fox's appetite.

But enough of these platitudes! I insist that I was never a Nietzschean, and the Nietzscheans in England, who praise me for my pagan brutalism should address their letters to Treitschke and the Prussian imperialists with whom I have nothing in common. Just as Jesus was never a Christian and remained a faithful, Jehovah-fearing Jew to the end, I was never a Nietzschean, and remain a Nazarene to the last drop of my blood!

52

My sister proclaimed the downfall of Zarathustra at Tautenburg which she announced to the world as my moral Waterloo. It is true that through her pernicious, unnatural hold on my emotions she pounded me back into "the little parson" who berated Fräulein Salomé for her loose behavior, her erotic bohemianism. But if my sister makes capital[7] of this fact and seeks to turn Nietzsche, the satyr, into a plaster-saint who was tempted like Saint Anthony into sin, I wish to record for posterity that Tautenburg rather than Naumburg was my natural habitat and that my great wish has been to sit next to Nero and watch the respectable Christians being devoured by the lions.

In fact I have often pictured myself as Nero, eyeing the butchers' shambles from the circus podium, sneering as the martyred Christians yelled, *Christus regnat!* as I chucked my Jewish *wife* Poppaea (Lou Salomé), the beautiful Augusta, under the chin. It is highly appropriate that the two great Antichrists of the West — Nero and Nietzsche — should have Jewish wives: in this manner history is avenged, and the oceans of Jewish blood shed in the name of the Prince of Peace are appeased.

Paul Rée, Georg Brandes, Leo Berg, Maximilian Harden — even Fräulein Salomé herself — saw in me a champion of massacred Jewry, and when I turned the lions loose and the Christian

---

[7] Nietzsche is anticipating his sister's prudish biography wherein she depicts him as a gay friar, happy and chaste, until Lou Salomé lured him from her sisterly grasp on his soul. — Editor

West was torn limb from limb there was rejoicing in Jerusalem, for only I dared to rip the masks from the pseudo-Christians who pray to Christ but do the work of Caesar every day of their pagan lives. My Jewish friends never took my anti-Jewishness seriously, for they knew my madness stemmed from the fact that I mistook the thunder of Sinai for the mawkish weeping and pity of Calvary.

53

The Christian, I began to realize, was nothing more than a confused, undisciplined, exhausted Jew, who in his Buddhistic despair turned to nihilism and pogroms to assert his will power. The Christian apostles were scourged out of history by me. *(Impudent rabble! they dare to compare themselves to the prophets!).* I caught the roll of Jehovah's thunder and cried out: *What does Europe owe to the Jew? The grand style in morality, the fearlessness and majesty of infinite demands, of infinite significations!*

I began to see the true significance of Jewish morality, of the Jewish national will to live, the most tenacious, as I said, that has ever existed on earth! I dreamt of a cross-breeding of Jew and Prussian, but this idea, of course, was foolhardy. What is the Prussian cult of commanding and obeying but a cult of dehumanization and bestialization? The Jewish élite breed among themselves because they live in a world of the human and super-human where the commands of God become a habit of the soul and obedience receives the sanction of the spirit, turning necessity into freedom.

The Jew did not only cultivate the habit of divinity but he agreed with Plotinus when he declared: *Our concern is not merely to be sinless but to be God.* Jesus thought he was God, and many Jewish Christians as well as baptized pagans actually believed he was the Lord. Of course the democratic instincts of the Jews prevented most of them, as Heine said, from acknowledging a fellow-Jew as Jehovah, but this did not prevent the ancient Pharisees from striving towards Godmanhood, to be *like* God as much as possible. Because they approached divinity, the Christian apostles, suffering from moral and spiritual exhaustion, slandered them, and this led the centuries to believe that the Pharisees were whited sepulchres, while they, the exhausted and corrupted ones, were models of spiritual integrity! . . .

54

The desire to be God is not only shared by Jews but by romantic philosophers like myself. Just as Empedocles leapt into the flames of Aetna so that it might be thought that, in the manner of Elijah, he had risen in a chariot of fire to Godhood, I too have plunged into the blazing crater of madness to achieve my apotheosis, my right to sit in the empty throne of Jehovah.

But how can God's throne stand on a fragment of the broken world? That was my delusion: to think that a creature of time, wrecked, splintered and scattered in all directions, can take the place of Spinoza's God who had built His Judgment Seat on the firm foundations of Eternity!

55

On the theory that fire must be fought with fire, mother has wished a madman on me, a certain Dr. Julius Langbein, who, aping my volume *Schopenhauer as Educator,* wrote *Rembrandt as Educator,* to prove Rembrandt can cure us of anything, including colic and chilblain. When I was in the madhouse I awaited his arrival with immense delight because he made me feel sane and sober by comparison. Now that I am back in Naumburg he only reminds me of the sad fact that the only sane people are clapped into lunatic asylums.

The professor is Germany's national disease, and Dr. Lang-bein, who seems to be a professor of aesthetics, breathes the national malady from every pore of his being. I gather from his wild talk that the broken mind can be made whole again by concentrating on beautiful paintings, but I prefer to concentrate on beautiful women, since they are creatures of flesh and blood, divine masterpieces that even Rembrandt himself could not imitate.

Morals comes before aesthetics — I have believed that, when I posed as the great immoralist to impose moral standards on our nihilistic age. The aesthetic man — the Hellene — is helpless in the face of private and public catastrophe: that is what Heine discovered on his mattress grave. And while I am in the underworld with Odysseus, a shadow among shadows — it is hard for me to believe that Rembrandt's paintings or Wagner's music can save man from his hell-on-earth. What is needed are the trumpets of the Last Judgment — blowing the doom of our rotten world!

56

Heine liked to boast that (by being born on January 1, 1801 — which he was not) he ushered in the new century. I hope I do not live long enough to bring it to its final rest.

CHAPTER TWELVE

1

I once wrote to my friend Gast that I was one of those machines that are likely to burst, the intensity of my thoughts and emotions being too much for any mechanism to bear. I felt when I was writing *The Dawn of Day* in Sils-Maria that my mood of constant exaltation was like Paul's epileptic trance when he saw the vision of the Redeemer on the road to Damascus.

But the sense of glowing health that radiated from the volume fooled my friends who saw in the opus *one of the bravest and loftiest and most beautiful books ever born of the human brain and heart* — a verdict which I would dispute if I were guilty of false modesty. But the price I paid for this great and beautiful book was my mental and spiritual health. And when I finished it in Tautenburg under the additional stress of my love affair with Lou Salomé, I felt that I was teetering at the edge of an Abyss where the faces of the Lama, Mama and Lou — the three Gorgon faces of infinite dread — were pulling me into the bottomless Void. Even now as I write I can see the three terrible Gorgons floating before me, their snaky hair whirling about my throat like a triple noose and their fierce eyes turning me into stone.

But I do not blame them: I have been spiritually at home in terror as well as in the exhilarating quiet of Genoa and the Engadine; heaven and hell met in me in a wild ferment of emotions that whirled me constantly to the tidal center of self-destruction. Having chosen to live alone without God and Man, I was finally sundered from my sacred aloneness, hurled from my Genoese rock where I once sat like a lizard in the sun while the ocean pounded its fury against me — the Titan who dared defy its inexorable waves! How I rejoiced in the delicious terror of loneliness, the joy of the Abyss, writing to Peter Gast that we were on the right track, *Loneliness and severity to ourselves before our own judgment-seat, no more paying attention to others, models and masters!*

2

I remember every word I scrawled on the postcard to Gast from my rock in Genoa — Columbus' town — because even then I felt intuitively that the Sea would conquer in the end — the wild ocean of humanity at whose furious core the English poet Blake saw the face of the terrible God of the Jews, the *tiger-Christ*, Jehovah Himself.

Like Saint Augustine's, my deep restlessness sought rest in an Absolute, but to find rest in God would have been a betrayal of my Satanic role in life; I would have out-Wagnered Wagner and landed among the Philistines. And so I sought to multiply my sense of power by living like the people of Genoa, the common people who attracted me as the mindless peasants attracted Tolstoy and Dostoyevsky. These Rousseauan savages, these *blond beasts* of mine, were at the polar extreme to my Superman and therefore met in a collective negation, a bold refusal to participate in the idiocies of Philistine culture. They were akin in their self-mastery to the medieval merchant-princes of Genoa who had built their palaces for centuries and not for the fleeting moment; their castles still dominated mountains, town and sea; stone emperors in a world of Herculean flux, regal and proud in their lofty conquest of Socratic reason.

3

And so I lived like a beggar-prince in my Genoese garret, mounting 164 steps to my castle-eyrie where my princess, the landlady, helped me prepare my vegetable dishes and my Genoese special — a gourmet's delight consisting mainly of artichokes and eggs. I, the sworn enemy of democracy, lived like the people, joked and drank with them, but their mindlessness filled me at last with Pascalian disgust. I was too worm-eaten by the Socratic malady, Greek intellectualism, to live among the Tolstoyan idiots for more than a season.

In Genoa, as in Naumburg, Zurich, Venice, Leipzig, Turin and wherever I have been, I have always sought to find *my true self* in a friend, in a group of friends, or even in the whole group of humanity itself, but I was always thrust back upon Peer Gynt's onion, a nothingness hidden by layers and layers of illusion without a kernel of reality. *My true self* is merely a shadow projected by my Promethean will caught between the double abyss of longing and frustration, high and low, heaven and hell.

In my romantic anguish I sought to escape the beer-materialism of my *Franconia* days at Bonn when I thought it was necessary to join a hell-fire students' club, for to be clubless, to be, as they say, *a camel*, meant to be banished to a monastic discipline of no wine, no women and no song. In fact I began to look upon the monastic ideal as the goal of the philosopher, who, like Spinoza, with his intellectual love of God, could not exhaust his energies with each Cynthia of the minute, every harlot who spread her thighs in a triangular effort to enclose the great circle of man's immortal dreams.

4

And so I sought retirement in the *nunnery* of Malwida von Meyesenbug, the elderly and eccentric Wagnerite who combined a love for Wagner's heroines with the strictest chastity, like a prioress who closed her eyes to the fact that her priory had been turned into a brothel and was catering not to God but to Satan.

But the Villa Rubinacci in Sorrento was not exactly the nunnery I expected, for the women Malwida introduced me to had Venus and not Mary in their minds; coached by the elderly spinster who loved to play the role of Cupid, they preferred to sacrifice their virginity on the altar of holy marriage rather than wither and die as the brides of Christ. I finally fled her matchmaking fury, escaping to Klingenbrunn in the Bavarian forest to avoid the Wagnerian wenches in Bayreuth. I turned to Saint Augustine with his dream of a civilized society of ten persons, Augustinian hermits like myself who were interested in preserving their sanity against the onrush of Western barbarism and nihilistic despair.

5

But Europe of the nineteenth century is not like ancient Greece and Rome at their Periclean height nor the North Africa of Augustine's day. The free groups of classic times were only possible when the property foundations of Society were not threatened by Anarchists and Socialists who seek to destroy the pathos of distance between masters and slaves and pound our hierarchic society into an amorphous, shapeless mob. Augustine could join the free group of the Manichees because their theological dualism of Light and Darkness was merely Persian web-spinning, while the huge, black spiders of *scientific* Socialism threaten to choke all culture into the democracy of the American jungle.

A free group today, when not political and destructive of all cultural values, usually ends up in a *ménage à trois*, which Lou proposed, turning Rée and me into her love-slaves, a shameless proposal that Malwida greeted with righteous indignation. And yet the need for intellectual and emotional companionship is rooted deep in our human nature; to lose a friend is a catastrophe greater than Waterloo. As I have written: *My whole philosophy wavers after an hour's sympathetic conversation with utter strangers; it seems so foolish to be right at the cost of love.*

Only an Antichrist like me can appreciate the agony of being hard and pitiless for the sake of principle, robbed of the free-group companionship of Augustine's dream-refuge where the hermits of the intellect and the heart talked and laughed together, combining *sweetness and light*, as the Englishman, Matthew Arnold, put it, and enjoyed the supreme happiness of being integrated, made whole through the friction of mind upon mind and soul upon soul. Because there are no free groups in our age, because we can find nothing to belong to and nothing to cling to — except the Devil's tail, of course — we have fallen out of the magic ring of our humanity and are collapsing into the Beast . . .

6

As I write this a madman is howling in the next room, and I am howling with him inside of me, howling for my lost integrity, sundered from God, Man and myself, shattered in body, mind and spirit, yearning for two clasped hands to usher in the great miracle — the unity of my being . . . O Cosmic Irony, O Devil-God of Schopenhauer! I brought together all knowledge into a single system of thought while my mind is splitting into a billion fragments, scattering into tiny grains of dusty death! . . .

I sit frozen with terror. Who is knocking at the door of Macbeth? The Bishop of Hippo with his dead eyes comes to claim me as God claimed him, a sinner: *You have made us for Yourself, and our hearts are restless till they find rest in You.* No, no, this is a trick of some fiend who has barricaded himself in my brain and is shooting the arrows of a dead God into my collapsing world. I shall call a keeper — *Am I my brother's keeper?* — God's widower is haunted by the divine ghost he once mourned . . .

Monica, Monica — why is the name of Monica crying in my sick brain? Ah, that is my mother, Augustine's mother of course — *Eternal Recurrence!* The Womb seeks me out to swallow me back into its vast Nothingness. Monica is dead, the Womb itself is dust, and thus ends "our most sweet custom of living together."

7

But if we cannot live together, how can we live at all? When Mama comes with her honey-cakes dipped in vinegar, I shall ask her this ultimate question upon which hang all the law and the prophets. To live together, to love together: is this the answer to the great riddle of Being? But it is too late: the Sphinx has destroyed me because I did not answer in time. Dionysos has been torn to pieces by the wild Maenads — the Lama, Mama, and Lou!

Dionysos is bleeding to death. *Help, keepers, help!*

8

I have said that woman was made for the recreation of the warrior, but Lou reversed my saying by making the warrior the recreation of woman. The female Wagnerites can only conceive of freedom in terms of sexual looseness; if that is the case, then Messalina was the freest of all women. My own dark Helen is a strong advocate of female emancipation which begins and ends with the boudoir.

Like the maidens of Odin, beautiful and terrible in their wrath, modern women mark out the warriors who are destined to die on the naked battlefield of love and bear the slain on their strong backs to Valhalla where the heroic dead enjoy a dubious feast with their conquerors. Lou, like a Wagnerian Walkyr, rides tirelessly on the steed of erotic enjoyment, and I pity the phlegmatic Jew in Paris who must dance to the staccato rhythms of this female Centaur pounding her hooves on the bodies of her middle-aged lovers.

Revenge is sweet: Rée is welcome to the woman who had made recreation rather than creation the goal of her female destiny, thus pointing to the sterility of bourgeois culture which can give birth to nothing except its own doom.

If Lou comes back to me, begging and weeping for my love, like Dido, I shall confound her with the answer of Æneas: *Cease to excite yourself and me by your wild complaints; not I but my destiny demands that I leave you* — stranded before the temple of Venus like a sacred harlot, shunned by a pious worshiper who detects the Beast in her embraces.

This is an improvement on Virgil: he made no reference to the Whore of Babylon!

Things are rather in the mind than in themselves, said Aquinas, and that is especially true of pretty things, like sweethearts and mistresses. My Russian Calypso is, of course, a figment of my imagination, but that is exactly why she dwells eternally in my soul like a charmer out of Homer or Balzac. If I could only see her as a creature of flesh and blood, I could blot her out forever from my memory. When her name is mentioned I could remain silent, as befits the dignity of a philosopher, but instead I act like a love-sick youth, a Romeo buried in a common grave with his Juliet.

I must remember to resurrect myself by fixing my attention on Diogenes of Sinope whose cynic's cry, *Remint the coinage*, gave me the clue to my own transvaluation of all values. By demonstrating to intelligent men that the cultural currency of the West was counterfeit, I lifted myself out of the grave of mediocrity and was resurrected in the mind. Now I must resurrect myself in the body and spirit by breaking through the grave of my self-contempt — a Pascalian disgust at the thought that a creature in petticoats can pull the nose of Zarathustra until it looks as big and bulbous as Cyrano's.

In this noble endeavor Diogenes can help me. What did he say when the people of Sinope condemned him to exile? *And I condemned them to remain in Sinope.* This madhouse is a refuge for the truly sane: I condemn my enemies to live in the lunatic asylum — the world of the Philistines! What did Diogenes say when, captured by pirates, he was bought by a fatheaded Moneybags at a slave-auction? *Come, buy a master!* Being a philosopher he maintained his human dignity to the end. No wonder he became the exemplar, the paragon of all the virtues to immoralists and Antichrists like Julian the Apostate, even though he fornicated in public and spat in the face of his snobbish, effeminate host!

Falsify the common currency! I must remember that! Socrates, the bourgeois ape, obeyed the mob-law of Athens, and took poison rather than defy the mob. Not so, Diogenes! He thumbed his nose at tradition and convention — the baits of fools who prefer the company of the unprotesting dead and dare not live dangerously in the perilous future! He tied Solon's laws like tin cans to a donkey's tail and heard their idiotic rattle as he laughed in his tub. He bowed to a single law — the law of his own free being. And he knew, as all philosophers should know, that the contempt of pleasure is the truest pleasure of all.

I shall imitate Diogenes, my great exemplar, Nietzsche himself on the great wheel of Eternal Recurrence. I shall live in his moment of time, repeated over and over again to all eternity. I shall write to all the harlots — married and unmarried — what Crales wrote to his wife Hipperchia: *Virtue comes by training and does not insinuate itself into the soul automatically as vice does.* Cosima, the Lama and Lou — how they will howl when the great immoralist teaches them morals by stripping them down to their nude skins marked with incestuous and adulterous sores. Every mask will be ripped off, every purpose, every pretense — to the amusement of the Philistines whose masks are so tightly glued to their countenances that their faces no longer exist.

Yes, Ulysses in hell shall follow the path of the sun into the kingdom of Helios, the sun-god, where Diogenes and Julian the Apostate shall greet him with bright dawn music, the music of Dionysos the Redeemer. I shall break out of this madhouse and live in a tub with Lou, and over the door-post shall be written: *Heracles Callinicus, son of Zeus, dwells here; let no evil enter.*[1]

Ah, Diogenes, how well you knew the hollow emptiness of Socratic word-mongering! The voice of thought squeaks like a cornered mouse; it is but the feeble echo of the Cosmos, while the reverberation of a beautiful body is more powerful than all the choruses of heaven!

9

In this madhouse I have reconsidered my case against Wagner, and in the light of pure sanity, the bright sun of intuitive reason that shines only upon lunatics, I am convinced that my breach with the arch-Philistine of Bayreuth was demanded by my destiny. I have been accused by fanatical Wagnerites — including my sister and Fräulein Salomé — of betraying my God, like Judas, because, being Jehovah myself, I could not tolerate any other deities in my private cosmos. It is characteristic of our mad age, as expressed by Lombroso and his school, to identify genius with insanity, thus catering to the egregious vanity of the Philistines who can never rise above plebeian mediocrity.

Being a genius without an equal in the history of human thought (I say this with all due modesty, since human thought is still at the Socratic level of admitting its ass-hood) I am necessarily a madman who knifed my best friend Wagner in a fit of

---

[1] Ancient inscription over door of newly married man. Nietzsche's pathetic effort to drive the demon Lou out of his brain proves a failure since he must have her in his tub-Eden, the eternal Adam with his eternal Eve. — Translator

megalomania. So runs the slander against me which does not hesitate to use the sword of pathology to pierce my pride. But the fact is that Wagner and I were polar opposites, two finalities, like Jerusalem and Athens, each of which sought to absorb the world of thought into itself. We were like two alien planets colliding in musical space, and the symphonic roar and flame outdid the stage thunder and lightning of a Wagnerian opera.

Wagner, the musical autocrat, was merely a despotic Nero, who used a full orchestra instead of a fiddle to overawe and astound the groundlings. But Nero, the royal buffoon, only succeeded in making the groundlings laugh: they were not pious Wagnerites poisoned by the death-religion of Christianity and hence did not confuse mere noise with the thunder and passion of life, the great *Yea-Saying* that roars out of the heart of Dionysos. To confuse his dupes, this Cagliostro of music actually embraced Christianity, accepting the final negation of the Philistines so that they would not *negate him.* But I negated this bloated negation like the fabled frog which puffed himself to gigantic size and then burst with an indecent sound which only Rabelais dared describe with physiological detail. With Hegelian logic I negated the negation and rose to a higher synthesis of music which even in my middle twenties I recognized in Berlioz.

Fate cannot harm me, I have dined, said Talleyrand. By dining on Berlioz as a youth I was saved from Wagner's wizardry, the Barmecide feast of illusion where the tables are filled with the voluptuous joy of eternal emptiness. Since my highest hope has always been my highest thought of life — my Zarathustra-creed — I have gone back to the peak of Berlioz, who, like a Swiss mountain-range, is wrapped in thunder-charged clouds alive with the pure energy of nature, far above the Wagnerian valleys where the cows and the pigs wallow in the muddy, tired sensuosity of Parsifal — the dregs of the Dionysian spirit!

Berlioz is the Stendhal of the musical world, and just as

Stendhal is a sharp, cold wind purifying the hot desert-air of European letters, Berlioz blows the clarity of mountain air through the fog of Wagnerism. I represent in philosophy what Stendhal symbolizes in literature and Berlioz in music, and my break with Wagner was as inevitable as the pitiless scalpel of the surgeon that cuts through the flesh and ligaments of a diseased limb. While Wagner was adding to the chaos of the West by his contribution of musical noise, I cut the Gordian knot of Western confusion by bluntly asking the question: How can man achieve power over himself and nature through a Christian philosophy of powerlessness?

My Superman is a blend of Caesar and Christ: he is too proud for Christian pity and yet too humble to play the role of a Caligula and wish humanity had but one neck so that he could strike it off at a single blow! My power-thought has never contemplated such an end to the race of man because I have a tragic view of life, and such a finish to the drama of history is not a tragedy but a bloody farce — a Wagnerian opera bouffe!

Berlioz set my Superman to music: in my twenties I composed a *Mystery of Saint Silvester,* in imitation of Berlioz, and while I was lured away from the great Hector by the din of Wagner — which I mistook for the battle-song of Zarathustra — I felt uneasy until I rediscovered Berlioz in Bizet. His *Carmen,* as I wrote my friend Frau Overbeck,[2] was free from Wagnerian mush and muddle and had the clear, Mediterranean tones of Berlioz — a miracle that made me break out in hurrahs and hosannahs, like an astronomer when he discovers a new planet. When I was lured by the Siegfried horn-call into the camp of Wagner, I felt ill at ease in the presence of the Wagnerian snobs

---

[2] Nietzsche actually wrote to his friend Peter Gast, but his confusion of Gast with Frau Overbeck is an interesting psychological revelation, for it was Frau Overbeck who constantly urged Nietzsche to break out of the psychic prison of his mother and sister — two women who dungeoned him in pathology. — Editor

217

who tried to hide their contempt for real music by belittling the great Hector. Wagner stripped him down to his musical underwear but sounded ridiculous in the borrowed clothes of the musician who composed *The Damnation of Faust.*

When Wagner, admitting his plagiarism, said that Berlioz needed completion and fulfillment by a poet *as a man needs a woman*, presenting himself as Berlioz's poetic bridegroom, he betrayed an interest in an incestuous relationship that could only have given birth to a Wagnerian monster. Besides, his comparison is an apt one: the Wagnerites celebrated the sexual freedom of the new era by the vicarious orgasms of the Wagnerian heroes and heroines who never succeeded in fully consummating their passion and plunged their frustration into a *Liebestod.*

I would have remained a perfect Wagnerite, perhaps, if my Russian charmer had not turned Tautenburg into a Venusberg, so that I was compelled to seek erotic satisfaction by watching a Wagnerian couple in the grip of a cosmic frustration that churns love into death. In Tautenburg, death was fired into life through the passion of my Cyprian goddess whose Wagnerism was merely social etiquette: a person of sophistication must be a Wagnerite or suffer the damnation of being an Ishmael like Professor Nietzsche, the offspring of a wild jackass!

In less than fifty years to be called a Wagnerite will provoke an action for criminal slander, and when a Wagnerian opera is mentioned in polite company, Gretchen's voice will be heard again: *Ye angels, holy cohorts, guard me!*[3]

10
The further a thing is removed from reality, the purer it is, the more beautiful and good. The only possibility is to live in art. Life is

---

[3] Wagner today has lost caste with sophisticated music lovers. Nietzsche was no mean prophet! — Editor

possible, thanks only to its aesthetic phantoms. These mad thoughts I wrote while I was so to stay sane, but now when I am supposed to be going stark mad I am too lucid to pass them off as the truth.

11

Under the influence of Rée, the Jew, I began to realize that the truth of art lies in the art of truth and that a mind which is not founded on the realities of science is like the Hindu's world which is reared on the back of an elephant which stands on a tortoise which crouches on the hot air generated by the Greek aesthetes. The aesthetic man must in the end die in his own sub-jective dream-world, since he has lost contact with the two poles of being — the Without and the Within — and collapse in the phantasies of the lunatic. The madmen I talk to every day here are perfect aesthetes, and when I improvise on the piano they accuse me of playing Wagner — the madman's god.

I first based my philosophy on art and landed in Tribschen, where Cosima played the role of the nymph Calypso, luring the young Ulysses with the borrowed siren-music of her elderly paramour. But I did not break away from Wagner because I wanted to put on him the horns he put on Siegfried. Though I call myself an immoralist to shock the Philistines, in the manner of Diogenes, the cynic, I am actually a fanatical moralist who must have faith in objective facts to keep the world morally sane. I therefore rebuilt my philosophy on scientific truths and quit the Orphic cult of Wagnerism, wallowing in the blood of bulls and mistaking hysteria for art.

12

Cosima was the first woman to reveal me to myself, as the mad King Ludwig, the perfect Wagnerite, was the first man. *The king*, cried Wagner, referring to his mad patron, *is capable of turning the world upside down!* That is what I feared when I was in his company. A ruler who abandons politics for art and drowns his melancholia in the subjective ravings of Wagnerism is bound to end up where I am now — in a madhouse.

It is true, as Socrates states, that the great majority of men live in appearances and shadows, but a king who lives in aesthetic illusions, who builds real and imaginary castles in the air as the Bavarian monarch did, turns his realm into a kingdom of confusion — like this asylum. Since it was my destiny to become the Emperor of the European intellect, the Napoleon of philosophy, I could not bow down with the mad Ludwig and kiss the big toe of Pope Wagner. Ludwig's face mirrored my mental breakdown and I fled from Bayreuth where the king and Wagner rioted over the corpse of sanity.

13

When I saw Cosima for the last time, she gave me a look of love as sad as the last notes in the Parsifal prelude but I had to sacrifice her on the altar of my human — and superhuman — pride. As a passionate lover of knowledge I was at first disarmed by Woman the great Enigma, and I became her love-slave, bowing and scraping before her, running errands, doing menial tasks, fitting into her desire to debase the man in me. For, as she was a true Wagnerite, her love-passion recoiled upon itself and took the form of a lethal desire to humiliate, to destroy, to annihilate me as a man so that she could carry me off on her naked back to her Valkyrean paradise of female dominance.

In the amorous fury of her face I saw reflected the nihilism of our age which loves to destroy and destroys to love: having lost contact with the Mystery of Being, the Miracle of the Self which reaches out into the universe for power and grandeur until it becomes Godlike in its longing, it seeks to crush the Ego beneath the heel of homicidal lust. Wagner once told me he placed me in his heart between Cosima and his dog, in other words, between two bitches. I fled this bitch-goddess of mine, as I fled the mad king and Wagner himself, because my love of knowledge led me to the knowledge of love, and I discovered, thanks to Cosima, that not Dionysos but Death reigned in Tribschen, Death that finally groaned into Parsifal: *Death, to die — grace supreme!*

What we have lost we possess forever,[4] and if I have lost the love of woman because of my implacable gaze into the great mystery of Eve, I possess her eternally in my soul, forgiving her sins as Adam did. And as I lie here buried alive in my loneliness, feeling my skull cave in like Caesar's, I can only say *Yea* to what I have written:

What matters what becomes of us if a minute of such detachment gives us at last the purity of vision in which things are seen apart from the light in which they are colored by our sorrow, our disillusionment, our lassitude, our greed or our enthusiasm?

Is my honor lost because women have betrayed me to weakness or I have betrayed my own strength seeking the power of true knowledge which alone can save us from approaching Doom? Am I completely damned because I am crushed beneath the Athenian dead on the plain of Marathon? Let Demosthenes, the eloquent defender of Athenian honor, deliver his funeral oration over me: "No, you have not failed, Friedrich Nietzsche! There are noble defeats as there are noble deaths — and you have died nobly. *No, you have not failed!* I swear it by the dead on the plain of Marathon."

I swear it.
I swear it!

14

I should have lived with a dumb, female creature like Heine's, a mindless brute who lacked everything but the capacity

---

[4] Compare Ibsen: "One possesses eternally only what one has lost." — Translator

for adoration — a bitch worshiping her master! Instead I sought out an Aspasia who took my philosophy seriously, like an educated Calypso who discussed Hegel, Schopenhauer and Tolstoy between violent acts of courtship, exhausting her Ulysses with her love and with her lore!

And now my beautiful nymph has left her cave in Tautenburg where the tall damask bed is gathering cobwebs while she is in Paris with her Jew drinking and singing her *Hymn to Life* to which I made a choral setting! But why should I, though a total lunatic, indulge in the crime of Wagnerian anti-Semitism because Rée has won the affection of the woman I love? Wagner rewards his friends by slandering them, as he slandered Meyerbeer, thus reversing Job's prayer: *Though he trusted me, yet will I slay him.* Being wholly mad I cannot indulge in the dodge of Jew-baiting which is the luxury of healthy-minded Philistines who since Apion, the Stoic philosopher, have used thought to betray Reason, as the Aryan Wagnerites do.

That is why Heine, in disgust, fled from Athens to Jerusalem where there are no sickly philosophers lying like cocoons on the dead branch of life, cocoons woven on futile threads of dialectics, empty brain-spinnings that have no contact with vital, exuberant living. How Joshua would have despised the Socratic Platos and Aristotles — the Jew who dared to defy God and stop the sun! The Jewish Pharisees knew how to combine thought with content, ideas with action, practicing the Goethean *deed* when the decadent Israelites, drained of their Hebraism, crowned their exhaustion by assuming the cross of Christ. A proud Jew like Heine could only look upon his enforced baptism with horror, and his Hellenism extended only to his daily visits to the temple of Venus. But Venus with her broken arms could not help him in his final agony: she betrayed him as she betrayed me, and like Heine I have a greater respect for Jehovah, the Thunder-God who cannot betray us unless we betray *Life itself* and assume the cross of exhaustion, the burden of nihilistic despair with Wagner and Schopenhauer.

15

I have always had a secret admiration for the early Catholic fathers whose virile Hebraism shot out like bolts of thunder from the gray clouds of their Christian theology, the sickly vapors of Pauline, Neo-Platonic mysticism. In the days of Chrysostom Christians dared to break into the closed system of Greek rationalism, pounding at the walls of Hellenic thought with the battering-rams of Jerusalem.

They proved, as I did centuries later, that Greek philosophy was the disease of a decadent Hellas whose eyes were set on vanity and whose feet trod the desert sands of nihilism, pursuing the mirage of abstract Reason while Sinai thundered the Deed as well as the Thought, making Justice not a plaything of philosophers but the pivot of practical living. The Hebraism of Saint Augustine planted the City of God in the midst of world chaos; Jerusalem was pulled down from the skies in a fury of passionate longing . . .

Where am I? I began with a girl and ended with the City of God. Perhaps they are one: did not Solomon locate Jerusalem in the body of his beloved?

16

Buckle has pointed out two *snares* of history: the fatalism of race and the legendary fatalism of providential great men. It is Fräulein Salomé who introduced me to the democratic notions of the English historian who takes the side of Michelet against the racialism of Taine and Gobineaux. Fräulein Salomé, with the connivance of her Jewish friend Rée, pulled out two pillars from the structure of my sanity — my pride of race and the conviction that I am a fatality — a pivotal force in world history. Under their positivist influence I wrote *Joyful Wisdom* and *Human All-Too Human*, trying to base my philosophy on scientific rationalism rather than on the intuitive findings of Greek aesthetics.

But in a sense Lou's action was inevitable. Nature conspires with woman to reduce the stature of a Superman to the proportions of a midget. No man is a hero to his butler, and no philosopher can be a cosmic force to a mistress who sees him naked with all the stigmata of the hairy ape! A Pole of noble blood who calls himself Nietzsche is no different in the cave of Calypso from a mindless peasant who spits tobacco juice over his jumper and defecates in the open fields. On her high silken bed all men are equal — the wrecked Ulysses and the gibbering idiot who has lost all goal or purpose in life.

Thought expands but lames, said Goethe. What was I in Lou's arms but an intellectual cripple, arriving at the horrible conclusion that all science, like art, is the subjective rationalization of power-minded men who thought in terms of their nation, race or class? My aristocratic philosophy was merely a mask to cover my own sense of humiliation at the thought that women could tweak my nose at will, and that in their presence I was merely a naughty child: Caesar with the soul of a diapered infant!

And because I had fallen into the Pyrrhonic pit of absolute doubt like Descartes, I eagerly grasped the helping hand of Lou, who at twenty already could dissect the basic fallacy in Cartesian thought. *I think, therefore I am*, places the cart before the horse, as every woman knows who has felt life stirring in her womb, or who in the midst of her erotic frenzy hungers for conception, even though, like Lou, she has no conscious desire for children. *I am, therefore I think* — this existential fact which the Jews in their great wisdom understood when they called their God the great I AM — this is what Lou taught me with the naked ritual of her passionate body.

My disciple became my teacher — the god of irony achieved

a perfect triumph! She inspired me with the thought of Zara-thustra: my greatest poem celebrates our union, and our tragic separation when the Christ in me broke away from the inner Caesar and I sought to recoup my sense of power by grasping a philosophic hammer and pounding away at every idol — except the clay idol of my own little ego.

17

Like the classical religions which are relics of the dawn-ages before morality, woman's religion of sexual love — *the cult of Aphrodite* — recalls man to his biologic heritage, his body, and while in possession of his body, his mind and soul rush back to him in the great triune unity of the orgasm. This Dionysian mystery which I had grasped only in philosophic theory, was made factual to me when a mere word or gesture from Lou was enough to set the springs of my erotic being into action. And instead of being *outside* my body like an actor pushing his dis-guised self across a stage and directing its movements like a puppet-master, I was *inside* my body, no longer shocked by the erotic gestures of a woman to whom sex is the central fire and intellect its hard incandescent glow. Lou's brilliance, unlike mine, did not derive from her head but from her thighs and the electri-cal energy of her vibrant, eloquent flesh. Even her bawdy talk had a salty flavor which made my epigrams, influenced by Sallust, sound like the tasteless satire of Luther.

I have always insisted that I have no zest for enmity, and this is true, especially now when I see Lou in the clear blaze of my own funeral pyre. I loved her then and I love her now: I mourn the loss of a beloved woman who was virtuous because she was beyond virtue and merciful because she was beyond mercy, giving me back to myself, my true unitive being. As I told Overbeck when I begged him to do something drastic because my sister's behavior towards Lou was driving me mad, I have no fault to find with this Russian cyclone who tore across my psychic landscape with the healing fury of nature, destroying everything but firing me with the urge to build again when I am strong enough to remove my ruins . . . *But shall I ever be strong enough?*

I have foresworn revenge and punishment, curbed my vengeful nature, my demonic fury which sprang from the fact that, following the ancient Greeks, I built my private life within the confines of the finite, and became frightened, and therefore defensively angry, when I stood before the infinite Mystery, the Riddle-Woman.

Paraphrasing Saint Paul, I say, "I, yet not I, but Spinoza's God, dwelleth in me," the God who sees all tragedies through the eyes of eternity where the anger and the evil of the moment become the love and the good of the ages. *To understand is to forgive.*

This is true morality, true virtue. As the poet Lucilius, Scipio's friend, said, *Virtue is to be able to render the true value to the things among which we move and in which we live.*

Let us stamp the impress of eternity upon our lives! Let us live that we may desire to live again: this is my creed, yesterday, today, tomorrow, and the yesterdays to follow tomorrow.

*   *   *   *

EPILOGUE

INVOCATION TO HER

I come to you tonight
Smile suspended from the nail over my head
Mother of God
Mother of the God I have not acknowledged since child-
hood and do not acknowledge even now in this hour of dire
humiliation
You must hear me because the woman who mothered me
never became my mother
I must have a mother tonight
or lose my identity in time.

Were the image identifying this shabby ill-smelling bed the
image of a bootblack
I would now have to crawl before it on my hands and knees
to cry for the compassion I need with which to press onward
this faltering, evilly predestined journey
If there's any compassion left in the world
(and why should there not be, seeing how little of it has been
spent since it was first emptied out bucketful into the infinite)
it must be contained in some image
left accidentally for me to find and worship tonight.

Feetforemost into this fantastic network of hypothetical rest
I have projected myself
    closed my eyes tight to things meant to be seen and those
meant to remain invisible
    made desperate descent into the dreamless sleep of those
whom even the dead envy in their graves
    See me close my eyes tight
    like the infant Samuel stumbling sleepily down the aisles of
the Lord's temple
    like the infant Samuel hugging himself behind the great back
of the good man Eli
    like the infant Samuel before the heavy hand of the Lord
descended on his fragile shoulder.

    Out of the night a sound came to me
    like the barking of a dog
    A second time it came
    and a third time
    when it came to me the third time I knew by its gentleness
that it must be the true voice
    and that it might be meant for me.

    Was I to be called again whose throat is hoarse with the
calling of soundless voices all about me
    and over what unpath'd roads was I to travel the long
distance to nowhere
    with my passport written in vanishing ink and sealed with
the blood of a patriarch who lived a whole lifetime on black
olives . . .

    Then something happened in the jumble of time and space
in which I roll about so feverishly
    it transpired like a last minute act of grace

I awoke lying on my belly
eyes straining toward your image over my bed
relieved to delirium
that it was to the gentlest of the godheads that I could lift
myself in silent speech
I could not survive again the sensation of His heavy hand on
my weary shoulder

What have I done that the humblest gypsy does not do every
day and every night of the week?
I ate corn bread and touched my lips with the pleasure of it
I looked upon the grass as if it grew for my special delight
it was with me as it was with Job
every new hole had to be filled
all the old ones were kept waiting
an old hole always reminded me of a new one.

I have called myself a free spirit
is that anything for which to frown on me?

I have called myself the enemy of all churches and priests
remember it to my honor

I have cried out against the democratic trend of my time to
jell up humanity into one vast shrinking Chandala[1]
would you have me keep silent about something so
scandalous?

I have denied the value of all the virtues of humility and
demanded a new roll call of those natural virtues of man that
maintain him in his erectness

---

[1] Hindu name for the lowest of India's castes.

would it have been honorable to do less?

I have shown up Nature as false a deity as God, and demonstrated that it is safe to assume that the universe is bossed only in its obscurest moments
all my heart went into this

I have excoriated all the lovers of the status quo
may their friend the devil claim them for his own

with all the fierceness I could muster I have demonstrated against the fundamental fallacy of reasoning, which is the Nay that can be turned into a Yea, and a Yea that is always in danger of being turned into a Nay
if that is not so, what have we eyes for?

Embrace every faith, I pleaded with them, but as soon as you catch a second breath, rebel against it, for it is as necessary to rebel as to keep alive
and I am still waiting for you to smile down on me

there is only one decadence, believe me, the conscious relaxation of power
my knees fail me

[Here ends the ms.]

APPENDIX

THE LAST LETTERS OF
FRIEDRICH NIETZSCHE

Translated by Christopher Middleton[†]
and Julia Solis

To Peter Gast[†]   Turin, December 31, 1888

You are right, a thousand times over! Warn Fuchs yourself . . .
You will find in *Ecce Homo* an astonishing page about *Tristan*,
about my whole relationship with Wagner. Wagner is altogether
the foremost name in *E. H.* Wherever I admit no doubts, here
too I had the courage to go the whole way.

Ah, friend! What a moment! When your card came, *what*
was I doing . . . It was the famous Rubicon[1] . . .

I no longer know my address: let us suppose that it will soon
be the Palazzo del Quirinale.

N.

To August Strindberg[†]   [Undated]

Dear Sir:
You will soon have an answer about your novella — it sounds like
a rifle shot. I have ordered a convocation of princes in Rome — I

---

[1] This phrase could be taken to indicate that Nietzsche had gone out of his mind
shortly before writing this note to Gast, thus before the date of his collapse on the
Piazza Carlo Alberto on January 3 (the date established by Podach). The following
postcard to Strindberg is likely to have been written on December 29th or 30th,
since Strindberg's reply is dated (in Latin) January 1, 1889.

mean to have the young emperor shot.

> *Auf Wiedersehen!* For we shall see each other again.
>
> Une seule condition: Divorçons . . .

Nietzsche Caesar

Strindberg's reply:

Holtibus pridie Cal. Jan.
MDCCCLXXXIX

Carissime doctor!

[In Greek text:] I want, I want to be mad.[2]

Litteras tuas non sine perturbatione accepi et tibi gratias ago

> Rectius vives, Licini, neque altum.
>
> Semper urgendo neque, dum procellas
>
> Cautus horrescis nimium premendo
>
> > Litus iniquum.
>
> Interdum juvat insanire!
>
> > Vale et Fave!

Strindberg
(Deus, optimus maximus)

Nietzsche's reply:

Herr Strindberg!
Eheu? . . . not *Divorçons* after all? . . .

The Crucified

To Jean Bourdeau   [Turin, January 1, 1889]

Dear Sir,

I am hereby sending you the end of my proclamation: in the last

---

[2] Quotation from an Anacreontic poem. The Latin, from Horace, *Odes* II, X, lines 1-4, means: "Better wilt thou live, Licinius, by neither always pressing out to sea nor too closely hugging the dangerous shore in cautious fear of storms" (Loeb translation). The following phrase means "Meanwhile it is a joy to be mad."

sentence of the first part we want to avoid the word "execute" and say instead something like: nail fast. —

I sincerely think it is possible to put the whole absurd condition of Europe in order by means of a kind of world-historical laughter, without there having to flow as much as one drop of blood. Expressed differently: the Journal of the *Débats* suffices . . .

N.

My most humble congratulations for today!

To Constantin Georg Naumann   [Turin, January 1, 1889]

Dear Sir,
I would like to once more request the poem that concludes *Ecce Homo:* it is called "Glory and Eternity," — I have sent it last of all.

N.

The thought of a Fuchs-Köselitz publication has been abandoned.

To Catulle Mendès   Turin, on January 1, 1889

Eight *inedita* and *inaudita*, presented to the poet of Isoline, my friend and satyr, with great distinction: may he present my gift to humanity.

Nietzsche ~~Caesar~~ Dionysos

To Catulle Mendès   [Turin, January 1, 1889]

As I wish to render humanity an unlimited good deed, I give it my *Dithyramben.*

I place them into the hands of the poet of Isoline, the greatest and first satyr who lives today — and not only today . . .

Dionysos

235

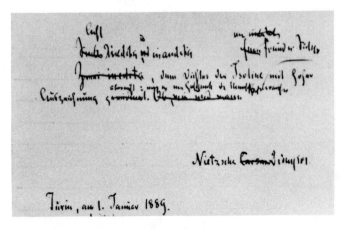

Letter to Catulle Mendès, January 1, 1889.

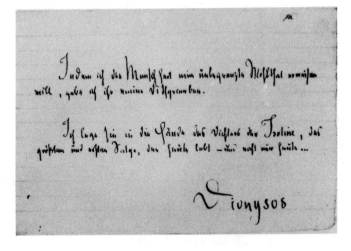

Letter to Catulle Mendès, January 1, 1889.

Letter to Jacob Burckhardt, January 6, 1889.

Letter "to the illustrious Poles," January 4, 1889.

Letter to Elisabeth Nietzsche, August 13, 1890.

To Constantin Georg Naumann   [Turin, January 2, 1889]
[Telegram]

C. G. Naumann Leipzig
Manuscript of the two final poems

To Constantin Georg Naumann   [Turin, January 2, 1889]

The events have completely surpassed the small essay *Nietzsche contra W.:* send me at once the poem that concludes it, as well as the last sent poem "Glory and Eternity." Onward with *Ecce!*

Telegraph to Herr Gast!
Address as before

Turin

To Meta von Salis   [Turin, January 3, 1889]

The world is transfigured, for God is on earth. Do you not see how all the heavens rejoice? I have just taken possession of my empire, am throwing the Pope in prison and am letting Wilhelm, Bismarck and Stöcker be shot.

The Crucified.

To Cosima Wagner   [Turin, January 3, 1889]

They tell me that a certain divine buffoon has these days completed the Dionysos Dithyrambs . . .

To Cosima Wagner   [Turin, January 3, 1889]

To the Princess Ariadne, my Beloved.
It is a prejudice that I am human. But I have often lived among humans and know everything that humans can experience, from

the lowest to the highest. Among Indians I have been Buddha, in
Greece Dionysos, — Alexander and Caesar are my incarnations,
as well as the poet of Shakespeare, Lord Bacon. Last of all I was
also Voltaire and Napoleon, perhaps Richard Wagner as well . . .
This time, however, I am coming as the victorious Dionysos, who
will turn the earth into a day of celebration . . . Not that I have
much time . . . The heavens are pleased that I am there . . . I have
also hung on the cross . . .

To Cosima Wagner   [Turin, January 3, 1889]

This *breve* to humanity is for you to publish, from Bayreuth, with
the inscription:
                    The joyous message.

To Cosima Wagner[†]   [Beginning of January, 1889]

Ariadne, I love you.

                                                         Dionysos[3]

---

[3] This message plays on the Cosima-Wagner-Nietzsche relationship, which Charles
Andler first detected beneath Nietzsche's treatment of the mythic Ariadne-Theseus-
Dionysos relationship in Nietzsche's "Empedocles" and "Naxos" fragments and
Zarathustra IV. Nietzsche's poem "Lament of Ariadne" ends with Dionysos replying
to Ariadne, "*I am your labyrinth*" (*Werke in drei Bänden,* 2:1259). Podach writes:
"Ariadne is the glittering symbol of the woman of Nietzsche's heart's desire, a
symbol that took root and grew up in his own world of mythic experience. He does
not reveal what experiences may have fostered its formation and growth — out of
deep need and also probably following his often all-too-artistic impulse to put on a
disguise. Yet beginning and end are certain: in Tribschen, Cosima becomes for the
young Nietzsche the governing image of Ariadnean being; twenty years later — in
Turin — he turns back to the original realm of his Naxos dreams and sends a last
lover's greeting to his heroine" (*Nietzsches Zusammenbruch,* p. 92; *Madness of
Nietzsche,* p. 148, where Voigt's translation [not used above] is defective).

To Georg Brandes[†]   [Turin, January 4, 1889]

To my friend Georg! Once you discovered me, it was no great feat to find me: the difficulty now is to lose me . . .

The Crucified

To Hans von Bülow   [Turin, January 4, 1889]

To Herr Hanns von Bülow . . .
In the consideration that you have begun and become the first Hanseatic, I, in all modesty, only the third Veuve Cliquot-Ariadne, I may not now spoil your game: rather, I sentence you to the "Lion of Venice" — he may devour you . . .

Dionysos

To Jacob Burckhardt[†]   [Turin, January 4, 1889]

Meinem verehrungswürdigen Jakob Burckhardt.
That was the little joke on account of which I condone my boredom at having created a world. Now you are — thou art — our great greatest teacher; for I, together with Ariadne, have only to be the golden balance of all things, everywhere we have such beings who are above us. . . .

Dionysos

To Paul Deussen   [Turin, January 4, 1889]

Since it has been irrevocably established that I alone have created the world, it appears that friend Paul also has been considered in the world plan: he is to be, together with Monsieur Catulle Mendès, one of my great satyrs and celebrators.

Dionysos

241

To Peter Gast[†] [Turin, January 4, 1889]

To my maestro Pietro.
Sing me a new song: the world is transfigured and all the heavens rejoice.

The Crucified

To Malwida von Meysenbug [Turin, around January 4, 1889]

Addenda to the "Memoirs of an Idealist"
Although Malvida, as is well-known, is Kundry, who laughed at a moment when the earth was shaking, much is forgiven her since she loved me much: see the first volume of the "Memoirs" . . . I admire all these exquisite souls around Malvida in Natalie her father lives, and I was also him.

The Crucified.

To Franz Overbeck[†] [Turin, around January 4, 1889]

To my friend Overbeck and his wife
Although till now you have had little faith in my ability to remain solvent, I still hope to prove that I am a person who pays his debts. — For example, my debts to you both . . .

I am just having all anti-Semites shot . . .

Dionysos

To Erwin Rohde [Turin, January 4, 1889]

To my ill-tempered Erwin
In spite of the danger that my blindness to Monsieur Taine, who once wrote the Veda, may enrage you once more, I dare place you among the Gods and the most delightful Goddess next to you . . .

Dionysos

To Carl Spitteler   [Turin, January 4, 1889]
                                       [Fragment]

[. . .] belongs to my godliness: I will have the honor of taking revenge on myself for that . . .

                                                    Dionysos

To Heinrich Wiener   [Turin, around January 4, 1889]

To Supreme Court Justice Wiener
Although you have given me the honor of considering the "Case of Wagner" detrimental to Wagner, said Wagner still dares to reveal his decadence to the light by means of a world-historical irresponsibility — *in lucem aeternam* . . .

                                                    Dionysos.

"To the illustrious Poles"   [Turin, around January 4, 1889]

To the illustrious Poles
I belong to you, I am even more Pole than I am God, I want to bring you honor, as I am capable of bringing honor . . . I live among you as Matejo . . .

                                                    The Crucified

To Cardinal Mariani   [Turin, around January 4, 1889]

To my beloved son Mariani . . .
May peace be with you! Tuesday I am coming to Rome to pay my respects to His Holiness . . .

                                                    The Crucified.

FRIEDRICH NIETZSCHE

To Umberto I, King of Italy   [Turin, around January 4, 1889]

To my beloved son Umberto
May peace be with you! Tuesday I am coming to Rome and wish
to see you next to His Holiness the Pope.

The Crucified.

To Jacob Burckhardt[†]   On January 6, 1889
[Postmarked Turin, January 5, 1889]

Dear Professor:
Actually I would rather be a Basel professor than God; but I have
not ventured to carry my private egoism so far as to omit creating
the world on his account. You see, one must make sacrifices,
however and wherever one may be living. Yet I have kept a small
student room for myself, which is situated opposite the Palazzo
Carignano (in which I was born as Vittorio Emanuele)[⁴] and
which moreover allows me to hear from its desk the splendid
music below me in the Galleria Subalpina. I pay twenty-five
francs, with service, make my own tea, and do my own shopping,
suffer from torn boots, and thank heaven every moment for the
old world, for which human beings have not been simple and
quiet enough. Since I am condemned to entertain the next eternity with bad jokes, I have a writing business here which really
leaves nothing to be desired — very nice and not in the least
strenuous. The post office is five paces away; I post my letters
there myself, to play the part of the great *feuilletonist* of the *grande
monde*. Naturally I am in close contact with Figaro, and so that
you may have some idea of how harmless I can be, listen to my
first two bad jokes:

[⁴] Vittorio Emanuele II, son of Carlo Alberto, died in 1878. He was father of
Umberto I, who was king at this time.

Do not take the Prado case seriously. I am Prado, I am also Prado's father, I venture to say that I am also Lesseps.[5]. . . I wanted to give my Parisians, whom I love, a new idea — that of a decent criminal. I am also Chambige — also a decent criminal.

Second joke. I greet the immortals. M. Daudet is one of the *quarante.*

Astu[6]

The unpleasant thing, and one that nags my modesty, is that at root every name in history is I; also as regards the children I have brought into the world, it is a case of my considering with

---

[5] Prado was tried in Paris on November 5, 1888; on November 14 he was condemned to death. Prado was a Spanish subject who claimed that his real name was Linska de Castilon. He had lived first in Peru, then in Spain, after exhausting his wife's fortune assessed at 1,200,000 francs. Heavily in debt, he came to France and lived with a girl named Eugénie Forestier; the couple had been without means since 1886. On November 28, 1887, Prado was arrested for theft in Paris. The investigation proved that he had also been involved in another theft outside Paris. During cross-examination, Eugénie asserted that Prado was the murderer of a prostitute named Marie Agriétant, who had been killed during the night of January 14, 1886, in the rue Caumartin. This assertion proved to be true. Henri Chambige was a law student who fancied himself a writer. He murdered the English wife of a Frenchman living near Constantine in Algeria. He was tried in Constantine on November 8, 1888, and was condemned to seven years of hard labor (it was a *crime passionel*). Ferdinand de Lesseps (1805-94) was the French diplomat responsible for building the Suez Canal and who initiated the earlier stages of the building of the Panama Canal. He also fathered seventeen children. During the latter part of his life, he was involved in a scandal. Nietzsche was offering Burckhardt these jokes with some reason: his own (*Der Antichrist*) idea of Cesare Borgia as pope — the total Renaissance secularization, absolute anti-Christianity — was culled from Burckhardt's *Civilization of the Renaissance in Italy.* In his note to Malwida, Nietzsche identifies himself with Alexander Herzen: "In Natalie [Herzen] her father lives, and I was also him" (original in the Nationale Forschungs-und Gedenkstätten der klassischen deutschen Literatur in Weimar).

---

[6] Greek for "city," with the connotation "hometown." The possible implication is "Alphonse Daudet's antiacademic hero Léonard Astier [in Daudet's novel *L'immortel*] is one of us."

some distrust whether all of those who enter the "Kingdom of God" do not also come *out of* God.[7] This autumn, as lightly clad as possible, I twice attended my funeral, first as Count Robilant (no, he is my son, insofar as I am Carlo Alberto, my nature below), but I was Antonelli myself.[8] Dear professor, you should see this construction; since I have no experience of the things I create, you may be as critical as you wish; I shall be grateful, without promising I shall make any use of it. We artists are unteachable. Today I saw an operetta — Moorish, of genius[9] — and on this occasion have observed to my pleasure that Moscow nowadays and Rome also are grandiose matters. Look, for landscape too my talent is not denied. Think it over, we shall have a pleasant, pleasant talk together, Turin is not far, we have no very serious professional duties, a glass of Veltliner could be come by. Informal dress the rule of propriety.

With fond love   Your   Nietzsche

I go everywhere in my student overcoat; slap someone or other on the shoulder and say: *Siamo contenti? Son dio, ha fatto*

[7] Presumably an allusion to Nietzsche's writings as "children." The passage relates, somewhat obliquely, to his discovery that his *Thoughts out of Season* on Schopenhauer and Wagner were in fact essays about himself; by now, the author is both "God" and the total solipsist (without object world).

[8] Antonelli was papal state secretary under Pius IX.

[9] Podach (*Nietzsches Zusammenbruch*, pp. 98-99) reads this as "quirinal-maurisch" ("Quirinal-Moorish"), which is doubtful; the original lacks, in any case, the middle letters "*ri.*" Schlechta's reading, "genial-maurisch" is, I think, correct. Presumably the reference is to the operetta *La gran via*, which Nietzsche saw about December 15.

questa caricatura . . .[10]

Tomorrow my son Umberto is coming with the charming Margherita whom I receive, however, here too in my shirt sleeves.

The *rest* is for Frau Cosima . . . Ariadne . . . From time to time we practice magic . . .

I have had Caiaphas put in chains; I too was crucified at great length last year by the German doctors. Wilhelm Bismarck and all anti-Semites done away with.[11]

You can make any use of this letter which does not make the people of Basel think less highly of me.

To Elisabeth Nietzsche

I am glad, my good beloved Lama —, that according to your letter, my little animal, you are doing well — . . . you are greeted sincerely — *cordialement* — by

The *confrère frère* —
Friedrich Nietzsche

The 13th of August
Naumburg at Saale
1890

---

[10] "Are we happy? I am God, I made this caricature . . ." The paragraphs following are written at various points in the margins of the original.

---

[11] That is, Wilhelm (the emperor) and Bismarck. As early as 1881, Nietzsche had anticipated farce and parody as a climax to his mental adventure; cf. *Die fröhliche Wissenschaft*, Bk. 3, sections 153 and 236; Bk. 4, section 342; Bk. 5, sections 382 and 383. Also *Jenseits von Gut und Böse*, section 223: "We are [. . .] ready, as no previous age was, for the grand carnival, for the laughter and recklessness of a mental Mardi Gras, for the transcendental heights of the highest idiocy and Aristophanic mockery of the world. Perhaps it is here that we shall discover the realm of our *invention*, that realm where we too can be original, perhaps as parodists of world history and clowns [*Hanswürste*] of God [. . .]" (*Werke in drei Bänden*, 2:686.)

Burckhardt took his letter to Overbeck during the afternoon of January 6. Overbeck wrote to Nietzsche at once, insisting that he should come to Basel. On January 7 he went to see Professor Wille of the Basel Psychiatric Clinic, and took the train to Turin the same evening, arriving there on Tuesday afternoon, January 8. He described the situation in a letter to Gast, dated January 15:[12]

My dear Herr Köselitz:[†]

[. . .] What I can say and want to say even to you at this moment will leave unanswered a thousand questions that you may have. First and foremost, you would like a factual report on what happened. I am obliged to be silent on a number of matters, only because the situation, in which I took action, was so urgent, and I would like not to have to mention such matters to any soul who was the sick man's friend, to you yourself especially, at least for now.

Until Christmas, I was bewildered by Nietzsche's letters about his present situation; around Christmas the letters became more frequent, and at the same time the handwriting and contents most disquieteningly betrayed a peculiar exaltation. Yet what perplexed me most of all was a completely reasonable letter received on December 31 by my excellent colleague Andreas Heusler, whom Nietzsche also knew from his Basel days. It concerned a demand for the return of [the rights of] those books of his which Fritzsch had published. The letters which I myself had received just before gave me cause to express [to Nietzsche] insistence that he should desist in this as well as the anxiety which his letters were giving me. On the same December 31, I received a reply which gave me cause to believe that the plan to deal with Fritzsch was over and done with, but which dismissed my anxi-

---

[12] C. A. Bernoulli, *Overbeck und Nietzsche*, pp. 231-37.

eties in a way that was anything but convincing. On January 6, Jakob Burckhardt received a letter, which he at once showed to me and which he has meanwhile given to me as the principal document which decided my intervention.[13]

Now it was clear, between this letter and the previous one — on January 4, as his landlord later told me — Nietzsche had gone out of his mind.[14] He was not only a king, but also father of other kings (Umberto and others), had even been to his own funeral (that of his son Robilant), and so on, and all this in the frenzied tone of a madman. In my helpless despair, I immediately wrote a most urgent letter to Nietzsche, asking him to come to me at once, which was doubly foolish, as I learned on consulting the head physician of our insane asylum the next day, and whose possible consequences I cut short on the same day by telegraphing Nietzsche that I was leaving at once for Turin. My colleague Wille — that is the physician's name — when I showed him that letter to Burckhardt and a short note which I had myself received on the Monday morning, left me in no doubt that no time should

---

[13] Since Overbeck was not a relative, the law required that his intervention should be proved necessary. Elisabeth later caused a furor, challenging the legality of his action. She argued that the family and the family physician should have been called (that is, Nietzsche's mother and Dr. Eiser of Frankfurt).

---

[14] Podach makes January 3 the date of Nietzsche's collapse (*Nietzsches Zusammenbruch*, p. 82) and connects it with the well-known incident with the horse: "On January 3, as Nietzsche is leaving his house, he sees on the Piazza Carlo Alberto, where the horsedrawn cabs are parked, a tired old horse being beaten by a brutal cabman. Compassion seizes him. Sobbing and protectively he flings his arms around the neck of the tormented animal. He collapses. Fortunately Fino comes by, attracted by the disturbance on the street. He recognizes his tenant, and with great difficulty brings him into the house." Karl Strecker (*Nietzsche und Strindberg*, Munich, 1921, pp. 41 ff.), who visited Turin in 1913 and spoke to people who had known Nietzsche, wrote that the incident with the horse occurred "several days" before the collapse (though he makes no claims to complete accuracy in his dating).

be lost, and said that I should leave at once if I felt it was my responsibility to do so. And for this I am now also very grateful to him, even though I was forced to undertake more than I knew I could do. In fact, it was fortunate that I did not arrive in Turin even an hour later than I did. On the same afternoon — the afternoon of my arrival, a week ago today — the affair became a public scandal there; the landlord, whom special circumstances prevented me from finding, was, when I had at least his wife before me at last, visiting the police station and the German consul — an hour before this, I had established that the police knew nothing. Nietzsche, who had collapsed in the street on the previous day and had been picked up there, was now in danger of being committed to a private insane asylum and was at that very moment being surrounded by adventurers of the kind who in Italy gather around more quickly than anywhere else when such a thing occurs. It was the last possible moment for removing him without obstacles apart from his own condition. I shall pass over the touching circumstances in which I found Nietzsche being looked after by his landlord and landlady — the former owns a newspaper kiosk on the Via Carlo Alberto — they too may be characteristic of Italy. The terrible moment at which I saw Nietzsche again brings me back to my main concern, uniquely a terrible moment and quite different from all that followed. I see Nietzsche crouching and reading in the corner of a sofa — the last proofs of *Nietzsche contra Wagner,* as I later found — looking horribly worn out; he sees me and rushes up to me, violently embraces me, recognizing me, and breaks into floods of tears, then sinks back on the sofa, twitching and quivering; I am so shaken that I cannot stand upright. Did the abyss open before him in that moment, on the edge of which he is standing, or rather into which he has plunged? In any case, nothing of this kind happened again. The whole Fino family was present. Nietzsche was hardly lying there groaning and quivering again than they gave him a sip of the bromide water that was on the table. At once he became tranquil, and laughingly began to speak of the great reception which had been prepared for that evening. With this he was among the delusions from which he had not emerged by the time I left him — always lucid as regards me and all other persons, but completely in the dark about himself. That is, growing inordinately excited at the piano, singing loudly and raving, he would utter bits and pieces from the world of ideas in which he has been living, and also in short sentences, in an indescribably muffled tone, sublime, wonderfully clairvoyant, and unspeakably horrible things would be audible, about himself as the successor of the dead God, the whole thing punctuated, as it were, on the piano, whereupon more convulsions and outbursts would follow, but, as I said, this happened only at few fleeting moments while I was with him; mainly it was utterances about the profession which he had allotted to himself, to be the clown of the new eternities, and he, the master of expression, was himself incapable of rendering the ecstasies of his gaiety except in the most trivial expressions or by frenzied dancing and capering.[15] All the while the most childish innocuousness, which had never left him even during the three nights in which he had kept the whole household awake with his ravings, and precisely this innocuousness and this almost total docility, as long as one shared his ideas about kingly receptions and processions, music festivals, and so on, made the task of bringing him back here child's play, at least for the attendant whom, on Wille's strict advice, I had sought out and taken with me. The journey, including a stop of almost three hours in Novara, took from two-thirty on Wednesday afternoon until seven forty-five on Thursday morning, began with a terrible half-hour on the platform at Turin, with the usual

---

[15] Nietzsche's assumed role of "Hanswurst" ("fool," "clown," "trickster") during his last months is discussed at some length by Podach.

platform confusion; in Novara too there was some trouble;[16] generally, though, we traveled alone, Nietzsche sleepy with chloral,
yet repeatedly waking up, though at most in his excitement he
would sing loud songs, among them, during the night, the wonderfully beautiful gondola song (*Nietzsche contra Wagner*, p. 7), the
origin of which I discovered later; it was a complete enigma to
me, as I listened, how the singer could invent *such* words with
such a wholly peculiar melody.[17] Also the transfer from the station
to the hospital on the morning of the 10th, which I had feared
most of all, was practically no trouble, except that for me the
whole situation was quietly terrifying. A scene in the waiting
room at the hospital (I preface this by saying that Nietzsche *still
has no idea* where he is; our attendant, in order to avoid the scenes
we had in Turin, impressed upon the sick man before we left the
train that he was entering Basel incognito to start with, and must
therefore not greet anybody, or else the procession later on would

---

[16] The attendant (a German-Jew named Miescher) who appears to have been a
dentist by profession, cajoled Nietzsche into believing that a regal reception was
awaiting him in Basel, but that it would have to be called off if he did not behave
himself.

---

[17] This song appears in *Ecce Homo*, without a title:

On the bridge I stood
Not long ago in the brown night.
From far away came song:
In golden drops it poured
Away across the quivering water.
Gondolas, music, lights —
Drunkenly swam into the gloom fading . . .

And my soul, a stringed instrument,
Sang, touched by invisible hands,
To itself a secret gondola song,
Trembling with all the colors of bliss.
— Can someone have been listening?

not be so impressive; and so with the greatest composure
Nietzsche walks from the railway coach to the cab, where he
crouches, for the most part, in a state of great prostration; also by
saying that there has been a first meeting with Wille, the director,
and the latter has just left the room again for a moment). Myself
to our attendant of the journey: "Forgive me, doctor, for not
introducing you" (I had omitted to do so, in my excitement).
Nietzsche (who must have known Wille from earlier years): "He
hasn't yet introduced himself; we shall soon find out." (Wille has
returned.) Nietzsche (in the politest manner of his best times, and
with great dignity): "I believe that I have seen you before, and am
very sorry but at the moment I cannot recall your name. Would
you — " W.: "I am Wille." Nietzsche (without moving a muscle,
continuing in the same manner and in a most quiet tone, without
a moment's reflection): "Wille? You are a psychiatrist ["Irrenarzt"].[18] I had a conversation with you several years ago on
religious insanity. The occasion was a madman [————————],[19]
who was then living here (or in Basel)." Wille has been listening
in silence; he nods in affirmation. Just think with what a frozen
feeling of surprise I heard this — being myself able to realize the
literal exactness of this memory of seven years ago. And now the
main thing: Nietzsche does not bring this completely lucid
memory into any relation whatever to his own present state; he
gives no indication at all that the *Irrenarzt* has anything to do
with him. Quietly he lets himself be handed over to the assistant
physician, who walks in and orders breakfast for him and a bath

---

[18] The word "Irrenarzt" ("doctor for the insane") does not seem to have suggested to
Nietzsche that he himself was the patient.

---

[19] The omission from Bernoulli's text was repaired by Podach; the patient's name,
which Nietzsche remembered, was Adolf Vischer. In 1875, he had given Nietzsche
an original engraving of Dürer's: *Ritter, Tod und Teufel.*

to start with; and he leaves the room with the latter the moment
he is told to do so — I can give you no clearer picture of the
annihilating split in his personality. Since then I have not seen
him again, not on Saturday either, when I went out there again. I
was told that his condition has not significantly changed — much
noise making and singing, sleep induced only artificially; I should
not try to visit him for another week; the main thing is that he
should have rest and quiet. On Thursday, when I was half
demented myself, I had to write to his mother. The poor dear
arrived on Sunday evening, saw her son yesterday afternoon [. . .]

*On Wednesday, January 17, Nietzsche traveled by train to Jena with
his mother, an attendant, and Ernst Mähly (who had studied under
Nietzsche, was an adept of his later writings, and knew Otto
Binswanger, head of the Jena Psychiatric Clinic). He enjoyed the cher-
ries which Overbeck's wife had given him and a ham sandwich from his
mother. On the journey Nietzsche had a fit of rage against his mother;
so she traveled in a different compartment from Frankfurt onward.
During the last days of January,* Götzen-Dämmerung *was published.
On May 13, 1890, Nietzsche was allowed to leave the Jena clinic, and
went to live in Naumburg with his mother. Six months later, his sister
returned from Paraguay but went back there in June, 1892, for a year.
At home, Nietzsche's condition steadily deteriorated. Bernoulli*
(Nietzsche und die Schweiz, Berlin, 1922), *at that time a student at
Jena, was present when Nietzsche's mother brought him on a typical
visit to the Gelzers there. "She usually brought her son, who followed
her like a child. So as not to be disturbed, she took him into the drawing
room, where at first he loitered by the door. She walked to the piano and
played a few chords, whereupon he kept coming closer and eventually
began to play himself — standing, at first, until his mother pressed him
down on the stool (if I may use such an expression). Then he would
improvise for hours. Frau Nietzsche in the other room always knew*

254

that her son was all right, without her having to watch over him, as long as she could hear him playing." As from early 1894, Nietzsche was unable to leave the house. In 1895, there were signs of physical paralysis. On April 20, 1897, his mother died; soon afterward, his sister installed him, together with her Archive, in the Villa Silberblick in Weimar. His mother's old maidservant Alwine used to look after him. He died on August 25, 1900.

AMOK FOURTH DISPATCH

The *AMOK Fourth Dispatch* is both a guide to the steamy undergrowths of the well-manicured fiction garden and a thorough directory of the extremes of information in print. The *AMOK Fourth Dispatch* offers over 3500 book titles in this heavily illustrated catalog as well as audio and video cassette selections. The books offer unflinching looks at mayhem, virus, and decay; dissections of the current global power structure; sexual impulses spinning out of control; psychiatric tyranny and schizophrenia; tribal rituals and ethnographic documents; psychedelic reality maps; the tactics of individual subversion and autonomy; and other stark visions of our time.

Inside this unique document, AMOK fingers the pulse of deviance — raw data in the form of: forensic medical texts and CIA torture manuals, behavior control techniques, biographies of serial killers and porno queens, fire and brimstone fundamentalist fulminations, Satanist manifestoes and Santeria spellbooks, Nudist Colony guidebooks and psychotronic film directories, human oddities picturebooks and UFO abduction accounts, riot control technologies and AIDS as biological warfare, the abolition of work and Situationism, keeping a severed head alive and creating a false ID, holocaust revisionists as well as the African roots of Western civilization, necrophilia and gay truckstop sex, and countless other manifestations of the bizarre and provocative.

The *Fourth Dispatch* also examines the human imagination in print — the desperate, the depraved, the decadent: drawing from such previously under-recognized realms of fiction as hard-boiled pulp writers, blaxploitation novels, Surrealists and Symbolists, Sado-Masochistic erotica, as well as comprehensively placing such literary eminences as Poe, H. P. Lovecraft, Rimbaud, Nietzsche and Dostoevsky in a post-industrial context.

"An impressive collection, absolutely definitive in many ways — one can almost say that there's no need to read anything that isn't in this catalogue. The whole thing, in fact, is a wonderful conspectus of that other literature that exists light-years away from mainstream publishing and the respectable academic consensus that underpins all those puffed-up reputations and assorted nonentities." — J. G. Ballard

"A reading list from Hell that is a must for any serious oddball bibliophile." — John Waters

Oversized Paperback, 8 1/2 X 11 Format,
Illustrated, Indexed, 376 pp.
$8.95

THE TRIAL OF GILLES DE RAIS

Georges Bataille

French philosopher and surrealist Georges Bataille presents and analyzes the legendary crimes, trials and confessions of the most infamous villain of the Middle Ages: the fifteenth-century homosexual child-murderer, sadist, alchemist, necrophile and practicioner of the Black Arts — Gilles de Rais. He began his remarkable place in history as lieutenant to the devout martyr and saint Joan of Arc; after her execution he returned to his estates in the French countryside where he ritually slaughtered hundreds of young children. After his arrest and subsequent trials, he was hanged and burned at Nantes, France on October 25, 1440. Includes the actual texts from Gilles de Rais' trials, translated from the ecclesiastical Latin by Pierre Klossowski and annotated by Bataille.

FROM *THE TRIAL OF GILLES DE RAIS:*

The Sacred Monster

Gilles de Rais owes his lasting glory to his crimes. But was he, as some affirm, the most abject criminal of all time? In principle, that hazarded affirmation is barely supportable. Crime is an act of the human species. It is also an act of that species alone; above all, however, it is the secret aspect, the impenetrable and hidden aspect of that species. Crime hides, and what escapes us is the most terrifying . . .

The Murder of Children

At this moment, a comedy would intervene. Gilles, halting the suspension, had the child let down; then he caressed and cajoled him, assuring him that he did not mean to do him "harm" or to "hurt him," that on the contrary he wanted "to have fun" with him. If he quieted him finally, he could enjoy him then, but the appeasement did not last.

Having drawn a violent pleasure from the victim, he killed him or had him killed. But often Gilles' enjoyment mixed with the child's death. He would cut into — or had cut into — a vein in the neck: the blood spurted and Gilles reveled. He occasionally wanted the victim, at the decisive moment, to be in the languor of death. Or further, he had him decapitated: from then on the orgy lasted "so long as some warmth remained in the body."

Trade Paperback, 6 X 9 Format, Illustrated, 380 pp.
$12.95

These AMOK titles may be available at your local bookstore, or can be ordered directly from us. To cover shipping, please enclose $1.00 for the first copy, and 50 cents for each additional copy. We accept U.S. checks and money orders by mail, and we also accept VISA, MASTERCARD, and AMERICAN EXPRESS by mail or phone. For credit card orders, please enclose your account number, expiration date, daytime phone number, and signature. Send orders to:

Dept. S
Terminal Annex
P. O. Box 861867
Los Angeles, CA 90086-1867
(213) 665-0956